READERS' RESPONSE

I0210923

What an experience!! I will read this book again and again.

– Ansie, Personal Assistant

I could not put this wonderful book down, it was so exciting and inspiring. It is one of those books that you think about for a long time after reading, and which has a positive influence on your life in general. I love the honesty, vulnerability, and openness. It has given me renewed hope and inspired me to carry on trying and working, and not to let past hurts and disappointments hold me back.

– Lisa, Energy Healer

I am overwhelmed by this book! It is so amazing! I enjoyed every page and made notes so that I can refer back to it.

– Janie, Businesswoman

What a mind blowing journey. Simply amazing.

– Janette, Lawyer

This book is incredible! It is absolutely mind blowing.

- Françoise, Kinesiologist

I have enjoyed this book thoroughly. What an incredible journey. I take a huge amount of comfort from many of the words in the book, which I feel have really helped me to grow in terms of how I am thinking about and handling issues.

– Lise, Businesswoman

I have found this book informative and honestly enjoyed every page. It also gave me some insight regarding my past lives.

– Priscilla, Journalist

I have read the book for the second time and I found 'things' in it that I had totally missed the first time round. I guess that is what happens when we read any of these deep and profound books on Spirit and Enlightenment.

– Alicia, Entrepreneur

By the same author:

The Infinity Trilogy:

Book 1 - *The Puppet Master's Secret (2023)*

Book 2 - *Choosing to heal – A journey through time into eternity and back (2015)*

Book 3 - *The Master's Touch (2025)*

Blog Collection:

Magical, Mystical, Miracle Life - It just is

Dedicated to all those who helped me

choose to heal

Choosing to heal – A journey through time into eternity and back

Copyright © 2015 Cathy Mc Donald

Publisher: Cathy Mc Donald – www.masterstouch.co.za

First edition, first impression: 2015

First edition, second impression: 2018

First edition, third impression: 2024

ISBN: 978-0-620-68532-0

ePub: First edition, first impression: 2018; second impression: 2024

ISBN: 978-0-620-78351-3

N.: 312234246
WWW.WORKSCOPYRIGHT.COM
ALL RIGHTS RESERVED

COVER: Pikkie Wolmarans

EDITORIAL PANEL: Madeleine de Swardt and Andrea Campbell

AUTHOR PHOTOGRAPH: Nellis Rietmann

www.masterstouch.co.za

CHOOSING TO

HEAL

A journey through time into

eternity and back

Book 2 of the Infinity Trilogy

Cathy Mc Donald

©Copyright 2015

.

FOREWORD

In every life there comes a time to heal. Not all of us are fortunate enough to know when that time comes. I have been one of the lucky ones, because I felt pain so deeply that I had no option but to try to find healing. Once I found healing for the first time, I continued to discover new wounds that needed healing. In the end, I realised that life is often a journey to healing. I share this journey with those who read these pages, because nothing ever helped me along more than the words I discovered in the pages of so many books, which seemed to have been written for me to find when the time was right; usually just in time, when I needed them most. I have little interest in going deeply into what lies beneath my own old wounds and scars, long since healed. I chose to heal long ago, and I write this book with the sole purpose of providing words of encouragement to anyone who has made, or is facing, that same choice. What I share in these pages, is the pure magic I found on this journey. I am deeply grateful to those whom I have been privileged to accompany on parts of their own healing journey. It is my fervent wish that this book will sow the seeds of hope, love, trust and faith in the hearts of all who read it; these will grow, once you choose to heal - that I can promise you.

TABLE OF CONTENTS

Cathy Mc Donald

CHAPTER 1: Introduction

For many years I had been under the impression that I was on a spiritual journey, trying my level best to change my world for the better. I thought that, since I had stopped blaming the world and those around me for all my woes, I was getting this spiritual journey thing right. Except that I was in fact not quite managing to achieve my goals. This bothered me a little, but I put it down to the fact that I was living in 'the real world' and suffered from the same human fallibilities as everyone else. So each day I would try again and hoped for the best. Committed to building the future I wanted, I kept reading all about life changing strategies, the dynamics of relationships and anything remotely related to 'how life works'. This meant that I regularly had to change my general approach, incorporating some or other new technique I had read about, in the hope of getting closer to the life I wanted.

This process assisted me greatly in understanding myself and other people a lot better. I found a lot of common ground in self-help books when it comes to belief systems and the struggles people grapple with, which helped me to realise that I was certainly not alone in my misery. Somehow I just did not yet have the knowledge I needed to hone the skills that I thought were required to build the life I was dreaming of.

However, I eventually realised that although I had managed to expand my mind and my thinking, I was beginning to get bored with it all, because it was starting to feel very much as if I was not really making progress. In hindsight, this is not surprising. I knew what I wanted and I wanted my journey to produce exactly that. And when it did not, well then ... what was the point? Clearly, all the stuff I had been entertaining myself with was actually just a whole lot of nonsense.

And so it came that I just gave up on my spiritual journey. Despite growing up in a loving family, my childhood had given me more than enough baggage to carry around and more than enough issues to grapple with and to try to fix. It seemed to me that most people were in pretty much the same boat and that, with the exception of a few special people, most people were also having a hard time sorting life and its issues into neat little packages. So, in solidarity with my fellow man, viewed from my limited perspective, I abandoned my spiritual journey, just as I had abandoned my religion a few years earlier to search for answers elsewhere. Even though I had given up playing the victim years ago, I now felt that we are all victims of a system that is simply not going to work and we just have to keep going, survive, toughen up, and not expect too much.

Of course few people agreed with my thinking and so I learned to keep my views to myself. Well, for the most part. Some of my very patient friends would every now and again have to listen to what I believed to be my well-reasoned explanations as to why I thought things were what they seemed to be. They would hear me out, mostly without comment, knowing that it was quite pointless to argue with me about things that clearly only made sense in my mind. In my own defence, I can say that I was totally honest about how I felt at all times. If something did not make sense to me, I did not pretend that I was okay with that. My logical mind, shaped by many hours of studying mathematics, physics and the sciences in general, insisted that there should be order in the spiritual world, just as there is order in the material world. Those beautiful natural laws that govern our planet and the rest of the universe somehow had to resonate in the living world where we exist inside our heads, as well as on this planet. Why would our emotional and spiritual lives not also be governed by such laws? And just imagine if we could understand those laws and then apply them. Maybe then I would be able to fix my world … Although I had stopped searching for ways to make it real, I never lost my dream of changing things for the better. My earnestly searching soul had failed to create and manifest into my life what I had wanted most, so how on earth was it going to give me the dream of a better world and a better life for all, where we had it all figured out?

But going around in circles in one's mind gets really boring and proves nothing, especially when no one is particularly interested in the argument or its conclusion. People around me seemed to be happy to accept things just as they are and to continue with their lives. Eventually, the hopeless conclusion of the futility of it all that I had come to some years earlier, could not quench the thirst for authentic answers. As time passed, I got a little tired of settling for my unsatisfactory conclusion and listlessly acknowledged that there might be more work to be done on the spiritual front. I did indeed need some answers. The scientist in me would not shut up long enough for me to find some peace. This time around, however, I set some strict boundaries for the new journey, because some realities, as I interpreted them at the time, were simply not acceptable to me and would accordingly be ignored. Yes, I can imagine what you are thinking as you read this, but at the time I really thought this plan could produce a good result.

The universe, of course, had a plan of its own brewing on the other side of my newly set boundaries, which was bound to attract my attention where I sat in my safe cocoon, believing I could control what I would be working on and what not. I was in for a very big wake up call.

For some insane reason, I had some years before, and for all the wrong reasons, chosen a profession that taxed me more than anything else I had ever encountered. Practising as an advocate had slowly, but very surely, sucked the life and the health out of my body. I remained unaware of this for many years, but as I entered the new phase of my reluctant and now neatly controlled spiritual journey, I became aware that my hours were filled with what I perceived to be very unreasonable people. Each and every case I was dealing with presented a 'problem' person. Either my opponent was out to make as much money as possible out of his or her duty to 'follow client's instructions', or my instructing attorney could not see where to draw the line and stop fighting on someone else's budget. If I was lucky enough to have a sensible instructing attorney and a reasonable opponent, my client would turn out to be stubborn and completely unable to hear the common sense advice that I was convinced I was giving. At other times everyone would be reasonable and willing to follow advice, but my opponent's attorney would refuse to contact his client to take an instruction, refusing an offer simply because he or she claimed to 'know' that the client involved 'would not go for that'. Let me not even mention the dynamics once a judge gets involved.

The unreasonableness of those around me seemed to be contagious. On any given day I would have to speak to at least ten people about some or other matter in which one of the participants, in my view, needed to wake up. My levels of frustration were almost unbearable and this started to affect my body. A diagnosis of high blood pressure and a trip to the emergency room were initially dealt with effectively by taking four holidays per year. But the day came when I finally realised that the level of unreasonableness around me was escalating. What did this mean?

And so I did what I always do when I get stuck in a bad place. I went to see someone about it. I am the problem solving type, usually happy to admit that the source of the problem is somehow within me, as I had at least learned that much during my first and eventually abandoned spiritual journey. So when I went to see Eric Pannaye that day, I had no pre-conceived ideas of what the problem could be. I knew that I am a very reasonable person, yet somehow I was attracting unreasonableness into my world. How I managed to do this, I had no idea. At the time I was beginning to realise that I was sick to death of practising law and I hated my days at the office. It was as simple as that. The hype and adrenaline rush no longer excited me. What had once been a stimulating career, had become a boring experience. I had to resolve the same conflicts and problems over and over again, dealing with an endless line of seemingly immature grown-ups acting like children. I represented some wonderful people through the years and worked with colleagues that I admired greatly, but for some reason this changed at some point and fewer of the people in my work environment were easy to be around, in fact they were in the minority. All the cases started to feel the same. They all had one element in common: unreasonable people. I no longer wanted any part of this.

As always, Eric, a former electro-mechanical engineer in the nuclear industry, now doing what he terms 'energyneering', was patience itself as he listened to my long explanations detailing precisely how heavy my burden was. Who could be expected to try to do a good job with so many unreasonable people around? He looked at me with his kind eyes and asked: "So, where in your life are you being totally unreasonable?"

When tears come to my eyes, you know that you have me. As I rummaged through my handbag for a tissue, I felt a heaviness sinking in, as if all the energy had just been drained from my body. All the incidents of unreasonableness around me were but reflections of what needed to be healed inside me; little red flags pushing me firmly over the neat boundary I had set to keep the universe out of my spiritual journey. I was not going to deal with my anger as there was no explanation that could ever make the anger go away. Of this, I had convinced myself. As I sat facing Eric, I could almost hear the words in my head: 'So what took you so long to figure that out?'

"But Eric, I have contained my anger. I am not taking it out on anyone and it has no effect on how I feel or how I spend my days," I mumbled miserably. I had to try. What self-respecting lawyer just gave up on an argument? He was unimpressed.

"Come now," he said. "You know physics. You know that your anger, even if it is 'contained', as you call it, has an imprint. It affects your view of the world, which creates your reality."

And so I left there that day realising that there was no way out. I was going to have to face my anger and deal with it, or the unreasonable people would stay in my world and drive me to an early grave, if not to prison. I could already see the headlines: 'Irate advocate strangles attorney.' I relished the particular thought for a few moments while driving home.

When I got home, I walked straight to the cupboard where I had packed away all my self-help books some years previously. Those books had once helped me through nightmarish times. Applying their contents could not produce the result I had wanted then, but I did not know where else to start. And so, that same night, I started reading from the top of the stack.

CHAPTER 2: Starting out

I soon remembered why my books got me through so much trauma in earlier years. They gave me hope that there is a better world to be unlocked somewhere. Once again, I felt like a treasure hunter looking for clues on a deserted island in the middle of the ocean. The belief that the answers had to be somewhere, slowly stirred the old curiosity about how things 'worked'. My passion for energy dynamics was rekindled and I was back on track.

As I once again read the story of Catherine, as told by Dr Brian Weiss in his book *Many Lives, Many Masters*, I knew that this time, I would not give up again. This time I had no agenda, no marriage to try to save, nothing of or in this world to gain. I knew with certainty that I was carrying something inside me that was poisonous to my soul. The reality was that I now had come too far to bury that truth somewhere convenient and out of the way. The only problem was that I knew that my anger was authentic and very, very real. To shift it, I would need help, as I would most certainly not be able to get around my carefully constructed and, to my mind, well-reasoned arguments. My case justifying my anger was rock solid. This did not make me right; that much I knew. But knowing that I was wrong in my thinking, made little difference to the fact that I was stuck. I would need to replace the anger with something authentic; if not with true understanding, then at least with peace in my heart. My mind would accept nothing less and I would not be able to fool myself in any way. I would always only accept what made sense to me.

Re-reading Dr Michael Newton's books, *Journey of Souls* and *Destiny of Souls*, reminded me of the extraordinary hypnotherapy sessions I had with psychologist Christie Els, many years before. I remembered the incredible power of the human mind to bring us the information we need in order to heal our lives. I also remembered that the combination of the therapy I had with Christie and the information I had found in the books of Dr Weiss and Dr Newton, had once before helped me to hope that I was more than just a miserable person, stuck in endless cycles of pain and grief, unable to break free from pain so deep that I did not even know its source.

I had started the initial leg of my spiritual journey some years earlier, because I simply had to stop the pain. I wanted to be healed. Eventually, I indeed managed to shift a lot of issues and to change my life completely. The pain left my world and I did become stronger, but I felt that the pain should not have been there in the first place. I still had no answers as to what the point of it all was and the answers phrased by the wise ones of the world, did little more than to irritate me.

And thus the anger remained. Convinced that I had done all I could and that living without pain was good enough, I forged ahead and built a life I was happy with. I labelled the anger I felt 'Unexplained' and packed it away. This lasted a number of happy years, until the unreasonable characters started showing up in my perfect little world, reminding me of what I had all but buried.

This time, I knew that wanting to heal was no longer going to be good enough. There would have to be more. I took out the notes I had kept of my sessions with Christie so many years ago. As I read them in astonishment, I realised that every word of the imagery and symbols produced by my own mind during those sessions, had come to pass in the intervening years. While the aim of the therapy I had received at the time was to help me to heal, my real intention was to save my marriage through healing myself. I never did believe in trying to save my marriage by changing my husband. I knew that the answer lay within me. I thought that if I changed through healing myself, the dynamic within my marriage would have to respond to the changes in me and that then my husband and I might be happy together. When that did not happen, I just pushed it all aside to make space for the grief and sadness of loss, not knowing that I was already living a miracle.

I am beyond grateful for the fact that I am almost obsessively detailed. My habit of keeping record of therapeutic sessions had preserved the treasure of information I had unknowingly gathered years ago. I continued making careful notes of every single thing that happened from the moment I chose to heal, which finally enabled me firstly to understand and make sense of my journey, and then to share it. Because this time, it was a choice to heal, not just a need to do so. And this, as it turns out, was the key that would unlock the door to inner peace, happiness, joy, health and the ability to see that I am living a magical, mystical, miracle life, no matter what my circumstances are. I used to feel perplexed as I observed people who seemed to love life and were happy to be alive. How could they be so happy with all that was going on in the world? Were they blind? Or was I? Happily, I was the one not yet able to see.

CHAPTER 3: Meditation - 8 April 2013

Over the months that followed, I would come to understand that the choice to heal is not a magic wand. Nothing falls into place immediately. Choosing to heal is a daily choice, one we have to affirm almost minute by minute. As we heal aspects of our bodies or our lives, other issues surface, demanding to be cleared, bringing our attention each time to a form of turmoil or pain that we managed to hide away or seal off in the deep recesses of our multi-layered beings. Healing takes time and a lot of effort. Actually, total dedication is probably a better way to describe what is needed for the life-altering facets of the choice to heal to become apparent.

Having made my way over the first hurdle and accepting that some effort was going to be required, I set about to find out how I was going to fix things in my life and in my mind. For this, I was going to need to unlock the amazing symbolism and secrets of my own mind; sort of like a treasure hunt of the soul. I have to admit that I did feel a little excited. Re-reading all those old books had set the scene for a fresh effort to fix my life. Getting into my own mind, meant that I had to create the space to meditate regularly. Thinking back over the years, I feel sad that I had allowed the pain and grief that I felt after my divorce to consume me. I was so engrossed with completing the grieving process, intent on getting up and moving on, that I never took the time to turn in and connect with the resources of my soul. Or perhaps I just did not want to hear my soul's quiet whisperings.

My meditation and self-hypnosis skills were a little rusty, given that I had not meditated for about four and a half years. I need not have worried. Meditating is like riding a bicycle. Once you know how, it remains a natural skill, ready to be called up at a moment's notice. My refreshed memory of the powerful sessions with Christie left me in no doubt that I would be using the same technique to work on my new shift. Christie is one of those incredible souls, born to heal those who cross her path without even trying. She taught me all that I ever needed to know about the essence of hypnosis, the trance state and the rich symbolism that helps us make sense of who we are. I knew the extent of my own abilities, as I had become quite adept at using self-hypnosis and meditation after the conclusion of my therapy with her. Once able to do this, I needed no help to slip into trance easily, yet remain able to guide the process, or rather to follow what my mind brought to me. On coming out of trance, I would immediately type up my recollections, because the memory of these sessions fades almost instantly if it is not recorded straight away. I now knew the value of making notes as re-reading the notes I had made on my sessions with Christie so many years down the line again, produced incredible insights.

In hypnosis sessions, use is often made of a 'special', 'favourite' or 'safe' place. In my case, my safe place turned out to be a white gazebo in the middle of a lovely garden, with white and pink roses growing all around it and even creeping up the trellised sides. Inside the gazebo, plush white furnishings invited me to relax. It was all just perfect. I often wonder how this place came to be my special place, as I certainly did not imagine it. It was simply an image that my mind presented to me in response to a prompt after entering trance, namely 'What do you see?' From the beginning I had the sense that this place was somehow real.

I was seldom alone in my gazebo. Someone would always come to talk to me. The first person ever to come to my gazebo during trance sessions was a man, or rather a guide, that I still think of, and shall refer to in these pages, as my guardian angel. He wore a white satin suit, with a pinkish shirt and pink satin tie. His shiny blonde curls and piercing blue eyes probably resulted in my seeing him as an angel, but the most important thing about this person was the fact that I felt completely safe, understood and supported whenever he showed up. I still use this technique in meditation sometimes and just go to my safe place to sit there for a while. My guardian angel always joins me and just sits with me, not communicating at all. Somehow, I always come out of the meditation feeling better.

Apart from his appearance, there is another reason why I tend to think of the man in the white suit as my guardian angel. I have a very strong impression that he 'has my back'. Sometimes when I journey inward, using the image of a staircase in order to deepen my level of trance, stepping down into the deeper levels of relaxation, he appears and walks down the stairs with me. I am never alone and that loving presence is always with me, no matter how dark the day may seem to be.

During one of my hypnotherapy sessions with Christie, my guardian angel and I attended 'a meeting' in my gazebo with certain other entities who also arrived to help me in my process. These entities did not tell me who they were, but as time went by, they kept appearing during sessions. Sometimes they would all be together and at other times only one of them would come to communicate with me. As with my guardian angel, I had intuitively assigned roles to all of them. I have come to think of these entities as guides, although I have to admit that I used to get irritated when people loosely threw around phrases like 'the guides are telling me' this or that.

The reasons for my irritation, I suspect, were simply that way back at the beginning of my spiritual journey, it all sounded so arrogant to me. I wondered what made people think that invisible guides actually communicated with them? If these beings were real and were there to help and to guide us, would they not communicate with all of us? Because they were certainly not chatting to me, no matter how many self-help books I read. A further cause of irritation was the fact that, to my mind, 'spiritual people' often without actually saying so, intimated to those less informed or less adept, like myself, that they were special in some way. Perhaps this was just my perception and not their intention. No one had explained to me that they did not actually 'see' these guides, but rather that these guides were perceivable in the mind's eye. The lack of that little detail caused me a lot of unnecessary confusion until I entered hypnotherapy.

Let me be very clear at this point. Each and every one of us has the ability to communicate with our guides, if we believe they exist and should we wish to, or need to. If we do not feel the need to do this or do not believe they exist, it certainly does not present a problem. All humans are assisted and guided in some way, regardless of what we believe or who we believe is protecting us and whether or not we are aware of this protection and guidance. A presence is always there, dropping hints into our minds, communicating in a softly whispering voice warning of some peril. When 'something tells you' that you should be doing this or that, or if you have acted on a sudden feeling and have managed to avert disaster, you know that those who watch over you are near. So, the purpose of this book is simply to share. There is nothing special, or unique, in my experience that cannot be repeated by anybody else who really wants to communicate with their guides if they feel the need to. It is not necessary to do so either; it is a choice and I believe that if the techniques I describe in this book would be beneficial to you, you will feel drawn to try them, whether on your own or with the help of a facilitator. If not, then I am pretty sure that you will still be looked after, by your guides or by whoever you believe is watching over you. We all eventually find our way, even though it might not look like that to others, or even to ourselves.

After my hypnotherapy sessions, I eventually accepted that there is a phenomenon, whether real or imagined, which involves entities (that despite my earlier misgivings I also came to think of as guides) coming to assist us when we ask for help and guidance. Once I had been in contact with them through hypnotherapy, I could no longer doubt the phenomenon and so I shall refer to these entities as guides, whom I believe to be available to all of humanity, regardless of belief systems.

Of course it is true that guides might be imaginary characters, yet I would not have conjured up such a phenomenon even if I had been given permission to create any fantastic story that I wished. The thing is, these guides would never tell me what I wanted to hear. They would tell me things that I would sometimes only understand years later. Mostly, they 'showed' me things in symbolic form, which generated feelings from which I could deduce a message. All communication was telepathic. It also took me a while to realise that fact. This method of communication is another thing I would not have dreamed up. I have a vivid imagination, but for the life of me I cannot come up with a plot for a novel, or even for a short story.

On the day of my first meditation after many years I was determined to tackle the issue of my anger. I was already familiar with the white gazebo in the rose garden, although I had not visited it for quite some time. As I imagined myself stepping down the staircase to find my special place, I was therefore not surprised when my guardian angel joined me, nor was I surprised, upon entering an altered state, to find that I had arrived back at my gazebo.

Meditation 8 April 2013: As we arrived in the rose garden with the white gazebo, where I had been many times before, I somehow felt that this place no longer suited me. I wanted a different meeting environment. I was instantly in a different place, which appeared to be a lookout point at the top of a tower which offered a view in all directions high above an endless forest. The roof of the tower rested on round grey pillars, in turn resting on a wall that was about waist high and encircled a stone floor. A guide soon joined me. I had not met him before. He wore a white robe and had longish, grey, curly hair. His name was Akaron. The scene changed, in the sense that the round tower room suddenly expanded into an additional round space. The top of the tower now represented a figure of eight. I moved from the original round room to the newly opened room where I found, instead of a stone floor like in the first room, a black and white chequered floor with large chess pieces standing around. The floor was circular and there was an ornamental pillar in the centre. It occurred to me that it would be hard to play chess on a round chess board with a pillar stuck in the centre, to which thought there was an instant response in my mind that the reason for this intricacy was that the game being played was the Game of Life, which was not supposed to be easy. It took me a moment to work out that this response came from the guide communicating with me telepathically. I moved further into the room to stand on one of the black squares. The black tile under my feet suddenly sank down through the floor to the bottom of the tower where I walked out onto a beach. A person came walking towards me along the beach. I recognised him as my primary soulmate. He had a sheep dog with him. I looked out over the ocean where a massive tsunami wave appeared, but something appeared to be holding it back. The man told me that he was the only thing that stood between me and the tsunami. I did not understand what he meant and suddenly I was surrounded by water up to my ankles. There was no sign of the tsunami anymore, but the water seemed to have flooded the beach and continued to rise until it had not only submerged the doorway of the tower where I had exited, but came level with the top of the tower. I now saw that the roof of the tower was in fact a rock. I rose with the water, which reached up to my waist and was pushed up to the level of the rock. I stepped onto the rock and from there onto another black and white chequered floor, which was covered with a thin film of water. I could see mountains in the distance and the sun was rising behind them. I turned back to see that the man and the dog were now both in a boat floating on the water, waiting by the rock. I continued to walk towards the light of the rising sun and reached the jagged edge of the chequered floor, which appeared to represent the border between my reality and what I somehow knew was the spirit world. There was what I can only describe as a consultation desk, where I sat down. Akaron, the guide whom I had met earlier in the tower, was sitting opposite me. I realised that this was my one opportunity to complain to the spirit world about the heaviness that I felt about being on earth and the terrible anger about it that I was trying to deal with. I explained to him that I was really angry, because I felt that this life had no purpose. It was impossible to live and to survive here without any purpose, without any joy and without any hope. I did not know the purpose of this life, but I did know that I had no hope and no dreams. I felt as if nothing that I really wanted would ever come into being. It was almost as if good things were not meant for me this time around and I did not have anything to keep me going, quite apart from the fact that I did not agree with what was happening on this planet, or the entire plan for our souls. The reality of having to grow through suffering seemed cruel.

Akaron said: "You have a problem. You are angry, because you do not have all the information, but we cannot get the information that you need to you, precisely because you are angry. The anger affects your vibration and prevents you from reaching up and it prevents us from reaching down to you. We will now lift the anger in order to help you, but you are required to do the work to reach up and download the information you need." Suddenly my primary soulmate was there. He was dressed in human clothes again, though not the same clothes he had been wearing on the beach. He had black, curly hair and blue eyes. It appeared that he and Akaron had decided that he and I should spend some time together. He took me out into a garden and we talked. He told me that everything would work out. I just had to hold on for a little while, as it was almost over.

After the meditation I felt a deep sadness that would extend into the rest of that day. Somehow I did not quite know how despondent I had been and how sad I had felt at being on this planet. Despite my primary soulmate's efforts to console me, I did not feel particularly comforted, but I knew that my opportunity had come and gone and that I had at least been heard. In the months to follow, I would come to know that my primary soulmate would always put in an appearance when the going got tough. There was no way that I would have been able to know the significance of the experience I had just had. I did not know that I had met my teacher guide Akaron. I would only fully comprehend the full symbolism of this meditation two years later, at the time of writing these pages. I had walked into a miracle, but it would be a while before I would be able to see it for what it was. What I would 'download' over the next two years, would forever change me in ways I could never have fathomed.

It was not easy to connect to an old emotion that I had tried so hard to suppress. Everyone around me seemed to love life and to think that life is a gift, regardless of whether they were happy or unhappy. I did not have that ability. I only saw the horrors people live through every day and could not find it in myself to be happy about the good things in my life when the world is filled with such ugliness. What did it matter that I had a loving family, food and a warm bed while a baby gets raped every few minutes? Other people's ability to look at the bright side enraged me. How is it possible to be happy in your own selfish little world and not be saddened by what goes on in the lives of innocent people? I felt that people were so in love with themselves that no one else's misery mattered to them. As long as their own lives were happy, life was beautiful. This is of course not the whole story, as there are people with miserable lives who still think that life is beautiful. I had eventually given up trying to understand why other people thought life was a wonderful gift, regardless of their circumstances. I only knew that I felt differently. There were those who would agree with me, but they were few and far between and, like me, they had learned to keep their views to themselves.

The reconnection to my sadness about humanity's plight, which had always been at the root of my anger, pushed away any immediate true understanding of what the session meant. I typed up what I recalled of the session immediately afterwards, but as I felt so deeply sad, I did not give it much thought until a few weeks later when I read the transcript of the session again. It always amazes me that I seem to forget the contents of even a significant meditation almost immediately. I was grateful for my habit of recording my sessions in detail without delay, while the memory is fresh in my mind. As I read the transcript, I suddenly realised that the deep, old and familiar anger was gone, and had been gone since the day of the session, as the guide had promised. The sadness that I experienced after that afternoon's meditation did not fade away and harden into anger the way it always had in the past. The anger simply did not return. In fact, in its place was a renewed interest in meditation and regression work with self-hypnosis. I was ready to download.

To this day, I have never again been able to get in touch with that anger. I used to feel it in my body, where I had tried to isolate it. Over the next two years after this meditation and the guide's promise, every aspect of my world would change in ways I could not have imagined. It was as if my soul had been released from prison and was finally free to grow. The journey was by no means easy or comfortable and growing, as always, remained painful. It involved loss, upheaval, stress, fear and a whole lot of worrying as my safe haven fell away and the foundation of my very existence was shaken by my own authentic decisions. I would come to understand where the anger had come from and that it was, in fact, an essential part of my journey.

I had chosen never to take my anger out on anyone, but it had reflected itself to me in the mirror of the unreasonable people who flooded my world. I am grateful that I was able to accept that truth when it was pointed out to me. I am even more grateful that I was given the tools and the guidance to tackle the issue head on. I had assistance throughout the process. After I had been freed of the anger, I was in time given all of the answers I could possibly require. I now know that this was nothing other than grace, because things usually work the other way around. In the normal scheme of things, I would have had to relinquish my anger before I would be given answers. Yet in this instance, I was assisted. The anger was lifted for me, before I was required to do any other work. With infinite wisdom my helpers must have understood that I would not have been able to let the anger go without their help. My logical mind would not have allowed that. I am eternally grateful that those who guide me appear to know me so well, that they knew what I truly needed to be free and that unconventional assistance would be required to extricate me from my prison.

The assistance I was given did, however, come with a responsibility on my part to reach up and to download the information I needed to stay free of the anger. Had I not continued meditating and making notes, reading as much as I could about every imaginable technique to reach for my soul, or had I decided to sink into the sadness I had felt at the end of my meditation that day, not bothering to type it all up, I would not have managed to put the anger behind me. I would not have been able to reach a space where I am not only able to choose to heal my life every day, but to want to make this choice. It would also have been impossible to share what I had learned in the hope that somewhere, someone in a dark place like the one I had been in, might be able to find enough hope in the pages of my story to help them turn in to find the wisdom that rests inside each of us.

And so it came that I was grateful for the difficult people in my practice. Their presence led to a revelation that I was, fortunately, guided to accept. It is amazing how much assistance we are given the minute we open up to receive it. From that first day in Eric's office, to the day when I entered into the meditation during which I met my teacher guide Akaron and my primary soulmate for the first time, I was guided to re-read a pile of old books, which inspired me to try old techniques afresh and to reach up once more. The moment I did so, someone was waiting to help. What changed me forever was the respect with which a truly negative emotion was handled. I was not reprimanded for being angry. My honest views were respected for their authenticity and the help I required was not withheld simply because I could not get my head around things.

One of the things that I would discover during the two years that followed this meditation, was that there is a little more to the notion that we create our own reality and that if we are ill, there is an underlying emotion or thought pattern that forms the root of the illness. In my case, these roots were fairly easy to find, but I soon discovered that they were underpinned by an attitude. When our attitudes are revealed to us, they can be very, very difficult to accept. And how do you change an attitude when you pretend not to see it? Our hidden attitudes are seldom nice testimonies to the kind of people we are and so we bury them deep within ourselves. And should we come across them again, we just arrange for a re-burial, leaving them free to poison us for as long as we choose to harbour them within.

In my case, although the anger appeared to be the root cause of many of my difficulties, it was in fact my attitude that had given rise to the anger. Digging deeper into this issue was easier to do after the anger had been lifted. The attitude that I found hidden in the depths of my mind, was that of a victim. Had the anger not been lifted, there would have been absolutely no way I would ever have discovered the hidden attitude lurking in the depths of my mind, as I was certain that I had put down that particular burden a long time ago when I first chose to take responsibility for my own life many years before and stopped acting like a victim. Our attitudes cannot be hidden. They are obvious to others and they show up in the world we create for ourselves. We are the only ones who have difficulty seeing our attitudes for what they are. They are very obvious to others. Sadly, even when we do become aware of our own attitudes, we quickly justify and rationalise them, and with that, all recognition of a possible path to healing is gone. That is why we have to make a choice on a daily basis: a choice to heal.

As it turned out, the recognition of my hidden attitude was going to be crucial to my survival over the next two years, as I would repeatedly have to adjust my thinking in order to find my way through turbulent times. No wonder my teacher guide thought it best to lift the anger that covered it. Without this, these pages would never have been written.

CHAPTER 4: Self-hypnosis Regression - 13 April 2013

Although I had not yet worked out that my anger had gone, I felt chirpier over the days following my meditation. I was so used to suppressing and isolating the anger that I seldom thought of it and my good mood was not really out of the ordinary. I energetically continued reading my pile of old self-help books and kept finding little gems of information that renewed my interest in especially the physical benefits of trance work.

A friend of mine invited me over for a casual birthday dinner one evening. It took the form of a good old South African *braai*, or barbecue. *Boerewors* sausages were already sizzling on the grill by the time we arrived. As her guests were making themselves comfortable, my friend emerged from the kitchen with a small mountain of soft, white bread rolls, ready to be piled high with the hot sausages and our choice of the fillings she had prepared.

I had been battling with food allergies since roughly the age of forty five and these had been getting worse over time. After having had myself tested, I had discovered a year or so before that I was, let us say sensitive to wheat products. Eating white bread would result in my nose starting to itch within minutes. I gradually developed sensitivities to other things as well, like white wine and yellow cheese. More and more foods started affecting me and I was at my wits' end by the time I attended the birthday *braai*.

I have never liked offending people when it comes to food preferences and so, on the evening of 6 April 2013, I did what I always do. I thoroughly enjoyed the meal, as I knew that I could simply take an anti-histamine tablet to deal with the effects of consuming the delicious, fresh bread roll. This time, however, the anti-histamine tablet had no effect. By the time I got home a couple of hours later, I was sneezing violently. I know how this sounds and I readily admit to being a bit of a drama queen at times, but there really is no other way to describe the almost convulsive sneezing fit I had. I barely had time to breathe in between. Mercifully, the sneezing fit eventually passed, as it always did, but my plan was clearly no longer working.

The following weekend, my sinus cavities still felt quite sensitive after the ordeal of the previous Saturday. During the week I happened to read one of my favourite books on past life regressions that resulted in the healing of physical ailments in certain patients, so when I once again woke up with my head feeling as if it had been stuffed with wool, I decided that this was as good a time as any to attempt a self-hypnosis session, regressing myself to see if I could find the answer as to why wheat products were tormenting me so much. I was forty nine years old and after four years of battling allergies that had appeared out of nowhere, I had had enough and was ready to try anything. It was a lazy Saturday and the thought of finding a regression therapist to help me, did not even enter my mind. I was in the mood to play around with my latest interest and was not about to wait for an appointment with someone who could facilitate a regression.

I did not use any form of assistance to guide me into trance. Given the focus that it takes to not only enter into trance through self-hypnosis, but to then guide the regression oneself, the regressions I do for myself tend not to be overly detailed. I seem to be able to hold on to what I see for long enough to register the impression and the intuitive knowledge of what is happening, but I am not able to explore the scenes in greater detail, as one is able to do in facilitated regression sessions while working with a therapist.

Given that I was feeling desperate, but also curious about and interested in the phenomenon of healing through exploring past life memories, I did not take any of this too seriously and went into trance with no real expectations. Basically, I was playing a bit. What did I have to lose?

Self-hypnosis regression 13 April 2013: I was a forty five year old Franciscan monk in Spain in the year 1413. The name 'Barbao', or something similar, was repeating in my mind. I could not make it out clearly. I was not sure if this was my name or the name of a place. I lived in a small harbour town in the north of Spain. I was agitated and was on my knees, praying in a church with lead glass windows. I had a small bag made of rough cloth hanging over my shoulder, containing all my worldly possessions. I left the church after finishing my prayer and then walked out of the town, making sure that no one saw me. I was going into hiding. I was running from someone and it had something to do with the fighting between the Moors and the Basques. I found a hiding place in a deserted barn, adjacent to a mill, somewhere in the countryside. Wheat from the fields had been stored in the mill and the barn, but there was no one around. I stayed there for five days before the soldiers eventually found me. [*I could not determine whether they were Basques or Moors and could not focus on their faces. I also could not* *determine why they were looking for me.*] They dragged me outside before they burnt down the barn and the mill, along with the wheat. While the wheat was burning, I was tied to a wooden cross with coarse ropes. The soldiers then all aimed their arrows at me, killing me with a number of arrows shot into my heart.

Ever the scientist at heart, I grabbed my cell phone when I came out of trance to record what I could remember. The next step was to ask Google what it knew about some of the details I managed to remember about the area and the name. To my utter astonishment I found the following reference: *'Bilbao is one of the twenty five boroughs in the Greater Bilbao comarca in northern Spain. It is also the capital of the province of Biscay in the autonomous community of the Basque Country.'*

The name Bilbao was very similar to the one I vaguely heard in my mind during my regression. The information is often more 'imprinted' or 'understood' than actually heard. It feels almost like telepathic communication. The thing is, before my regression the sum total of my knowledge about Spain and its history was that there had once been wars between the Moors and the Basques. That is it. I certainly had no idea which harbour towns were situated in the north of Spain and had never heard of the Basque Country or where it was situated within Spain, let alone anything about the Franciscan Order.

According to Google, the Franciscan Order had indeed been active in that region of Spain during the relevant period I visited in my regression. The Moors and the Basques had also been fighting in the north of Spain for many years, including during the period of the monk's life I had visited.

Once again, after adding the interesting bits of information regarding Spain to my record of the regression, I forgot about it. Just as I had done five days earlier after my visit to my teacher guide in the spirit world. Life carries on and my busy law practice did not leave much time to ponder the weird and wonderful.

Perhaps I should mention that I have little interest in proving that past lives exist. I am and have always been a healthy sceptic, but one who nevertheless does believe in all kinds of wonderful possibilities. Too many times in our history have we believed that we knew it all, only later to be proved to have been limited in our thinking. However, trying to prove that these lives are real takes the focus away from what really interests me, namely the effect of these past life regressions on our bodies.

A few days later, on 18 April 2013, the very same friend whose birthday I had attended, invited me over to her home again. And ... there they were. Fluffy, fresh white bread rolls. I hasten to say that I have had many, many meals with this friend and none of these meals, before or since, ever included white bread rolls. Yet on these two occasions, twelve days apart, they seemed to form part of some synchronistic plan to help me along my journey. Imagine that!

And again, I ate them, expecting the worst and deciding that this time I would simply take two anti-histamine tablets subsequently. I had not touched any wheat products since the birthday *braai* and so I had no way of knowing whether the regression had had any effect on my condition. In any event, the Franciscan monk had already been all but forgotten. I was hesitant at first to acknowledge that the bread rolls had no effect on me that evening, yet I went home without having needed to take an anti-histamine tablet. By the next morning, I could barely contain my excitement. I woke up without a blocked nose and my throat did not feel like someone had dripped acid into my nostrils while I had been asleep. It was time to test the apparent miracle. And I kept testing for weeks after the event. It was clear that I was no longer sensitive to wheat products. At the time of writing these pages, almost two years to the day have passed and the sensitivity has never returned. In fact, I used to be similarly, but far less severely, sensitive to yellow cheese and white wine before the regression. Although I still have a minor sensitivity to only certain white wines, eating yellow cheese and drinking most wines no longer have any effect on me. The only exception is *quiche*. No matter who prepares it, *quiche* makes my nose itch. Here and there I will encounter something in a restaurant that causes me a little discomfort, but in general, I can eat whatever I want to.

As you can imagine, it does not matter to me whether I have ever lived as a Franciscan monk in northern Spain. What matters is that I have a huge chunk of normality back in my life and that, as a human being, I shall never be the same again.

If there is one thing that I always felt to be missing from our world, it is magic. This is probably why I love J K Rowling's *Harry Potter* books and movies and never missed an episode of the television series *Once Upon a Time*. I am a realist and to me 'happily ever afters' have always been a myth that does no one any good, but I am a complete sucker for a happy ending which involves relief from pain and suffering. To me, that is magic. If I had a magic wand, I would use it to give myself wings and then I would fly around finding pain and suffering in the dark corners of the world, waving it all away into oblivion and replacing it with health and laughter with a second wave of my magic wand, while pretending that I was not interfering.

And now I was beginning to feel like I had been given a magic wand, early edition admittedly, which is probably why it had been modestly packaged in the form of two white bread rolls. I started thinking about what else in my life I would like to disappear magically.

CHAPTER 5: Facilitated Regression - 26 May 2013

Once I got over the excitement of being rid of my sensitivity to wheat, I suddenly remembered the meditation I had done a few days before the self-regression that introduced me to the Franciscan monk. I read the transcript of the meeting with my teacher guide again. Where was my anger? For the second time in less than a month, I felt something stir inside me. It was hope, I think. I slowly but surely went through that particular day, waiting to reconnect with the anger and the dark thoughts that justified its existence. No connection was possible. In the same way that my problematic internet connection sometimes maintains that it cannot connect to the server, I simply could not connect to the source of my anger. I even tried explaining to myself why I used to be angry. I could still follow my logical reasoning that had before made it impossible for me to let go of the anger, but I simply could no longer feel it.

It was time to take my meditation and regression work seriously. I had managed to get rid of two enormous burdens in less than a month. What else was possible? After talking to a friend, who had training in hypnosis and who was more than familiar with regression work, I decided to tackle another issue I had been wondering about, this time with the help of my friend who would be facilitating the regression. I felt that the particular issue might need more detailed exploration than what I would be able to do while in a self-induced trance. I also thought that some work might be necessary to address the issues arising in the past life and that I was not yet skilled enough to do this on my own while holding trance.

Dr Newton, author of *Destiny of Souls* and *Journey of Souls*, in discussing altered states of consciousness in his book *Life between Lives Hypnotherapy for Spiritual Regression*, explains the usefulness of the various altered states. The Beta state is the fully awake conscious state. The Alpha states involve light, medium and deeper trance levels, with the lighter stages typically used for meditation. The medium stages are generally associated with recovering childhood memories and past trauma and are useful for behaviour modification, such as to quit smoking and to lose weight. The deeper Alpha states involve past life recovery. The Theta state is as deep as we can go before losing consciousness. According to Dr Newton, it uncovers the area of the superconscious mind that reveals our spiritual life between lives activity. Dr Newton explains that questioning by a facilitator stimulates the regression subject's power to reason, since both the conscious and unconscious minds are engaged.[1] I presume that this is the reason why I have been able to do self-regressions, but as stated above, what can be achieved in such a session is limited and facilitation just makes things a whole lot easier. Playtime was over and I now wanted to do some serious work.

I have had an interesting life. Without including any of the boring details, let us just say that I have had to start over a number of times. I have come to view these experiences as periods of enormous growth and I am certainly not complaining, but there comes a point when one simply has less energy to start over than one had, say, twenty five years earlier. There was also the reality that very often the necessity to start over had either been caused or helped

[1] Michael Newton Ph.D., *Life between Lives Hypnotherapy for Spiritual Regression*. (Llewellyn Publications, 2004), pp 19 and 24.

along by something that appeared to be out of my control, like the decisions other people made, for example, the decision to retrench me as an employee at a time when I was in the middle of my final examinations during the second last year of my studies towards my LL.B law degree. Then there was the time when I was forced to share an office with three chain smokers before the use of tobacco was regulated in South Africa. The result was that I had to have a sinus operation, this time in the middle of my final examinations in my final year of studying towards my law degree. And so there were countless episodes in my life that literally ripped apart my plans and depleted my resources, leaving me with nothing other than my strength and determination. I was fortunate to have loving friends and family who assisted me through these tough times. The problem was that having to start over was a pattern in my life.

At this particular point in my life, I was having grave difficulties in getting people to pay my accounts. I would put my heart and soul into a client's case, ostensibly under cover of a deposit taken by the briefing attorney to cover my fees. Unfortunately, many times over the attorneys who briefed me as counsel quite simply lied to me about having taken a deposit or the ability of the client to pay my fees in the end. I had just received a call from an attorney about a client who had passed away leaving my fees unpaid. The attorney had little difficulty in simply pretending that he had never told me that he had my fees covered. And for that particular month, it was the third disaster of this nature. Essentially, I had lost two full months of income, a tall order for anyone. In this way, quite apart from the many hours of *pro bono* work I had done over the years as a practising advocate, I had to write off hundreds of thousands of Rand in circumstances where I was, I believed, powerless to prevent this.

I had managed to attract these things into my reality. As I have stated before, I had, or at least thought I had, ditched the victim attitude a long time ago and I do not think anyone gets very far by pretending that things are 'being done to them' or that things are 'happening to them', without them having any control over such events. Things happen. And then we choose how to resolve them.

I was happy to take responsibility for creating these circumstances on some level, but I was getting tired of the particular pattern. I no longer wanted to fall down and then have to get up to start over. I try not to compare my life to the lives of other people, but it is hard not to notice that I have lived in sixteen different homes since leaving school thirty two years ago. As much as this gave me a wonderful opportunity to grow and learn, it was exhausting. I was beginning to feel that I somehow never really got to build a life for myself. Just when things appeared to be going well, some event that was apparently out of my control would start a chain reaction in my life that would rip everything apart like an unstoppable train crashing into suburbia. Each time I recovered and few people would even notice the hardships that I went through in the process, but it would be nice to settle down and to stay in one place for a little while.

It is against this background that my friend facilitated a regression session for me, using hypnosis to tackle the question as to why I never really got onto my feet financially and why, just when I was almost at the point where I could relax and just live, I would lose almost everything. I had recently been through a divorce, preceded by an extremely traumatic period which almost ruined my practice. I managed to claw my way back to health and was able to buy and furnish a new home, a home which, thanks to some of my briefing attorneys and clients, I was now struggling to hang on to. I was feeling that very familiar sense of powerlessness as I watched my life fall apart – again. I always had the strength to start over, but I never had the strength to stop it from falling apart in the first place. Something was not quite right.

Facilitated regression 26 May 2013: I was a young initiate priestess in a desert country somewhere in the region we know today as the Middle East. I had been busy with my training when I was asked to perform an animal sacrifice. I refused to perform the sacrifice and as a result, I was branded a failure and was banished from the temple and my homeland. I was sent away with a horse, some food and a flask of water. I would never be allowed to return home.

I was wearing a white dress and had an amulet around my neck. I am not sure why my robes and the amulet had not been taken from me. They were my only worldly possessions and were a small reminder of the life I used to have. After travelling a very long way, I arrived at a small rural village. I had green eyes and given the way I was dressed, in my misery still hanging on to my white dress and my amulet, the villagers thought that I was involved with something unholy and chased me away. I was too tired to continue travelling and just wanted to settle somewhere, even if only long enough to rest. I managed to find a cave in the hills above the village and moved in there. The villagers discovered this and they were enraged. They were too scared to come near me and so they set fire to the grass at the foot of the hill below my cave. The plan was to force me to flee before the fire in the hope that I would leave permanently. But the wind changed direction and instead of the fire driving me from the cave, their entire village was destroyed. The villagers lost everything. I stood on the hill watching and I felt that the villagers deserved what had happened to them. It was the price they had to pay for their prejudice. The villagers who survived the fire came to the conclusion that I did indeed have supernatural powers and believed that I was able to change the direction of the wind, causing their village to be destroyed. This belief made them even more fearful of me. Despite my initial reaction in thinking that they had got what they deserved, I felt deeply guilty, as I knew that it was my arrival that ultimately caused them to lose everything. Had I not arrived, they would not have started the fire and their village would have survived. I was the one who did not belong and I brought this on them, no matter how unfair they had been to me.

My friend facilitated a process whereby I could change what happened in that memory and in so doing heal the karmic pattern that was repeating in my world in various forms. We enlisted the help of my guide. *[This guide was not my teacher guide, Akaron. He was one I had 'met' a few of years earlier when I read a book on channelling using a technique described in the book on how to meet one's guide.]* He helped me to see that I should have tried to blend in a little more. I should have tried to wear clothes that resembled those of the villagers. Instead, I had clung to my foreign identity, because that was all I had left of my old life. To repair the energetic imprint of those events, my guide assisted me in calling together all the souls who had inhabited that little town. I gave them my version of events and explained who I had been and how I had ended up in their village. The villagers said that they now understood. They accepted that their own prejudice had caused them to want to get rid of me, instead of helping me and welcoming me. This did not work out well for them. They realised that I had in fact been totally innocent, except for the fact that I could have made more of an effort to blend in, in order to make it easier for them to overcome their prejudice.

The next step was for me to release my feelings of guilt. I helped the villagers to build new homes. They helped to build a home for me and they made some clothes for me that looked like theirs. I in turn used the small shells I had collected in my cave to make them each an amulet and I gave them some seeds that I had brought from my homeland, which they planted. After this, they experienced prosperity.

The process of making peace was symbolic and was done for purposes of removing the negative imprint that resulted in the pattern that repeated endlessly in my current life.

I asked my guide whether the resolution of the issues of that past life was sufficient to break the pattern. It was not. I entered yet another life. I was an Eskimo and entered the life at a stage where I was on a sled that was being pulled by a team of dogs through the icy landscape of Alaska. One of my hands was bleeding, apparently from a knife wound. I had been involved in a fight over fish in a small town the night before. I made a living from catching and selling fish, but strangers had entered our world, trying to take over the local market, resulting in the fight. I left town after I was wounded in the fight, but the strangers followed me. A snowstorm was brewing and I thought that I had managed to escape and leave them behind, but I fell into a fissure in the snow that I had failed to see in the haste of my flight. The sled was shattered, my leg was broken and one of my dogs died.

I cut the remaining dogs in my team loose and set them free. They managed to find their way out of the deep crevasse in the snow. I tried to crawl out, but only managed to get back to the surface after one of the dogs turned back to try to help me. When I finally pulled myself out, the dogs were all still there waiting for me.   Unfortunately, my pursuers had seen the agitated, waiting dogs and they were also waiting for me. They laughed, took my dogs and just left me there. I lost everything I had ever owned, my sled and my dogs.

My guide helped me to see that I had died there feeling utterly powerless and filled with despair, unable to change the course of events.   As I died, I felt that something bigger than me had decided that I would lose everything.   I recognised the feeling, having experienced it over and over in my current life, when everything around me would come tumbling down due to circumstances that were not of my making and when I had done nothing to deserve such an outcome. Where I in my life with the villagers had caused them to lose everything by simply entering their world innocently, even if their own prejudice ultimately caused the destruction of their homes, it was my turn to lose everything in my life as an Eskimo, although I did not know it at the time of my death.

To release the imprint of the life as an Eskimo, the powerlessness I had felt when I was dying in the snow, was given a form. It stood in front of me like a massive demolition ball made of lead, which was ready to roll over me.   I visualised the ball being filled with white light, which broke up the lead.   My guide and I then pushed the ball down a hill and as it rolled down the slope, it broke into pieces, scattering the lead in all directions.

My guide explained that I would never again have to lose everything and that I have nothing to feel guilty about.

In the life as a foreign priestess I had caused others to lose everything they had, even though it was due to their own prejudice. My guilt, caused by the fact that I understood that if I had never come to their land, everything would have remained unchanged for them, left an imprint that carried over to my life as an Eskimo. In that life, the roles were exactly reversed in that foreigners had come to my land and tried to take over the local fishing industry which had been my only source of income. I lost everything in circumstances where I had displayed no prejudice of my own, as I was the one who was attacked. I did not realise in that life that I was merely restoring the karmic balance which had been carried over from another life and so at the time of my death, I felt powerless because of the unfairness that caused me to lose everything. Feeling like this, I died of exposure, causing an imprint of its own which carried over to my current life in which I had been repeating the pattern of losing everything I have, in circumstances that seldom appeared to be of my own making (economic downturn, retrenchment, sickness, difficult marriage, etc.), feeling utterly powerless to prevent disaster.

It is all too easy to miss what is happening in our lives. The disasters in my life always came dressed up in masks, making it appear to me as if my misfortune had been caused by people 'doing something to me' or by things that were 'happening to me'. Yet the reality is that it is much more likely that the imprints my soul carried into this world for resolution in this life, were then and are now drawing events to me, constantly alerting me to patterns that I need to break.

Something else that I realised after this session was that in my current life, as an adult, I have managed to blend in everywhere I went. As a child, I had great difficulty in blending in with certain groups. Mostly, I felt a thousand years older than all the other children and felt as if I was carrying a very heavy, very old burden. It was like a dark knowledge, just there on the edge of my consciousness. I could not explain it and I could not put the burden down. In time though, I came to understand the path my life had taken and why. This session helped me to recognise that I had somehow learned to use my 'different side' for the benefit of others and ultimately for myself, without upsetting everyone else as I became much more able to blend in. Perhaps some ancient wisdom from that long ago life has filtered through to help me find my way.

A couple of weeks down the line, I started noticing that I no longer felt as cold as I used to do. I was always cold, no matter what the season. We reached mid-winter four weeks after this session, but I had not yet pulled out my winter blankets and had not once switched on my heater or my electric blanket. Normally, these cosy comforts were switched on in my home almost all the time during the winter months. A few weeks later, I went for a regression session with another regression therapist who mentioned to me that, after releasing an imprint of a previous life where she had frozen to death, she stopped feeling cold all the time. I had not mentioned my life as an Eskimo to her, but when I drove home that evening after the session I had with her, I remembered that in my life as an Eskimo I had been left to die of exposure in the icy landscape of Alaska. I could not help wondering whether releasing the imprint of my life as an Eskimo approximately a month earlier could, as was the case with the regression therapist who had frozen to death in another life, explain why I no longer felt so cold.

The reason why I had tackled this session in the first place was that I was trying to avert another crisis in my life, due to people not paying my fees on time. Over the months that followed the regression, I received work from new and more reliable attorneys, who were more responsible about things like paying counsel's fees. I also finally managed to get payment from some of the attorneys who had previously failed to pay my bills. All in all, things were looking up and I felt that I had somehow averted disaster.

I did not know it at the time, but the next time I would face difficult times, it would not be due to events that were ostensibly out of my control, but would be due to circumstances of my own and very deliberate creation. Eighteen months later, at a time when my legal practice was very successful and busy and my attorneys were paying my bills on time, I would change careers and would go through a very difficult period, because I would choose to follow my soul path and put down a burden that I no longer wished to carry. The imprints from the lives of the initiate priestess and the Eskimo no longer dictated what was happening in my world. Though the usual stragglers of non-payers did make their selfish contribution to the difficulties I encountered during the changeover in my career by paying many, many months late, and in one case not paying at all, they did not force the decision. In fact, despite their unscrupulous practices, my practice was flourishing at the time I closed its doors.

CHAPTER 6: Self-hypnosis Regression - 1 June 2013

It seems to me that there are two types of people: those who have long relationships that are apparently happy and those who have a series of relationships that appear to be less so. This is of course a gross generalisation, but this rough and very general distinction is helpful when one observes one's own relationship pattern. I have long ago stopped concerning myself with the contribution that the other person in a relationship I am in makes and how that person contributes to the end of the relationship. It just takes too much energy to worry about what is happening in another person's mind. I see myself as the only common denominator in all my relationships, so in analysing them, the best starting point is with me and what I contribute to each relationship dynamic.

I do not want to create the impression that the fact that some people have a series of relationships, as opposed to having one stable relationship, means that they are somehow at fault or too messed up to have a good relationship. Each and every person is different. There is a myriad of reasons why a person would end up in either of my admittedly general categories.

Basically, whichever category one finds oneself in, neither is necessarily always a comfortable place. I truly believe that the purpose of all relationships is for us to learn about ourselves. The category does not matter, only the journey. So when I decided to explore the issue of my less than happy relationships, I was very much aware that each relationship had been followed by a period of extraordinary growth during which I processed what had happened. I am eternally grateful that I have always taken the time to dissect things, to grieve properly and then to put the past behind me. I never just swept it all under the rug and jumped into the next relationship opportunity that presented itself. I understand that many other people can easily, and apparently with success, move from one relationship to the next fairly quickly, if not immediately, but to me personally a pattern like that would have been utterly destructive, merely because of the type of person that I am. There would have been no time to learn anything while bouncing around between the highs and lows, which I would certainly also not have been strong enough to cope with. Entering a new relationship in order to avoid feeling the low of a relationship that has ended, or to get back at the person who has hurt you, can also sometimes be a recipe for disaster, as I had learned from the facts of cases I handled over the years in my legal practice.

As I was now intrigued about the variety of things that I was able to explore on my journey, I decided to explore my apparent inability to sustain relationships. I was aware of an underlying belief that I was not lovable. Objectively speaking, this was nonsense, but that did not change the fact that whenever I gave the issue some thought and closed my eyes, I could literally feel the block in my gut. It was as if I had swallowed a steel rod that went right through my being. If I pushed myself and tried to argue reasonably that I was perfectly normal and not much different from others, something bubbled up, causing discomfort in my body and angrily screaming in my head that I was just not good enough to be loved. I felt a deep and inexplicable sense of shame for even thinking that someone might possibly find me attractive.

This I had to work on, because as happy as I was in my independent life, I was not happy with the emotions stuck in my cells and I was not about to get sick because a trapped emotion had not been released from my energy body. Little did I know that I was about to open a can of worms. I would need two years to get to the bottom of my relationship woes and they would not relate to any relationship I had had in my current life.

Self-hypnosis regression 1 June 2013: The entry was difficult and I felt agitated. I had to keep calming myself in order to stay focused. As always before regressing, I had asked for appropriate protection, especially as I was working alone and had no one to facilitate the session. Though the communication imprints were clear, I only saw flashes in quick succession and at times I struggled to hold on to the images. I suspect that this was due to the violence involved.

Upon entering a bamboo forest in Japan, I initially had difficulty determining which role I was playing in the scene as I could only sense fear and saw flashes of movement and people. There were Samurai all around. One of the Samurai was female. She wore no headgear, staring directly into my face. I had the impression that she wanted me to see her face. The name 'Wakachan' echoed in my mind. It was the year 1711. I was a young woman of oriental descent, but not Japanese. The female Samurai was extremely aggressive. I was tied up against the bamboo with my hands above my head. I do not know what was eventually done to me, because I was watching from behind and only saw my head and body shaking violently as the blows fell. The other Samurai were standing around watching, in full gear, while the woman with the exposed face continued her violent assault until I was dead – she wanted me to know who was killing me. Long after everyone had left the scene, another Samurai came along and removed and buried my body, leaving the grave marked by his own Samurai headgear. He was the brother of the female Samurai who had killed me. I think they were twins. I scanned back over that life before the death scene to find out who he was. I saw an older man, apparently someone whom the Samurai who had buried me respected greatly (it could have been the particular lord he served as Samurai or a leader of the Samurai). He spoke sternly to the Samurai. I was agitated through the whole session and could not focus enough to hear the conversation, but I knew that it related to me.

I moved further back to an earlier time in that life to see why I had been killed. The female Samurai had asked me to stay away from her brother, the Samurai who had eventually buried me, because I was 'not right' for him and I think the older man had told him the same thing. When we did not listen to them, I was taken and killed. I was too emotional to continue with the session and ended the process without getting much more detail, or even being able to do any healing work on the energy imprint.

Nine days later I returned to this life in another self-hypnosis session and cut the karmic link between me and the soul of the female Samurai. I told her that I regarded the imbalance she had caused in that life and which she again perpetrated against me in my current life, although fortunately to a much lesser extent, as balanced out and forgiven, as long as she stayed away from me. I do not wish to expose myself to this soul ever again.

Google revealed that the Samurai of Japan were active for many hundreds of years and that 1711 was about one hundred and fifty years before their modernisation. Wakachan is a female nickname in Japanese. I did not know any of these things. I knew little more than that the Samurai had existed. I found these details interesting, as it might explain why the sight of a Samurai in a movie had always stirred a strange reaction in me. I feel connected to them somehow.

I recognised the soul who, as Wakachan, ended my life in the past life we shared in Japan. Unfortunately, I cannot share the details of that same soul's involvement in my present life in these pages and I can only continue to tell my story if I disguise the current identity of not only that soul, but also the identity of two other souls. At the time of this regression, I did not realise that these three souls would continue to come up during my journey and as much as I would dearly have loved simply to omit all references to these individuals, their involvement in my current life, as well as in a few of my past lives, formed part of a pattern that I would only fully understand and resolve almost two years later.

For the sake of these three individuals, and for my own, I shall refer to them collectively as The Triad. Where I refer to them as individuals, I shall refer to The Bishop, The Pawn and The Rook. I shall also refrain from disclosing the true gender of these three people in their current lives. The intention is to share my soul's story, not to denigrate people who are still alive today. However, it would make it cumbersome to relay events without being able to assign any gender to these three people, so I will refer to them all as male.

In the game of chess the pawn is a piece on the frontline of the game. It is interesting that in respect of my soul's journey, The Pawn was also the first to make an entry as Wakachan, the female Samurai.

Four days after this session, I left my office to go and see a colleague in another building up the road. As I stepped outside, I saw a woman walking towards me. I recognised her immediately. Over two decades ago, this woman had been a good friend of The Pawn and I knew her well. But something happened to me at the hands of The Triad that required me to remove myself from their space and the woman walking towards me that day in the street was one of the people who were left behind in that space and who never learned the truth of those events.

After my departure, I was out of the way and therefore not in a position to stand up for myself and so The Pawn was free to tell The Triad's version of events. I shall not repeat the details of the slanderous explanation that had apparently been given to those who stayed behind in my former life, firstly because what had been conveyed to me is hearsay and secondly, because it is irrelevant. It would also disclose the identity of The Triad. I never saw most of the people I had previously known in the space I shared with The Triad and I must admit that I sometimes felt sad that I had never been able to set the record straight. Hopefully, given that they all knew me and also knew The Pawn, they would have been able to come to a few conclusions of their own. Nevertheless, I never had the chance to tell my side of the story.

So when I stepped out into the street that day and saw the woman I had known coming my way, I at first merely walked past her, as she had clearly not recognised me. I remember also having seen her in a shopping mall about ten years earlier, at which point she also had not recognised or even seen me. But as I walked past her this time, I heard a voice in my mind saying: 'This is your one chance to set the record straight. Go now!' And so I left the poor attorney who was with me at the time, standing on the sidewalk while I ran back towards my past. The woman was looking worried and had clearly just left the advocates' chambers where I was also practising. I introduced myself to her and she immediately knew exactly who I was, saying that someone had told her recently that I was living somewhere in Cape Town. It seemed that after all these years those I had left behind were still talking about me. I told her that I had been living in Cape Town for fourteen years at the time, practising as an advocate. I could see her slowly digesting this information. Clearly, someone wearing the label that The Bishop had put around my neck, which The Rook had so readily accepted and which The Pawn had made sure the world knew about, would not have been able to become an advocate. I felt sure that the news would eventually filter back to all those who used to know me. Somehow, I felt vindicated. It was as if my release during the regression had created an opportunity for me to at least set the record straight to a small extent.

If I have to make a list of all the things I am grateful for in my life, my profound gratitude at having been spared a life lived in the space of The Triad, would be right at the top.

The universe never intended for me to continue living my life around The Triad. The only purpose of our involvement had been to give me a chance to balance a karmic distortion; I just did not know it at the time. It would be more than two decades before I would find the answer as to why three people had been allowed to get away with their vicious actions in my current life.

CHAPTER 7: Self-hypnosis Regression - 10 June 2013

Although the session revealing my past links with The Pawn was powerful and resulted in an interesting opportunity to communicate something to someone I had known years ago, I felt no shift in my self-perception, because the judgments of The Triad had been totally irrelevant to me for many, many years. Their judgment of me does not define me; it defines them, as it did all those years ago.

I decided that perhaps this old injury had to come up so that my link with The Pawn could be resolved before I could delve deeper into the true cause of my less than desirable self-perception. This conclusion made sense to me, because what I had unearthed about my link to The Pawn, was an old pattern between us. It was not something that really had much to do with my relationships *per se* and so clearing our history was just that; clearing an old karmic imbalance between the two of us. The issue remained the same. I could not believe that anyone could possibly love me – in the romantic sense that is. The relationships I had drawn into my life up to that point, were less than desirable. People do not come into our lives to fix us or our beliefs; they come into our lives because of our beliefs. If our beliefs do not serve us, or if we are injured, those beliefs and injuries will draw people to us who will give us the often very painful experiences that are needed to expose the belief or injury to us, so that we can see it and choose to heal it. Or not.

And so I decided to repeat the process and see what would surface next regarding my relationship life. This process would take many sessions and many shifts in my world before I would eventually be in the right space to unearth the answer I was looking for. Fortunately, I did not know that at the time otherwise I might have become despondent. What surfaced next might appear to be unrelated to the issue of relationships, but it certainly formed part of the jigsaw puzzle.

Self-hypnosis regression 10 June 2013: Upon entering the life, I had the sense that I was the daughter of someone important. From what I observed (as I chose not to enter the body but just to watch from the outside) my clothing and my home resembled that of aristocrats around the time of the French Revolution. Although I during the session sensed that the year was 1814, I did not know my name or my age in that life, or even in which country I was living, never mind the year.

I saw myself staring blankly into nothing.   I was overweight and had dull brown curly hair and brown eyes.   I was clearly not of sound mind and was apparently nothing more than a big baby, all dressed up according to my station in life, but I doubt that I often left my room.

A chamber maid was looking after me and she was talking to some of the other servants who were busy cleaning the room. She complained to them that 'We cannot even marry her off as no one could possibly be attracted to her!' I recognised the chamber maid as the soul of a former friend in my current life.

The lesson in that life was that sometimes it is okay just to be.

Google confirmed that the French Revolution in France occurred between 1787 and 1799. I had probably learned these dates in school, but would not have been able to remember them consciously if anyone asked me today when the revolution had taken place. The girl I was in that life also did not know her name or her age, so I presume that the impression of the date was received from an 'all-knowing state' of awareness when one revisits these past lives.

In my current life, I had at some point 'looked after' my former friend, the French chamber maid in my past life, at a time when she did not have a place to stay and had just started working in the city that I lived in. She stayed in my home free of charge for a period of about ten months until she could get onto her feet. We were really good friends, or so I thought.

All my friends and family were aware of my inability to believe that anyone could find me attractive, much to the astonishment of many of them, simply because I am no different to any other ordinary person who is perfectly capable of finding a partner. My friend also knew about it. Unlike my other friends, though, she often made cruel and unnecessary comments about me and, in general, made me feel big and ugly.

Over the last months of our friendship, I had to speak to her twice about her habit of making unnecessarily mean comments, warning her that I could not continue in a friendship where her sharp tongue continually caused me pain. So, when she insulted me quite directly for a third time, I summarily ended the friendship. Given how she had lived her own life and her selfish actions while she was staying with me when she was dictating how I should run my own home, I had just had enough.

Ending a friendship in this way was out of character for me, but I think that from my side I had finally balanced the karmic scales by looking after her in this life, just as she had looked after me in the life we shared in France. In turn, she had a chance not to repeat the pattern of cruel words and to resolve the karmic issues which had been created between us as a result, yet she chose to continue the pattern. I believe that her utterance in that life so long ago may have contributed to the fact that I spent most of my current adult life alone, on some level believing myself incapable of creating a good relationship, because I believed myself to be unattractive and, as such, I was treated as being unattractive. Instead of releasing that old pattern and balancing the scales with kindness, my friend had continued to create an imbalance in this life. She had still not learned to curb her tongue. I reacted by ending the friendship, so that this time she was the one who was not 'good enough'. In so doing, I probably unwittingly set right the imbalance that she had perpetuated with her words. Hopefully, the dynamic between us is now in balance. Things need not have ended this way. We do not always have to address karmic imbalances by experiencing what we did to others. I truly believe that we can address such imbalances by changing our behaviour towards someone we have hurt before in other lives. We can choose not to do it again, but if we choose to repeat the pattern of hurting another, then the imbalance may have to be addressed by experiencing what we perpetrated against another.

Interestingly, while we were friends, a psychic once told my friend that she and I had been close in a previous life – one had been a servant and the other the mistress. Clearly, this was correct. I only remembered this after the session.

The lesson of being okay with an existence where one can just be, has come in handy in my current life. I had to be okay just to be, and to be just me, no matter what anyone else thought of me. And I was. I still am.

CHAPTER 8: Facilitated Regression - 19 June 2013

I do have a tendency to get bored with things quickly and I was now tired of exploring the relationship line. I had no wish to enter into a relationship ever again and to be honest, the two lives that had come up brought up less than pleasant memories. I had initially been curious about my inability to sustain relationships. Now I wanted to move on to more tangible things and, for the moment, I was in no mood to continue the exploration of my complex relationship issues. It was no fun, after all. There were more important matters to explore, all of which certainly had more relevance in my life.

I had been having difficulties with my throat and my neck for a while and now I happily directed my attention to a more measurable issue to work on. I developed throat infections constantly and sometimes these would be so severe that I would lose my voice for a few days. This somewhat hampered me, given that I was earning a living as a litigation lawyer. It became especially uncomfortable when I had to argue an opposed matter in court and I found myself without a voice. On more than one occasion I had to squeak my way through a discussion in the magistrate's office, or try to conduct settlement negotiations with an aggressive opponent in a whisper.

At some point I wondered whether the daily stress I had been experiencing at work could have triggered these infections, but that made no sense, as I had been practising for over a decade without any trouble. It would be many months later that I would eventually work out that at some point the scales had started to tip. My vibration was lifting and my body was no longer happy to be subjected to the negative energies of the legal profession.

And it was making itself heard. The fact that I was having difficulties balancing the negative impact of the profession on my body, does not mean that those who are able to do so are people with lower vibrations. It is not wise to compare people to each other, as we are all unique. I believe that it is quite possible for a highly evolved and awakened soul to function perfectly well within the profession, but I was sensitive to the extreme and daily discord that is part and parcel of a legal career and the impact on my body was not acceptable to me. Unfortunately, it turned out that my body would have a tough time convincing me to leave a profession that was strangling the life out of me. In a sense, I was my own worst opponent; that obtuse person who simply seemed incapable of using common sense or of seeing reason.

And so at some point during the reading of my stack of self-help books, I found myself thinking about perhaps learning more about hypnosis and regression work. Some small part of me dreamed of one day being free of a profession that, as I had started to acknowledge in my quieter moments, was not allowing me much room to live and to be happy. One day, I decided to dig around to try to find more information on the spiritual regression work of Dr Newton. The whole idea of visiting my soul's life between lives on earth fascinated me. Apart from wishing that I could go to America to undergo such a session myself, I was aware of a little spark somewhere inside of me that could, if it were allowed to do so, grow into a full blown dream of becoming a spiritual regression therapist. Without any training as a psychologist, I did not think this was remotely possible. Nevertheless, I searched the internet, just to see what I could find to read about Dr Newton's work. I discovered that one does not need to be a psychologist to perform hypnosis and, ultimately, spiritual regression work. The starting point would be a course in hypnosis. The little spark exploded into a dream in no time.

Two things happened around this time. Firstly, I made the decision to take a course in hypnosis and set about finding a teacher. I soon enrolled for a course which was due to take place in July 2013. Secondly, I discovered a registered life between lives therapist, who had been trained by Dr Newton and who was living in South Africa. There was no way that I could resist the temptation to go and see her, though it took a little planning and a few months' time to get to that point. One of the things she needed me to do before I could see her, was to go for a past life regression session with a trained regression therapist in order to ensure that any problems with blockages and other stumbling blocks were sorted out before attempting the journey into the spirit world with her.

So it was with great enthusiasm that I went to see a regression therapist in my area. I decided to focus on my neck and throat problems for the session, given that these issues seemed to be the most prominent aspects that were causing me discomfort at that time.

Facilitated regression 19 June 2013: I entered the life seeing myself staggering through a desert. My clothes were torn and I was barefoot. I had nothing with me. I was a travelling merchant in my early twenties and had been abducted by bandits. My name was Marcus and I came from a city with mud brick buildings, somewhere in the region which is today known as the Middle East, but I could not recall the name of the city I lived in or the name of my country. The bandits had taken all of my merchandise and my boots when they abandoned me in the desert. I was trying to reach a mountain range in the distance, but I did not make it there and collapsed in the sand.

I was found by another desert tribe. The women were wearing veils and I think they were Bedouin. They nursed me back to health. When I was well again, they gave me boots and one of their horses – it was black and adorned with small bells and sashes – so that I could return to my own land. I never made it home.

The next significant scene in that life was when I was standing at the gallows. I was to be hanged for stealing a Bedouin horse. I was clearly a foreigner and had no business riding a Bedouin horse. The punishment for horse theft was severe and immediate and I was sentenced to death without a trial.

After my death, I lingered a little and watched my body hanging there. I did not die immediately and the knot in the rope was tied on the left side of my head, just below the ear. I could see that my neck was stretched in a very straight line and throughout the time it took for me to die I remained hanging in this position. My head was also twisted to the right side.

The facilitator asked me where I went next and I told her that I was going home. I felt myself pulling away and just above earth I encountered a mist within which my now familiar teacher guide was waiting. The facilitator told me to ask my guide whether I could ask any questions and he agreed. I then became nervous as I had not prepared for such an eventuality and suddenly all of my questions appeared to be too frivolous to ask at such an important moment. Akaron said that he wanted to show me something. We were standing at 'the end of the mist'. I was in my present body and no longer connected to the body of Marcus. I got the impression that my present consciousness was being given a gift and some insight into the future of my current life while my soul waited to return home after the life of Marcus.

Akaron showed me the land below – it was a picture of the modern world the way I see it each time I look out of an aircraft window. He said that the world was my oyster, that I could do anything that I wanted to do and that I could be anything I wanted to be. I wanted to know whether I was at least on the right path, still not really knowing what questions to ask him. He laughed and said: "You are doing just fine. Keep going just the way you are."

After this there was another life to go to before returning to the present time. I found myself in Egypt straight away. I was male and working in a temple as an architect in my mid-thirties. It was my job to build the aqueducts which carried water to the temple.

In the next scene in that life I was called before the high priest of the temple. The other priests were in the chamber with us. The high priest was irate. He was an angry, small, scrawny man who accused me of having tried to poison him. Apparently, he had become ill from drinking the water in the duct I had built.

I was tried and sentenced to death. I was not killed, however, but I was thrown in a dungeon instead. I do not know the reason why. I stayed in the dungeon for a long time, probably until I was in my mid-forties, but I was eventually sold as a slave with about five other people. We had leather collars around our necks and were tied to each other by means of chains which connected the collars. We were made to walk through the desert behind men on horseback. Each time one of us fell, the person ahead of him would sustain a severe injury to the throat as the collar around his neck was jerked tight by the weight of the falling prisoner. After falling many times one of the prisoners did not get up again and he was cut loose and left there.

Eventually we arrived in a city where we were sold as slaves. I was bought by a really nice lady, who nursed me back to health. For the first few days I did not have a voice, but I eventually recovered. I lived out my life in her service and died of old age. It was a peaceful death.

In my current life, I had long ago lost the curve in my neck, probably due to at least two whiplash injuries which I sustained during horse riding accidents and show jumping. Although I never came anywhere near advanced levels, the adrenalin rush of the sport had kept me going through the many falls and injuries. My horse was wild, beautiful and black and the bond between us was strong and intense. My body was young and strong. After each fall I got back up onto a horse that was foaming at the mouth. Naïve as I was at the time, I never gave much thought to the effect that it had on my body each time when I was flung to the ground. My instructors were also keen to get me back onto the horse immediately after the fall before fear could set in to stop me from riding again. Ironically, it might have been better for me to have allowed the fear to set in, because then common sense might have prevailed before I ended up on crutches for a few months, finally ending my show jumping hopes.

I started having treatment for my neck around the time I stopped riding, which was in my early twenties, around the age that Marcus had been at the time of his death. Over the next twenty six years I had ongoing neck problems. For many years my skull X-rays looked a little unbalanced, almost as if my skull was tilted and sitting at an angle on my neck. The imbalance caused temporomandibular joint problems and my clicking jaw stayed with me until about four years before this session when my chiropractor managed to balance my spine. However, my most recent X-rays at the time still showed my cervical spine leaning to the right. Through treatment the curve in my neck had, from time to time, been restored to some extent, but my neck always reverted to the straight position. My neck and shoulders had been stiff for as long as I could remember.

The night after the regression session I slept soundly, which was a rare occurrence for me. A few days after the session, I discovered that I was able to start sleeping with a pillow under my head for the first time in many, many years. Before the session, I would wake up with a severe headache if I had slept with a pillow under my head while lying on my back. I am still able to use a pillow when I sleep.

In my mid-thirties I started having difficulties with my throat. I often developed laryngitis. Since the regular occurrence of sinus infections and food sensitivities kicked in somewhere in my mid-forties, my struggle with throat infections became worse and I often lost my voice for up to five days in a row. During the last seven months before this session I had developed throat infections twice, with the infections lasting about a week on each occasion. Each time I had to cope with a heavy work schedule at the same time. I was perfectly healthy and able to work, but totally unable to speak.

The interesting thing is that right from the beginning, each time I developed a throat infection, I happened to be working on a legal matter which involved someone who was not prepared to accept my professional advice. In some cases, it was the attorney involved and in others the client. On at least one occasion I also felt that I could not get through to a colleague.

Each time I was forced to act on an instruction that I knew to be wrong or not in the client's best interests, my voice would somehow stop working. If the people who were instructing me, or who were involved in the case, were taking a route that could only take them to a bad place, it was almost as if my body was communicating on some level that it had no intention of helping me to get them there. Unfortunately for my clients, I always turned out to be right in these particular instances. My gut feeling about a case never let me down in fifteen years of practice and the points that concerned me, in the end, were the same points that concerned the presiding officer. Not that anyone remembered the advice they had ignored by the time the judgment was handed down.

These uncomfortable experiences started occurring more frequently and I became concerned that I might damage my voice in the end as I often had to strain to squeak out a few words. I had to continue working to avoid cost orders being granted against my clients on such days, as their matters would have had to be postponed if I was unable to appear, requiring my clients to pay the other side's costs for the day. I recall that on one occasion I had to negotiate a settlement over a period of four hours while I was whispering to my opponent and the magistrate. The worst part about these times was the sinus drip. It felt as if acid was trickling down my throat, slowly eating away at the soft tissue. A few days after this regression, however, the sinus drip disappeared and I no longer had to sleep with a lozenge at the back of my mouth to sooth my throat at night.

Seven days after the session, the mobility in my neck had greatly improved, especially movement to the side. The tightness and stiffness had all but gone. However, there was one area in my problematic neck that had always been more painful than any other. The pain was sharper in that area. This particular pain had not been relieved during the regression session and remained unchanged. Ten days short of a year later, my neck would step up to deliver another message. It seems to me that sometimes a problematic area in our bodies carries more than one message for us and brings us more than one memory to heal.

By 5 July 2013 I was still processing the regression involving my past lives in Egypt and the middle-eastern country when I realised that in both of those lives, I had not been heard. In the first life, no one believed that I had not stolen the Bedouin horse I was riding and in the second no one believed that I had not poisoned the high priest through my work. Both incidents that led to my death and imprisonment respectively in those two lives, were work related. In my current life, in the two instances immediately prior to the regression when I had lost my voice, a particular attorney I was working with at the time simply did not hear me. He refused to let me speak to the clients and always advised them without me being present. A day before one of the hearings, my throat became scratchy and by the next morning I could barely utter a sound. It was one of those days that I had to strain my voice to get the job done. In the life as Marcus, when I had not been heard, my ability to speak was terminated by my hanging. In the second life as a slave, when I had again not been heard, my ability to speak was interrupted due to the injuries to my neck. My clients in both of these matters lost badly in court, as I knew they would and I was never given the chance to explain the reasons for the loss to them. I really felt that I had not been heard and I was very upset for the clients' sake as I knew that if I had been given a chance to talk to them, I might have been able to avert disaster, as well as spare my voice.

After the session, the throat infections disappeared for more than a year, before resurfacing in the very last days of my practice as an advocate at the bar. I had made the decision to leave the profession and closed my chambers at the end of October 2014. Unfortunately, one of the last matters I dealt with exploded at the last minute, because my enthusiastic opponents were unaware that their client was a pathological liar. They believed their client and followed her instructions. As a result, they filed a set of papers which was a complete distortion of the truth. I was called back to complete a mammoth document in order to set the record straight. The work involved took about five days and at the end I had to work for sixteen hours without a break. We demolished the other side and finally convinced them of their client's vicious lies, but my body was not happy with the experience. I had been looking forward to being free of the law for three months since making my decision to end my legal career. Being hauled back to the salt mines due to the lies of a mother without a conscience put strain on me in ways that I had not prepared for.

I was ready to move on, but I felt trapped in the thick mud of a profession I no longer wanted to be part of. I developed a fever and this time, I lost my voice for ten days. During these ten days of silence, I made the decision to cut my ties with the law forever. My body knew its power and it just switched off my voice until I this time listened to my inner voice and to my body, even if some people did not seem to hear me when I said that I would not be returning to practice law.

It was only when I was writing these pages and upon re-reading the transcript of the meeting with Akaron that took place in the space just after visiting the life of Marcus and before I moved on to the life of the Egyptian architect, that I realised the significance of the message Akaron had given me on that occasion. He told me that I could do anything I wanted to. It was as if he was giving the present me a message that I was going to need in the coming months. Eventually, I would have to believe that I could be anything I choose to be and that it would be safe to leave the law behind. Perhaps then already he was guiding me towards that decision. After all, the lives of Marcus and the Egyptian architect related to careers that led to a difficult death and imprisonment. It had been a most appropriate time for my teacher guide to help me see that I did not have to be tied to a career that I no longer wanted.

I cannot over emphasise the importance of keeping notes or journaling when it comes to regression work, meditation or any kind of symbolic work. You will benefit from your sessions without keeping careful notes, but you will most certainly miss the magic bits and the amazing insights into the tapestry that is your life.

CHAPTER 9: Self-hypnosis Regression - 22 June 2013

After my regression into the life of an architect in Egypt, I started thinking about all kinds of unanswered questions that had been floating around in my mind. I had run out of big issues to work on, but there were small, unimportant things that I had been wondering about forever. One of them was a 'connection' I had always felt with one of my colleagues. I could not explain it and I could not put a finger on it. Looking for an excuse to do another regression, I decided to explore this link after running into the particular colleague again one day. Again there was that strange moment of almost recognition. It is really hard to explain. Regressing myself using self-hypnosis had become quite easy for me by then, and so, three days after my facilitated regression into a life in Egypt, I got to work, soon to find myself in Egypt yet again.

Self-hypnosis regression 22 June 2013: Upon my entry into the life, I could see a group of people coming towards me in the distance. I was observing from somewhere in a massive desert canyon and watched the people walking down a dry riverbed.

Suddenly I was no longer observing the group, I was one of them. I was one of quite a few young Egyptian women who were being escorted to a temple by a group of soldiers. The year was 89 B.C. and the name Kendra kept reverberating in my mind.

The officer in charge of the soldiers stopped the column shortly before we reached our destination. He turned to me to ask if I was sure that this was what I wanted to do. I told him that I was. He then continued on to the temple and we were handed over to the priests to start our training. The officer left the temple and returned home. I never saw him again.

As he was leaving I realised *[as observer]* that he was in love with the young woman and that she had chosen her ambition to become a priestess over him. He did not mean that much to her, although she respected him. Although the officer was very sad about leaving her behind, he respected her wishes.

The officer was the person I knew as my strangely familiar colleague in this life.

I was fascinated. Although I have never been to Egypt, my fascination with that country borders on the ridiculous. The story of Cleopatra has always resonated with me and growing up I loved reading mystery novels and watching movies set in Egypt. The old movies about the Pharaohs in biblical times are still part of my favourite childhood memories. The fact that I kept ending up in past lives in Egypt made perfect sense to me. It felt so familiar being there; so right.

I could hardly contain myself as I started up the search engine to see what I could dig up about the year 89 B.C. on the internet. It turned out that the period 89 B.C. onward is referred to as the 'post-fall' era. The last Egyptian queen, Cleopatra, died in 101 B.C. I thought that I must have been approximately eighteen years old in my life as a young priestess in Egypt, which means that in that life I would have been about six years old at the time of

Cleopatra's death. Given the fact that it was a self-hypnosis session, I struggled to maintain a level of trance deep enough to explore more details about the temple I had been taken to and its location, but I did have a name to look into – Kendra. What I could find on the name Kendra was that in Anglo-Saxon and in American the name Kendra means 'prophetess'. In English the meaning of the name Kendra is 'knowledge'. Unfortunately, I have no idea how this name would connect to a young Egyptian priestess who lived in 89 B.C.

As always, the details of the lives do not concern me much. They are very interesting to mull over and it was awesome to find something that seems to link back to the history of another age, but ultimately, I am alive now and I want to heal my body and my mind as best I can to continue living my best life now. This particular regression did not impact on my body, but it gave me some very interesting insights into why we keep connecting with the same people.

I had always 'noticed' my colleague. He is a kind, brilliant, gentle person and an excellent teacher, always helping others and paying genuine attention to everyone he talks to. He is an exceptional person whom I had always found intriguing. I seemed to be very aware if he was around and had worked with him on a couple of occasions, yet I had never been able to figure out whether I was attracted to him or not.

This colleague treated me like he treated everyone else. He was friendly, respectful, kind and helpful. Although I remained puzzled by the fact that he was strangely familiar to me, he did not seem to have the same inexplicable interest in me. Perhaps one can describe his behaviour towards me as friendly disinterest. I had the impression that the Egyptian officer Kendra had turned down with a similar disinterest, was a good man. Perhaps I just had to experience that same disinterest that the young Egyptian priestess had so casually displayed in her life in Egypt.

CHAPTER 10: Self-hypnosis Regression - 23 June 2013

Maybe it was the trips to Egypt, but the two previous regressions opened up a whole new world of understanding to me. I just love to figure out how things work. Everything from the mechanics of energy healing to the dynamics of a relationship between any two people or family members absolutely fascinates me. Every now and again I come across a person in my world who simply acts in a crazy manner that baffles me. Almost as if some hidden force takes charge of them, making them act in ways that are so far removed from what a reasonable or remotely rational person would do, that it leaves my head spinning. It is also the kind of behaviour I simply have to understand. I find that if I can understand why someone acts in a certain way, it is much easier for me not to judge them and also to forgive them, should the issue of forgiveness be relevant in the particular circumstances, which it usually is when people do crazy things which affect me detrimentally.

One such person was a man I met through a friend a couple of years earlier, whom I shall refer to as the cyclist. After seeing him only twice, I started feeling extremely uncomfortable and emotional. I felt sad, vulnerable and miserable. In fact, I felt downright insecure. I sensed early on that if anything was going to come of our friendship, it would largely be a waiting game on my side. I felt certain that it would be nothing more than a game to him and that there was no real interest in me. I did not feel like playing power games and I was not going to sit around waiting for someone to make up his mind when I already knew where I stood with him. Besides, he was in fact not my type at all. My interest in him was somewhat baffling.

I did what felt safe to me. I ran. When I ended the still very new friendship, I was as honest as I could be under the circumstances about the reasons for my decision. The cyclist's reaction was weird. He was irate and it was as if the man had not heard anything I said, making things up as he went along. This was totally crazy. I could not understand that he was not to be placated by the fact that I ended things out of respect for both of us, because even though I was not really sure of my own feelings anyway, I was fairly sure that we did not want the same thing.

The cyclist made a point of being as hurtful as he could be; totally out of context. It took me a long time to get over this deeply hurtful incident and to shake off the sad feelings that this strange encounter had left me with. This was another thing I could not understand. It made no sense that it would take me such a long time to forget about the ridiculous business.

Now that I had discovered a really nice tool to understand relationship dynamics, it seemed like the ideal time to dig into the cyclist's weird behaviour that still so baffled me. In a way, though the unfortunate incident had taken place almost eighteen months earlier, it still caused me to feel a form of discord whenever I was reminded of the cyclist. It was like something uncomfortable I just could not shake off. Given that my last regression gave me a little insight into my own strange reaction to my colleague, I decided that it was time to head off into another life. It is quite nice to travel from life to life in the space of two days. One could make a list of things that bug one and then go and dig up the reasons for the dynamics of one's present day relationships with those who cross one's path all over the ancient world! Sort of brain or memory archaeology, only cleaner!

Self-hypnosis regression 23 June 2013: I was a medieval knight in shining armour taking part in a jousting event in England. Not only was I really good at jousting, I was also quite a handsome man. At the end of the jousting tournament, which I had won with ease (I got the sense that I often won these tournaments), I confided in my good friend, who was assisting me at the event, that my betrothal to a young woman was not entirely what I wanted from life. I wanted adventure and was not ready to settle down. My friend suggested that I should go on a crusade. I followed his advice and went away on some journey or crusade, while the young woman I was betrothed to waited for my return. She waited for me for a very long time and prayed in the church for my safe return daily. I eventually did return, but only to tell her that I would not be marrying her. She was heartbroken, but I told her 'At least I came to tell you!' This, of course, did not help her to feel better at all. The young woman was the same soul that I knew in this life as the cyclist.

According to Google, the history of jousting started with the emergence of knights as a fighting force in Europe of the Middle Ages in the tenth century. The decline in the practice of jousting started with the invention of the musket in 1520, while the crusades took place in the period between the eleventh to thirteenth centuries, making it possible that a young knight, skilled at jousting, could conceivably have left on a crusade for a while.

My regression into the life of an English knight helped me to make sense of the strange scenario that played out between me and the cyclist. Obviously, I had treated the young woman in England unfairly. It is cruel to make someone wait for your return in hope, when you already know that you have no intention of honouring your word.

I believe that I was supposed to address the imbalance I had created in that life in my current life. It was my turn to sit around waiting. I can see that had I not terminated the friendship with the cyclist, I would indeed have sat around waiting for nothing to happen, thereby feeling what the young English woman would have experienced and in so doing addressing the imbalance. On some level though, I must have known that it was payback time and I literally bolted from an experience that I was probably supposed to have.

And so the soul of the young woman had to move on to plan B. This explains why none of the details about the cyclist's behaviour made sense. The important thing is that it was precisely his crazy, illogical and unfair reaction that had caused me pain. In addition, it was done in such a way that the incident stayed with me for a long time. In a sense, I had to put up with the incident in my mind for about as long as the young woman had spent praying in an old English church.

This insight brought me immediate peace. I was now able to think of the cyclist with great compassion. More importantly, I was easily able to put the incident behind me, admittedly with a bit of a mischievous smile. Naughty boys do not get away with behaving badly it seems.

CHAPTER 11: Self-hypnosis Regression - 26 June 2013

With each self-regression, came more clarity. As I connected more strongly with my eternal soul, things started to make sense. The scientist in me was happily making notes of my 'research'. I loved every minute of this journey. The result was that I had no time to even wonder what had happened to the anger that I used to feel about being trapped on the wheel of time.

It was the middle of winter and therefore only natural to once again turn my attention to my physical ailments, which seemed more pronounced during winter months. I was getting older and no matter how young I felt or acted when I spent my summer weekends cycling up and down the beautiful mountains in Cape Town and surrounds, my knees were giving me hell, especially as I could not cycle during the wet winter months in the Cape, causing the muscles supporting my knees to weaken, exacerbating the condition.

My doctor had already told me a couple of years earlier that the X-rays of my knees showed the early onset of osteoarthritis. The condition was manageable, but would get worse over time. I was to take anti-inflammatory tablets as and when needed. The diagnosis had brought home the reality that I would eventually have to give up cycling and I would certainly have to move, because I would not be able to climb the stairs at home for much longer. I was in no mood to move house. I had just settled into my home nicely a couple of years earlier and had no plans to move again anytime soon. So I managed the problem and devised all kinds of plans, like putting groceries into a bag that I could carry over my shoulder so that I had both hands free to support my weight climbing up the stairs. Imagine that. The whole plan was just embarrassing and I soon got really tired of explaining why an apparently healthy woman needed to pull herself up the stairs by the railings. Going to shopping malls, in fact going anywhere had become stressful.

I had already successfully gotten rid of my sensitivity to products containing wheat, which was also something that I could previously only manage by popping pills, until these stopped working. I recalled how the problem had to get out of hand before I paid attention to alternative solutions. Perhaps the issue with my knees could be resolved in the same way. If we are diagnosed with some or other physical condition, it is all too easy to fully embrace that diagnosis and adjust life accordingly, limiting ourselves as may be demanded by the illness or condition. I was disturbed by what was going on in my mind after I had been made aware of the osteoarthritis. I constantly worried about how many stairs would be at any given place that I needed to visit. Eventually, I realised that in my own mind I now had 'a condition'. Of course I indeed did have a problem with my knees, but I was allowing it to define me. I was no longer a person; I was a person with knee problems. I could think of no better motivation for another self-regression.

Self-hypnosis regression 26 June 2013: I was an 88 year old shepherd by the name of Johann, living in a village in the Swiss Alps. Some soldiers came to our village looking for someone. We did not know where this person was and so we could not tell them anything. I was the oldest person in this village of peasant people and was dragged out of my little dwelling to explain things to the soldier in charge. He did not believe that we did not know the whereabouts of the person they were looking for. They roughly pushed me down onto my knees, very badly bruising them. I was begging for my life and was convinced they were about to torture or kill me. I was terrified. They did not kill me, but held me down and branded a symbol on my chest. The symbol was a circle, with four lines connecting the centre of the circle with its outer edge. Three of the four lines represented the letter 'Y', with a fourth line connecting the middle of the letter's fork with the edge of the circle, dividing the top half of the letter 'Y' into two halves.

On searching for symbols on the internet, I discovered that the symbol I had seen during the regression had since ancient times been connected to Satanism and actually began as a symbol of satanic benediction during rituals. The Christianisation of the Swiss Alps began in the late Roman period, in the third and fourth centuries. There are legends and stories of Christian martyrs and persecution woven into the histories of many towns in Switzerland. With the fall of the Western Roman Empire, Germanic tribes moved in. I found a reference to Germanic tribes using the symbol, attributing strange and mystical properties to it. Much later, in the 1950's the symbol was used in the campaign of a British nuclear disarmament movement and was referred to as the peace sign.

What had happened to Johann, it seems, was therefore not entirely farfetched. He certainly lived in the Swiss Alps long before 1950 and thus the symbol burnt into his chest by persons who could easily have been members of a Germanic tribe, had little to do with peace.

After completing this regression, I sat down thinking about how and when my knee problems had originally manifested. I could not recall having had any problems with my knees before injuring my right knee during kickboxing training about twelve years before this session. I eventually had to have an arthroscopy approximately five years after the incident. My knee was never really the same after that. Although the arthroscopy did resolve some of the original difficulties I was having with the knee, it certainly caused a new weakness in the knee that I did not have before. However, apart from being aware of the slight weakness and sometimes minimal discomfort in the knee, it did not hamper my lifestyle in any way.

A few years after the original kickboxing injury, I was briefed to handle a particularly taxing case during 2011 and we spent almost a month in court. My clients were electronic engineers. All the witnesses, bar one or two, were also engineers. I have a solid scientific background, having a degree in Mathematics, Chemistry and Physics and having studied Astro-physics subsequently and I have never had much difficulty in understanding the mechanics of things once they were explained to me properly. During this trial we had to spend long hours every evening after court had adjourned, ensuring that I understood the expert testimony as given that day so that I would be able to properly cross-examine the other side's expert witnesses the following day. This meant that on court days I would work from 07h00 in the morning until 23h00 at night. The first three hours would be spent preparing for the court day starting at 10h00 and the hours after the court day, which ended at 16h00, would be spent working through the day's evidence with my clients so that we could deal with the points that we were expecting to come up during the next day's testimony.

Naturally, what I ate during those weeks came from a shop or a restaurant and often there was simply no time to eat. I drank mostly water and coffee, but probably not enough of the former and too much of the latter. Standing on one's feet all day long, focusing and stretching one's mind around issues that are far removed from the principles of one's own profession, is taxing to say the least, regardless of one's background. I was exhausted, but I did not have the luxury of rest. There was simply too much at stake for my clients. The trial took place in August 2011. During that month, I celebrated my forty eighth birthday on a Thursday, which meant that the trial week lasting from Monday to Thursday, was over. This meant that I would be able to spend the Friday in chambers preparing for the rest of the case and would not need to go to court. So when a friend suggested that we have dinner to celebrate my birthday that evening, I thought that there would be no harm in taking a bit of a break as the next day would not require my presence in court and I could perhaps go to the office a little later than usual.

And so it came that I had two slices of pizza and half a glass of wine that evening. I was beyond tired and after dinner I went home to try to get to bed early. Somewhere in the middle of the night I woke up feeling very thirsty. I got up and walked to the kitchen to get some water. While I was standing at the kitchen sink drinking the water, I started feeling dizzy and realised that I was about to have a black out. I put down the glass and made the mistake of trying to walk back to my bed. I never got there. A few hours later, I woke up on the cold, tiled floor of the passage outside my bedroom. I was aching all over.

Upon examining my position on the floor and looking at the injuries I had sustained, I realised that I must have passed out on my feet. From the state of my two badly swollen knees, I gathered that I must have dropped onto my knees like a sack of potatoes. I had bruises on my collarbone, ribs and forehead. There was an abrasion under my chin and I vaguely recalled feeling a hard knock and being aware that my chin had hit the corner of what I suspect was my desk.

A visit to my general practitioner confirmed that drinking half a glass of wine in my state of complete exhaustion had probably caused my blood sugar to drop, which would have explained the thirst which sent me to the kitchen in the first place.

Given the bruising visible on my knees, it seemed that I must have collapsed onto the tiled floor with all my weight bearing down on my knees. The X-rays taken at this time had revealed the early onset of osteoarthritis as alluded to earlier. After this incident, my knees simply never really healed. The condition of my knees in fact deteriorated rapidly and eventually I could not walk if I did not take supplements containing MSM twice a day. Getting up the stairs at home became very painful and on some days almost impossible.

Obviously, I was distressed about this and after a while I went to see a specialist. He advised me to start cycling and to continue with the spinning classes in the gym that I had been going to for a while. A couple of weeks later I started cycling with a friend and although my knees soon benefitted from the exercise as the muscles became stronger, the deterioration continued slowly, but surely and by the time I decided to do this regression about my knees almost two years later, I was having severe difficulties with my knees, as I have already explained. Unfortunately, I had in the meantime also injured my left knee while I was cycling up a steep hill in Stellenbosch and I left a gear change too late. I had the option of getting off the bike, which would make cycling up the hill from a complete standstill really difficult, or of changing gear and possibly breaking the chain, or of using sheer muscle power to keep going until I could safely change gear. I chose to do the latter, which would not have been a bad option had I been twenty years younger. I got to the top of the hill, but I knew from the sharp pain in my left knee that I had perhaps not made the best decision.

When comparing my own history to the events I had recalled of Johann's life, I started wondering how and why certain imprints carried over from one life to another. It appeared to me that it was possible that traumatic memories can imprint on the soul while it is in a body and those memories are taken back home with the soul, only to manifest again in another body in a new incarnation. It seems as if such imprinting occurs during the times when we fear, or know, that we are about to die. Johann certainly thought that he was about to die and so did the Franciscan monk who was hiding amongst the wheat in a deserted barn in northern Spain. For an 88 year old man to fall onto his knees on a hard surface would have been very painful. I cringe when I remember how painful my throbbing knees were when I woke up on the tiled floor of my home. I was suddenly glad I had passed out on my feet and did not have to feel the pain of that fall.

I believe that when I fell onto my knees like a dead weight in my current life, the old memory that had imprinted on my soul when I, as Johann, feared for my life when I was being pushed down onto my knees, must have been triggered, possibly sparking the osteoarthritis in my knees. That memory would have been imprinted on my current body when my soul reincarnated, for purposes of clearing it in this life. It would also explain why the deterioration of the osteoarthritis in my knees did not appear to be age appropriate. The deterioration was drastic and fast. There were days that I felt as if I was, or at least that my knees were much, much older than my actual age. It made no sense at all, until I visited the aged Johann's life.

After working through all of these thoughts, the infection in my knees started clearing. Forty eight hours after the regression, it was markedly easier to climb the stairs at home without pain. Almost three weeks after the session I was able to stop taking MSM supplements and I was walking up the stairs pain free.

As the months went by the pain started to return. It would take two more releases to sort out my knee problems. I already knew that we are complex beings. Our difficulties often have layers. When something comes up and we deal with it, we feel relief. If the relief is temporary and the problem returns, it means that we have not yet completed the work. Something else still has to come up for clearing. It is almost as if our bodily injuries carry complexes of imprints, rather than one simple memory imprint. I was to discover in the months to follow that the clearing of imprints is not the full story, yet it is certainly a good start.

Interestingly, when it comes to my knees, the first thing that came up was the old injury which triggered certain problems in my current life. With that cleared, the way was open for me to end up on an extraordinary journey that would change my life forever, again involving my knees and the message that they had for me. Had I not started off by clearing the old body imprint, the remainder of the work would not have been possible. I have learned to be very grateful for the fact that my knees had more to teach me. It was worth the days of struggling up the stairs in pain. Our bodies talk to us. If only we learned to listen to them, they would guide us safely home.

CHAPTER 12: Self-hypnosis Regression - 27 June 2013

While still pondering what I had learned from Johann's life and having allowed a few days for the energy release during the regression back to the lives of Marcus the merchant and the Egyptian architect to settle, I decided to take another look at the area in my neck that still felt 'stuck', despite the relief I was feeling. I was wondering whether there was perhaps another memory imprint of an injury that needed to be released. Our bodies function in amazing ways and it is common knowledge nowadays that we all hold the power to use our minds to help heal our bodies. One only has to look at the different ways in which two people with the same illness or injury manage their respective processes. Some choose to do what I had done with my knees for a while, namely to accept the condition as inevitable and learn to live with it. Others refuse to allow the condition to limit them any more than it has to.

On our journeys it is also important to remember that healing is not the same as curing. If we manage to cure an ailment or improve a particular condition by utilising either conventional or more unconventional methods, we indeed have something to celebrate. But what if we do not manage to cure what ails us? Does that mean no healing took place? I do not think so. I would eventually come to believe that our ailments, illnesses and general discomfort are part and parcel of the tools we have available to understand ourselves and our paths in this world. In our efforts to cure ourselves a whole lot of healing takes place, although many of the wounds we might manage to heal along the way might in the end turn out to have had nothing to do with what we had set out to cure in the first place. Curing an illness is perhaps more important to who we are in our current lives, while our souls are more concerned with our overall healing and spiritual growth as seen from a broader perspective, even if we eventually die without finding a cure for what we had set out to rid ourselves of. But from where I stood in the winter of 2013 I was still gathering information, exploring the laboratory of my own body and mind.

> **Self-hypnosis regression 27 June 2013:** I was a black woman hurrying along a beach in the company of a European man. We knew each other well. My name was Wukata'an and his name was Jeffrey. We were agitated as we moved inland through thick vegetation. There were many palm trees. I had three children, whom I saw when we arrived back at my village. I moved forward in this life and saw myself and Jeffrey tied to a tree – one on either side. We had been captured by a tribe of cannibals. We were there alone; no one was watching us. We managed to get free from the ropes, but we were recaptured soon afterwards. The cannibals took us to their leader. Their bodies were painted white, blue and yellow. The last thing I saw was myself standing on my knees before the leader. I could not hold the trance and that was the end of the regression.

I encountered heavy blocks after entering the life I had regressed to. I felt very tired and could not hold the trance. As a result, I eventually gave up and never got to the culmination of that life. In the images that I did manage to retrieve, I found nothing significant. I realised that it might be that I was being too hasty and overly enthusiastic about how much work could be done on the same issue in a short space of time. After this incident, I decided to give the regression work I had done some time to take proper effect and to allow the energy that I had released during the regressions to filter through to the physical world. I could always take another look at my neck in a few months' time.

Thinking back, it is no coincidence that I was not able to do more work along these lines. It was time for a different journey that would unearth other things I needed to work through before getting to crossroads that would take a lot of courage to face, in circumstances that would be closely connected to both my neck and knee problems.

CHAPTER 13: First Channelling - 10 July 2013

The fact that I had decided not to continue with more regression work immediately, did not mean that I could stop poking around in my own head, trying to understand how things are connected. My life, mind and body had become my laboratory, while my thinking and the dynamics involved, were the subjects to be studied in my lab. I was loving every minute of the journey and had the time and the space to work on these matters, feeling so very grateful for the fact that I had no one who relied on me. I was not raising children and there was no partner around taking up my time and energy.

I had finally gotten to the last book in my pile of self-help books that I had steadily been working through over the last few months. I have to admit that there was a reason why the particular book was at the bottom of the pile. A part of me was still in my societal box and I can be pretty judgmental about things I do not really understand. I have often wondered why it is on occasion so easy for me to convince myself that something is nonsense, without actually having taken a really good look at things before delivering a verdict. We all have our flaws and it has been helpful to look at my own behaviour critically from time to time.

The book about channelling that I was now planning to read did not hold much promise of inspiring me when I picked it up for the first time in four years after originally purchasing it in 2009. In 2004 and again in 2005, before I got married, a friend of mine did two channellings for me. Both sessions were recorded and she gave me a typed transcript of the 2004 channelling, as well as the tape recording of the 2005 channelling.   At the time, the sessions did not bring me any answers and I found the information somewhat interesting, but not very useful. I had little interest in messages telling me that all was well when I literally felt my soul being torn apart.

I soon forgot about the channellings and I never listened to the recording of the 2005 channelling again until 2014, nine years later. I had filed away the transcript of the 2004 channelling and only discovered it again, quite by accident, during the writing of these pages, another year later.

In hindsight, most things are clearer. It is odd how we never seem to hear the special messages hidden amongst ordinary words. In the 2005 channelling I was told to learn to meditate. I do not recall even registering this suggestion at the time. It took eight years before I would in fact take up meditation in earnest and this was not because I remembered the contents of the channelling. Needless to say, the pages you are reading are about the results of a single meditation on my anger issues, which opened up a soul journey that still leaves me breathless when I think about it. It is tragic that my issues with channelling led me to ignore the solid advice I was given as early as 2005. I eventually got to the point where meditation changed my life, but I could have done so eight years earlier had I not been so busy judging the process of channelling and had I not been so absorbed in what I wanted to create in my world at the time. The relationship I was in back then consumed my reality and my focus and caused me to miss the open door that my soul needed me to walk through. But our souls are patient. Fortunately.

In 2007, about two years after the second channelling and after I had gotten married, my channelling friend and I exchanged treatments. I had in the meantime started to learn Reiki and gave her a Reiki session, while she did an energy balancing for me. At this point in my life I was very much caught up in the agony of being in a miserable marriage. I seldom experienced anything but sadness, pain and grief and barely had the energy to keep breathing. My pain blinded me to many things and I was not so much interested in learning as I was in getting rid of the terrible pain that was tearing me apart.

We did my friend's session first and when it was my turn, I relaxed and just listened to the beautiful music we used that day, namely *Temple of Healing* by Anthony Miles. I had my eyes closed and although I was not really focusing on anything, I was aware of my friend's position as she worked. At some point I could feel her holding my feet. I was covered in a soft blanket as it was winter, so I only felt the pressure of hands on my feet. When she touched my shoulder, my eyes flew open, because someone was still holding my feet! There was no one standing at my feet, yet the pressure remained. My friend explained that she was aware of the fact that a guide was working on me and that he was standing at my feet. She said that he was communicating to her that he was a new guide and that he was asking my permission to enter. Of course I agreed, but I was not ready for the experience that followed. I instantly felt my face, head and neck heat up. I started to panic as I had no idea what was happening. The heat in my face was incredible. My friend advised me to lift my head to ease the guide's entry and it seemed to work.

But being told that a new guide had entered my life and having had a momentary experience of something happening to me that I could not explain, did not help much. My despair at the time was just too deep, too thick for anything to really penetrate. The new guide, whoever he was, was not the talkative type. Or at least he did not communicate with me and after realising that the new guide had no presence that was perceptible to me, I soon put it out of my mind, focusing on survival. I had no use for a guide who would communicate with my friend and not with me. It obviously had something to do with the fact that after years of doing energy work my friend was able to perceive things I was not able to, but this hardly made me feel better.

About a year after my inevitable divorce in November of 2008, I was in the process of trying to repair the damage to my spirit. As I listlessly walked the isles of *Exclusive Books*, not able to believe that I was back to putting my life together after someone else had torn it apart on every level, I did what I always do when I feel that I am in trouble and there is no one that I can go and see about it. I went in search of a self-help book. On this point I should say that I have never read one such book that was a waste of time. These books were always 'sent' to me in a way. I always found something in the pages of a book that I could use to propel my life forward. The wisdom of others who walk this planet with me, is extensive. How privileged we are to be able to share each other's knowledge and learning. I had fortunately by then become very good at learning from others, something that has always served me very well.

The book that seemed to attract my attention that day in the bookstore was *Opening to Channel*, by Sanaya Roman and Duane Packer. At the time I vaguely recalled the channellings that my kind friend had done for me, but channelling is not something that ever really resonated with me and I am frankly, to this day, downright suspicious of channelled information. I have been a practising litigator for too many years to ever believe one word that comes out of anyone's mouth, including my own. Human beings are in my view incapable of refraining from interpretation and are only ever capable of telling you their version of the truth, despite their very best intentions. It never really is the same truth as that of other witnesses of the same event, no matter how honest everyone involved tries to be.

With channelling the same applies, I suspect. Whatever is channelled, goes through the unique filters of the human channel, although I have been told that channels cannot remember what they had channelled, hence the recordings. In reality, I simply do not know enough to challenge anyone on any aspect of channelling and as I have said before, I have a tendency to judge things I do not fully understand. Hopefully, one day I will learn to stop doing this.

My own experience with channelling up to that point had not changed my scepticism, probably because I did not get from the channellings what I had wanted at the time. My focus had been on getting what I wanted then, not on hearing what was actually being said. It would only be during the writing of these pages and with the benefit of hindsight that I would rediscover the advice I had been given in my friend's 2005 channelling, namely to learn to meditate. It does not help matters that I tend to want to see for myself that something works before I believe it. There are also some truly strange channellings out there, as a quick search on the internet reveals and for a sceptic like me that does not inspire confidence in channelling. However, given what I am about to share, I feel that it is important to explain that I remain sceptical, despite what I was to experience in experimenting with channelling myself, or perhaps precisely because of it, and despite the wisdom contained in the early channellings of my friend in 2004 and 2005, recognised only with the benefit of hindsight.

I first read *Opening to Channel* during 2009 when I bought it. It made little sense and unsurprisingly, did not resonate with me much. There were plenty of exercises in the book, none of which I particularly felt like trying at the time. There was one exercise that did look interesting though. It described a technique to meet one's guide. It reminded me of the strange experience I had had a couple of years earlier when my friend told me about the new guide wanting to enter and I thought that I might try the exercise.

I have already alluded to my irritation when people talked about their guides as if these entities lived at home with them, giving advice and insight to the individual who is clearly so advanced that this type of thing is 'normal'. The irony is not lost on me that I would eventually end up doing exactly the same, but at that point in time it was with a mixture of reluctant determination, a hint of scepticism and a little bit of excitement that I tackled the exercise to try to 'meet my guide'. Despite my lack of conviction and negative attitude, the exercise did work and a rather strange fellow 'walked out of the light'. He did not come closer and did not communicate with me, nor did he give me his name. He just stood there. I can only describe him as the twin of Spiderman, except that his outfit was blue. On his chest he wore a big, flat, yellowish crystal with five corners, sewn into the blue Spiderman-like suit he was wearing. The experience was somewhat interesting, but did not rock my world. I was getting really tired of these guides who did not communicate. What on earth is the point of having a guide? The book ended up in the cupboard where it stayed at the bottom of my pile of self-help books until I hauled it out in 2013 after my visit to Eric.

Given that the book never resonated with me, it was the last one in the pile that I had been re-reading since early 2013. I was fortunately a little more open-minded by then. My divorce had been finalised years before and my anger problem had miraculously been resolved, with the help of a very communicative teacher guide. The communication was finally two-way. I had successfully rid myself of my sensitivity to wheat and had discovered all kinds of other interesting things along the journey. Re-reading the book on channelling brought me the realisation that I had grown immensely since purchasing the book in 2009. It was not the same person re-reading the book at this time. The exercises that had appeared so boring in 2009, where now things I did on a daily basis anyway. Entering altered states of consciousness was no longer an obstacle for me and I certainly no longer needed to practise doing this.

When I came to the part where one is invited to meet one's guide, I realised that the guide, whom I had come to think of as the blue man and whom I had 'met' in 2009 already when I read the book the first time, had in fact pitched up in my facilitated regression work with my friend in May 2013 when I had regressed to the life of a banished priestess, trying to find a home in the village of foreigners. He was the one who had helped me to heal the situation and who showed me how to make my peace with the souls of the villagers who had lost their livelihood. He had actively guided me through those sessions and most certainly was communicating with me telepathically. He had a wonderful sense of humour too. For example, when my friend was taking me down stone steps and over the bridge of time to get to the past life I was visiting that day, he enjoyed ignoring her instructions, taking me through a tunnel instead where the two of us conspiratorially waited at the light at the end of the tunnel for my friend's facilitation to catch up with us. While waiting there with the blue man, I felt like I had my best friend with me and we were skipping school. We literally stood their giggling while we waited. You might ask how one giggles telepathically. I do not know, but although I could not see beyond the blue Spiderman-like mask, I could feel his laughter.

I had not yet finished re-reading the book, but once I had figured out that the initial exercises presented no problem to me any longer and that I had already met my guide, I suddenly felt an urgent need to try out the section where one opens to channel. Over eager is probably one of the most accurate descriptions you can give me. I had been working until midnight and merely wanted to read a few pages before going to sleep, but the need to try to open to channel became stronger. And so about fifteen minutes after midnight, I decided to give it a shot.

Feeling excited, I asked my guide to come in only if he was a high-level guide of the purest light and aligned with my path and best interest, following the procedure of opening to channel as set out in *Opening to Channel.* I put myself into trance and visualised my guide coming closer and entering my aura. I focused on the energy shining through him. I felt a small shift, barely noticeable. Then I simply started talking, asking a question about a dream I had the night before which I did not understand. In the dream I had an out of body experience where I had left my body, leaving me feeling scared. A voice said: 'You wanted to know what it feels like, and now you do.' This scared me even more and in the dream I returned to my body, only to find a clown waiting for me.

The answer followed immediately upon my question about the dream as I hesitantly started talking in a tone of voice a little lower than my normal tone. The words came in what I can best describe as broken waves. I asked my guide to slow down as some of the words were transmitted on top of each other, almost like 'hearing' two words at the same time. The waves of words slowed down immediately and I could follow them more easily. The connection became stronger as I went along.

It took a while to realise that I was in fact getting a message and I registered disappointment that I in my haste had forgotten to record it, as I did not really think it would happen. The channelling was short and I think my guide probably knew that I was out of my depth, over excited and actually had no clue what I was doing. This turned out to be fortunate as he kept the channelling short so that immediately afterwards I was able to record the entire message on my cell phone before the fast fading memory disappeared.

First channelling 10 July 2013: I asked: 'Explain the dream to me'. The answer, in a different tone, simply started flowing: *"It was I, precious one, trying to connect with you* (through the dream)*, but your fear was blocking it. I can help you to take all the steps necessary to do great things, pieced together from your dreams, and to see through the maze of information that is confusing you. Go forth in kindness and in love until we meet again."*

To say that I was excited is putting it mildly. The fact that there was an immediate and appropriate response to my request that the communication be slowed down, was probably the most convincing part of the experience. I had a new technique to work with and the possibilities of self-discovery were once again endless. What more could a curious soul ask for? The July course in hypnosis that I had so looked forward to, had in the meantime been cancelled and rescheduled for the following September, so I felt thoroughly disappointed and needed something to distract me. With the learning about hypnosis having been put on hold and the regression options seemingly having been exhausted for the moment, channelling seemed to provide just the right research subject I needed.

CHAPTER 14: Second Channelling - 11 July 2013

Apart from having fun and feeling excited about my experiences, I was slowly starting to feel a sense of sheer awe. I felt the need to connect deeply with the kind energy of the guides whose presence I was beginning to sense everywhere in my life. I wanted to express my gratitude for all the positive changes that I had seen in my life and for the efforts that I was starting to realise were being made behind the scenes, so to speak, to ensure that my life of learning was following its course.

When I set about preparing for my second channelling the next evening, I silently thanked my guides for their efforts and for all the changes that had come about in my life due to what I could only interpret as guidance. I felt humbled by it all. It made me want to change my life into one where I followed my soul's purpose. I wanted to live the life I was meant to live, not the one I was trying to live.

At this time and in the face of what is sacred, my deepest unhappiness finally surfaced in its raw ugliness. I found myself talking to my guides about how trapped I felt in my career. Earning a good income made my life easier and allowed me to do things for myself and my loved ones that I would not otherwise have been able to do, but unfortunately it had also trapped me as time went by, because the lifestyle I had become accustomed to had to be sustained. That *per se* was not the problem. I simply no longer wanted to earn a living through the practise of law. There was also an increasing interest in regression work and I could not then, and still cannot, imagine anything more interesting than accompanying other people on their inward journeys. Slowly the idea of perhaps eventually working as a regression therapist started forming more solidly in my mind. Despite this, I also felt the stirrings of doubt about the viability of this option.

For my second channelling, I had initially decided to try to focus on one issue and to merely ask for guidance in respect of ways I might still be blocking my soul's purpose and how I could release such blocks. I sensed that some of these blocks might be keeping me in a profession that is far removed from the soul path I knew I needed to travel. As so often happens with me though, my enthusiasm spilled over and my one request ended up being elaborated upon and I also expressed my curiosity about further exploring physical healing in my body through channelling.

Before I started the channelling, I suddenly remembered a strange phenomenon I had been wondering about for a few years and so this got added to my list of requests for the second channelling. Shortly before my marriage some years earlier, I had started hearing a tune playing in my mind. It was the first few lines of the song *White on White, Lace on Satin*. The lyrics of the song at some point continue on to say 'My little angel is getting married today'. I had heard that song as sung by Danny Williams many times during my childhood, but in the intervening years I had all but forgotten it as I had not heard it for over twenty years, perhaps more.

The odd thing about the tune was that it only played in my mind when I was in one specific spot, namely right outside the side entrance to my garage. After my marriage, I eventually sold my home after renting it out for a while and did not hear the tune playing in my mind again until a few years later. The next time I heard it, I was standing in front of the mirror in my bathroom, a couple of years after my divorce. At the time of this second channelling, I had again been hearing the tune playing in my mind every so often for about two years, and always only in the one spot, namely in front of the mirror in my bathroom. The whole thing remained an enigma and since I was now, in my view, already venturing into the realm of the strange, I thought there could be no harm in asking about this little detail that baffled me so much. While I was at it, I mentioned to my guide that I had noticed over the last few days that my dreams had become visually clearer, yet they remained as confusing as before. I had absolutely no idea what they meant, if anything.

Second channelling 11 July 2013: *The relationship with your ex-husband drained your energy to almost nothing. Breaking free from him in that state was very brave. Your most pressing concern is the bond between you that you have not been able to break and that relates to your need to still hold on. You cannot break free if you are still holding on. Grab the chance to break free the next time it comes and then everything else will fall into place. I know you have many questions and we will work on those, but I cannot choose for you and will not limit you by doing so. It is in order not to think of others so much at this time and to work only on your own issues for now. You have to go back in time. Follow the light as it will set you free. You are a golden bird, meant to fly. Trust me to shape the information you need to do so into a format that you can absorb and understand. I am always with you, we are as we have always been. Go forth in love and light until we meet again.*

Gentle as always, the guidance I received made it clear to me that most of the aspects I had asked about would be touched upon, but they would not necessarily be dealt with fully, or in a way I would expect. Instead of directly dealing with my holding on to the safety of my profession, I was told, I think, that I was holding on to my former husband. We still jointly owned a property that we had been unable to sell due to the collapse of the property market and this necessitated contact between us, which contact had been and remains very amicable since our divorce. Having to keep up the payments in respect of that property was one of the reasons why I could not simply walk away from my profession. Could it be that there was something underlying my inability to walk away from my career? Was I holding on to a property in order to hold on to a person, or an idea, or a memory? Sometimes we allow things to become embedded, hidden in the dark corners of our minds where we fail to see them wielding their power over our lives.

I also formed the impression that I was being gently coaxed to take it slow when it comes to asking questions. My curiosity about strange tunes playing in my mind was not all that important, at least for the moment. This question would eventually be answered, but my ability to receive the messages was still rudimentary and I doubt that I would have been able to hold a very long connection allowing for detailed answers to all my questions.

It was also clear that I was going to do all the work myself and that guidance is no substitute for figuring things out as you go along. What really felt good about it all was the way my need to grow and expand myself through digging into the processes involved was respected. I was not going to be given an easy way out, but I would be supported.

I understood the message to indicate that I should, for the moment, focus on my own soul work before thinking about embarking on a journey involving regression work with others. The reference to going back in time was a little ambiguous, but I assumed that perhaps some more regression work was in order. I was soon to discover that the information that needed to be shaped into a format that I could understand, would be given to me in the form of dreams.

After channelling that night, I could not fall asleep and tossed and turned for about two and a half hours. I eventually fell into a stressful sleep and, just before waking, I had a vivid, clear dream about my former husband. The content of the dream related to the major issue that resulted in the end of our marriage. The detail in the dream was astounding and very, very real. I woke up in a highly emotional state and I knew without a doubt that the dream had been sent to show me that I had in fact not recovered from a particular and repeated emotional injury sustained during my marriage. Thinking back, I know that I had made my peace with certain things and put them behind me, but they were too painful to go back to for purposes of trying to release the trauma. Perhaps it was time to do just that, which meant 'going back in time' as my guide had said I should do. How could I hope to heal my body if I was still holding on to pain on some level?

I was not entirely sure exactly who I was channelling and whether it was the guide I had come to think of as my teacher guide Akaron, or whether it was the blue man. I suspect it was the former. I am aware that there are a set of rules that those who channel abide by, one of these being that one has to be sure who one is channelling. In my case, I have no interest in channelling anyone other than my own personal guide or guides, and this is the intent that I set.

I now fully understood what my guide had meant when he said that he needed to shape the information into a format I could understand. He intended helping me by sending me dreams. Actually, the whole experience was just amazing. I had made contact with my guide who was responding to me in a way I had not dreamed possible. Given the painful dream of that night, all I could think of was that I was not looking forward to some of these dreams that I suspected might be flowing my way in future. Fortunately, as it turns out, most of them were helpful only and not as painful as that first very vivid dream, taking me back to an old and very painful place.

CHAPTER 15: Third Channelling - 15 July 2013

I was naturally very concerned that I might still be holding on to an old relationship without even realising it and so for the next channelling, I decided to explore what remained to be done before I could finally break the bond with my ex-husband. My guide, however, had other plans. During my next channelling, I received some more clarity on the issue of the use of dreams. My guide explained that it was easier for him to show me what he wants me to see through dreams and pictures, but that he understood my inability to understand the dreams he sent me. My difficulty, according to him, was the fact that it was hard for me to make sense of all the possible different interpretations of my dreams. He asked me to allow my heart to lead me in this, as I would then understand the dreams. He further explained that he uses dreams to guide me, as the guidance is clearer than if he had used words, because it is the feelings behind what I dream, 'the ties that bind' as he called them, that I needed to understand and release.

My guide pointed out that I seemed to receive the guidance that he sent me, but that I would forget all about it at the times when I needed to remember it most. He urged me to follow the guidance I received, because not to do so, would be a grave mistake. My failure in this regard would slow me down, which is contrary to what I had set out to achieve in this life.

I had noticed that since I started doing regressions a few months earlier, my dreams had become more vivid. After I started learning to channel, they became even more vivid, but also more intense. I now struggled to deal with the deep emotions that the dreams would evoke in me and often woke up quite upset.

The dream I had the night before my third channelling was so vivid and so painful that it helped me to make sense of the third channelling when my guide explained that he would not be able to put into words what dreams could convey to me. I felt my pain in that dream and when I woke up, I knew that I had not yet released it. There is work to be done there. Had my guide merely told me that I had not dealt with an old injury, I would probably have forgotten about it by the next day, despite the fact that I would have made a note of the words uttered. The dream was much more effective. It seems that human beings can be quite a handful and guides have to be imaginative to get through to us sometimes.

CHAPTER 16: Self-hypnosis Regression - 17 July 2013

I was still worried about my guide's assertion that I was holding on to my former husband in some way. Now alert to my tendency to forget the things I am told, I looked at the record I had kept of my three channellings. My guide had suggested that I should 'go back in time' when he was dealing with the issue of my holding on to things gone by. This time, I was going to do as I am told and decided to tackle another self-regression. I felt quite tired, but I was nevertheless able to maintain a fairly deep trance. The life I entered and its significant events, however, did not appear to relate to any relationship issues I was aware of.

Self-hypnosis regression 17 July 2013: I was on a battlefield somewhere in Flanders. My name was Richard *[Dutch pronunciation]*. After the battle, I walked into the woods and went up a hill where I prayed at what was either a grave or a monument. The tombstone or monument had a big, square base on which a Celtic cross had been erected. During my prayers, a group of mounted enemy soldiers arrived, accompanied by their leader and his general. *[I recognised the leader. It was the same soul who had incarnated as the High Priest in my life as an Egyptian architect, who was later sold as a slave.]*

I could not determine what they wanted from me, but I was beaten up and eventually stabbed to death. They left me lying at the foot of the monument.

I was utterly exhausted by the end of the regression and although I could still hold the trance, I decided not to try to delve deeper into the patterns of that life and to perhaps later return to the life to ask for relevant insights. I had the distinct feeling though, that the tombstone or monument at which I had been praying, might have held some connection to a loved one. The soldiers came looking for me there, because they knew how much that place meant to me.

I did not spend too much time digging around on Google, but I did find one reference to a Celtic cross having been erected in Flanders, where it was apparently out of place. My sudden lack of energy when it came to researching what I had seen in my regression, made me think that the break neck speed at which I was trying to complete my journey, was a little unnecessary. Being curious is one thing, but missing details because I was going through necessary processes too fast, was not worth it. I was getting tired and decided to give myself a break.

Two days later, on the morning of 19 July 2013, I woke up at 06h00 when the alarm went off. It was Friday and I did not have any court appearances or consultations scheduled at the office. One of the benefits of working for myself was that I could work when I felt like it, except when a deadline, court appearance or time constraints necessitated dragging myself out of bed. On this day, however, I was free to silence the alarm and go back to sleep and so I did just that, falling into a deep sleep that took me into an intricate series of revealing dreams. I could remember every single detail when I woke up, almost two hours later.

Dream 19 July 2013: I had an argument with a boyfriend. *[This was not someone I knew in this life.]* I was trying to communicate with him, but he refused to engage in any communication with me and kept turning his back on me. I ended the relationship, telling my boyfriend that I was not prepared to tolerate this.

I moved to a different scene where my sister had apparently arranged for me to sleep over at the home of somebody that we both knew. *[We both knew this person in the dream, but not in the real world.]* This person was very upset with my sister for having made the arrangement and she made it clear to us that it did not suit her to have me in her home. I reacted by telling both my sister and the woman that I really could not be bothered to stay where I was not welcome and I left.

In the next scene, I saw a piece of fabric that had been painted by hand. I loved it and I wanted my mother to make it into a dress for me. My mother refused and said that she had been keeping that piece of fabric for the woman who, in the previous scene, did not want me to stay over at her house (whoever she was). I threw the piece of fabric down and told my mother that I really could not be bothered to have something that she did not want me to have and I left.

In the next scene, I was in the process of leaving my home. I had it in my mind that I needed to find my own place, because I needed to be independent. Some children approached me just as I got into the car and tried to prevent me from leaving. I locked them out, but they managed to get into the car with me, through the roof. *[Don't ask!]* Eventually we all just fell asleep in the car, as they would not let me leave.

I moved on to another scene. I was sitting amongst people in an amphitheatre. We were to be trained as warriors. The leader of the warriors, who were to be our instructors, was giving us a preparatory talk before the training started. All the warriors were wearing warrior 'body suits', giving them fake muscles. I thought that if the muscles were not real, it was safe to assume that the training would not be too difficult either. When our group got up to leave for training in the dungeons below the amphitheatre, I was overcome with a very bad feeling about what was to come and I turned around and ran out. One of the others, a young man, followed me.

Later, the two of us turned back to watch the rest of the group jump from a cave opening into the sea below them, apparently as part of a training session. We watched as their instructor, after their swimming session, wanted the trainees to eat raw meat. One girl refused to do this and one of the other trainees, in an effort to impress the instructor, grabbed the raw meat from her and ate it. I could almost smell the fear the trainees all felt. Their need to impress their instructor was palpable.

My new friend and I eventually moved on and found two other trainees. They were being trained by two master teachers, one of whom was of oriental descent. *[I would again meet this oriental master teacher, during a life between lives facilitated spiritual regression some months later. I would also learn then that his name is Li Mang and what his true role in my life is.]* As the two of us joined the other two trainees and started walking down a passage behind the two master teachers, I almost turned back, as I had a feeling that the proper training that awaited me now, would be much more challenging and the instructors much, much more demanding. The oriental master teacher seemed to sense my hesitation and turned to speak sternly to me, so I stayed.

They took us to a garden and as we stood there watching, the roots of the trees came alive and grabbed us by the ankles. Our teachers instructed us on how to free ourselves from these traps and then continued to explain to us where these particular trees could be found, how to detect them and how to avoid being ensnared by them. We clearly understood how it all worked. *[In the dream the strangeness of the whole lesson did not occur to me. I felt as if I was learning a very valuable skill.]*

The dream left me feeling irritated. Annoyance flooded my mind as I opened my tired eyes. It turns out that it is really hard work to watch a vivid dream when one is supposed to be asleep. Once again I had no idea what the dream was about. I wasted no time complaining about this out loud, talking to the ceiling while I focused on the lovely chandelier hanging in my bedroom. Distracted by thoughts of interior decorating and other shiny, worldly things, it took me a couple of seconds to register that someone had responded to my complaint – in my mind: 'Did I not tell you to focus on the feelings you have in your dreams?' Well, my guide did complain that I tended not to listen to the advice he gives me. He was right. I had quickly forgotten what he had said about the feelings I have in my dreams, just a few nights before.

I stopped admiring the chandelier and focused on the details of the dream that I seemed to be able to remember very well, which in itself is a rare occurrence for me. I usually forget all about the contents of my dreams within seconds of waking up, except if it was a painful dream, yet this time I recalled all the scenes in the dream clearly. As I focused on the feelings I experienced in each scene, one after the other, I suddenly, and very clearly, understood the significance of each scene. In each of the situations depicted in the scenes, I had made very definite decisions relating to independence, standing my ground and walking my own path. In the end, I chose a difficult and lonely path, so that I could learn from and be taught by a wise master, instead of following the mainstream, popular and easier option that was available to me. I realised that my guide had shown me a symbolic series of choices I had made in my lifetime and how each of these had been to my benefit. He had shown me where I was at on my life path.

It all clicked into place. In the first scene I had walked out of a relationship in which my efforts to communicate were purposefully blocked, just as I had done in this life when I left my husband, for the same reason. In the second scene, I did not want to live in a house in which I was not welcome, as was the case when I was married. Next, I had given up on something that I cherished that was apparently not intended for me, exactly as I had done with my marriage. In the dream, I had tried to establish independence, but some children were holding me back. This feeling resembled how I felt about my career; in a way it was holding me back. In the dream I could distinguish between bad and good training and between a fake master and a real master teacher and mentor who was prepared to help me, to teach me in detail and to explain things to me properly. In this life, I certainly feel that a lot of what we are taught in our society is not only false, but useless and merely serves to trap us in fear. Yet sticking to the dictates of society can be tempting and can feel safe, as the true learning that our souls yearn for is not necessarily easy and so we do sometimes want to turn away from those who can truly guide us along the narrow path.

Clearly I was going to have to pay very close attention to the detail of the messages I received during my channellings. My guide could be relied upon to show me what he meant, as long as I stayed open to listen. My thoughts turned to the direct communication I had just had from my guide on this issue. This had never happened before and, apart from one more time a few days later, it has not happened since. Perhaps it was just that, for a short while, I had been able to reach up and access information that I needed. Perhaps my guide talks to me more often, without me realising it. In this one instance, I knew that the communication I had received had to have been from him, as we had been dealing with the issue of dreams as a vehicle for information or guidance during two channellings in a row. Given the many questions I try to squeeze into a channelling it might be for the best that direct communication between my guide and I is not the norm. My guide would not have a moment's rest if I am able to communicate directly too often. Besides, he had already told me that he would not limit me, which would certainly happen if I received too many quick solutions from the higher realms. Nevertheless, he seemed to know when to step in and that particular morning had presented an opportunity that he had taken at just the right moment. Despite not always having a direct line to my guide, I never again felt at a loss to understand my dreams. All I needed to do was to focus on how I felt during a dream and the meaning of the dream images would simply and instantly become clear.

CHAPTER 17: Fourth Channelling - 19 July 2013

Needless to say, the lack of energy I had felt a couple of days earlier was soon replaced by a renewed interest in what my guide might be willing to share with me. I now picked up on my true feelings about my career. I was still convinced that I would never realistically be able to escape my career and so I thought of perhaps asking for advice on how to make the whole experience a little more bearable. In essence, I was sort of seeking career counselling on how to save my relationship with my profession, which I had now totally fallen out of love with.

I also really needed to be sure that I had cleared all of the baggage on the relationship front. The thing is, if I was still carrying some relationship baggage, chances were that I would continue to draw relationships into my life that I would rather avoid. I was perfectly happy on my own and not entirely open to the idea of a new relationship. Perhaps, deep down, I knew that there were still a few things to clear and until I did that, what, or rather whom, I would draw into my life, would not be bringing me an experience I would necessarily like to have.

As always, I remained interested in healing my body, especially as my knees were slowly but surely starting to act up again, and so I added my knee problems to the list of things that I wanted to explore in my next channelling that same evening. What can I say, I am a slow learner when it comes to the need to take things slow. I suppose on some level I always worried that the connection would dry up at a certain point and that I would run out of opportunities to get the information I would like to have. Fortunately, my guide has infinite patience.

I had known for a while that more than one guide was involved in overseeing the course of my life. Whereas my guide referred only to himself in the previous three channellings, the '*I*' became '*we*' in all the channellings going forward. I never did get around to asking who the others were, as I was much more interested in getting answers. It still took tremendous amounts of energy and concentration on my part to hear the messages and in places I lost bits of the waves in which the information seemed to flow to me. Parts of the channellings, therefore, did not always make sense to me and the structure of the sentences was very different from my own speech patterns. Afterwards, while typing up the recordings of the channellings, I always had to stop myself from changing the style of the recorded words to match my own style. In part, I suspect that my guide simply uses words differently to the way I do and, secondly, I am very sure that I often miss certain words, or even get them wrong. As I said before, the words come through in waves as if one hears the whole phrase all at once. What follows, is a slightly shortened version of the message I received that night.

Fourth channelling 19 July 2013: *It is our understanding that you need simplistic answers in a way that you can interpret clearly to yourself.*

You cannot keep what you learn from others. It is essential for you to share your learning with them. It takes away from the power of what we give you if you cannot share. Mankind is in great need of assistance, as are you, at this time. You need help with understanding yourself and guidance on the way forward. We seem to be getting through to you, but it is not enough, not yet.

With regard to your question, you may seek help from us in practical matters. We are here to help and assist. Ask any question you need to ask now and we shall answer. [I asked: 'I want to know if there is a way I can make it easier for myself to deal with opposed cases and the stressful preparation before the time.']

Have you given any thought perhaps not to grapple with these issues so much? You interfere with your own ability to perceive the problem for what it is. It is a simple task to unravel the questions and yet you fear making a mistake so much that you believe you do not know what to do. You need to determine what you have to do each time. The next step is your research. After you have done that, you can attempt a draft of whatever it is that you are planning to do. Of course it will make it easier for you if you would listen to our advice when you receive it and trust it when it comes. But we understand your need to be sure what the source of the information is. We shall try to help with that.

We need to give you something to take forward on your other questions asked regarding your health and your relationships. Your health is good. You can deal with the outstanding health issues later. With your relationships all is well too. In time, under grace, it will all come to you when you need it most. Carry on the way you do now. Do nothing different. You are doing well in this world and in your space. Take care, dear one. Until next we meet, in health and kindness, go forth.

A couple of days later, on Sunday 21 July 2013, I went out for a walk along the beautiful canals around my home. I noticed some discomfort in my knees as I climbed a set of stairs and I wished that there was a way to stop it. I knew that I had now been told that these things could wait, but some relief would be so welcome. Immediately, I became aware of a very clear instruction in my mind, like I did two days earlier whilst staring at my chandelier. My guide told me that if I would stand still for a moment, he would show me how to carry my body by placing his energy over mine. Well, needless to say, I was not about to stop walking, looking silly by standing still for no reason. I continued walking, acutely aware that I was now probably ignoring my guide. I was not prepared to pass up an opportunity though, so I looked around to see if there was anyone else in the vicinity and walked on until I could pretend to rest in the shade of a tree. It was a beautiful, sunny winter's day and I hardly needed the shade, but it was the best excuse I could come up with. Apart from being worried about what other people would think, I had some trouble convincing myself that I was not losing my marbles.

And so I stood there in the shade, waiting. I could hardly believe it when I felt my guide's energy simply melt into me. Immediately, the way I carried my body was adjusted. I felt balanced. There is no other way to describe it. I left the shade of the tree and started walking. My feet moved differently and I was walking with a different gait. There was no doubt about it. I felt like a little girl learning to ride a bicycle for the first time. A little way down the road I had to climb a few stairs. So, up I went, this time, feeling no pain. I was astonished. Before, I tended to lean forward when climbing stairs. Now, my body was held a little more upright and I carried my head and shoulders differently. This seemed to relieve the strain on my knees. I was finally convinced that it had indeed been my guide's doing. He did say that they would try to help with my trust issues and my need to be sure where the information comes from. In moments like these, my soul expands and I become more than I had been before. Experiences like these changes one, forever. A year after this incident, a chiropractor would teach me this exact same body posture to help me strengthen certain muscles in my neck and improve my posture.

I remembered that I had been told that I would need to share what I am shown. As I sat down on my favourite bench near one of the bridges over the canal to watch the water running down a manmade waterfall, I realised that there was a reason why I had been driven to write down everything about my experiences so far. I was going to have to tell the story of my journey to wholeness one day. From that day onwards, I knew that I would one day be writing these pages. It was also around that time that I began hoping for a sabbatical, a time to write about the wonder I was experiencing and the gratitude that was beginning to flood my waking hours. One should indeed be careful what one wishes for, because one will get it.

CHAPTER 18: Self-hypnosis Regression - 21 July 2013

After my experience during my walk that day, there was simply no way of slowing down with the work that needed to be done. I did, however, realise that I might need to try to focus on just one issue for a while. Since I clearly had no clue what the most important issues were that I still needed to work on, I decided to keep my intention for my next self-regression as general as I could.   For the moment, I would try just to focus on, and therefore go to, the entry point of my most pressing issue, the issue that is holding me back the most at present. This took me back to the relationship line I had been following and that I had abandoned some weeks earlier.

Self-hypnosis regression 21 July 2013: I was a young woman, running through a forest wearing a white dress with a black mantel. I was blonde with blue eyes. My name was Anabelle. I did not want to be seen and I hurried through the forest. I went to a little hut on the edge of a lake to meet my lover. His name was Philip. It was 1793 and we were somewhere near Aberdeen – the scenery resembled that of the British Isles.

I was pregnant and Philip was the father of my child, although no one knew the identity of the father of my child. We spent the day together and were sitting at the edge of the lake when my father's guards arrived. Philip was killed and I was taken back to my father's homestead. He was a land baron.

Due to the trauma of what had happened to Philip, my baby girl was born prematurely and I called her Abigail. She was taken from me and I never saw her again. I fell into a deep depression and had no interest in living. I did not have a mother. My father was an angry man whom I had shamed.

I asked for insight into the events of that life. It seems I could have done things differently, by negotiating a better situation for Philip and me, instead of rebelling and falling pregnant. I also could have given up on Philip at the right time, instead of putting him in a position where he could be discovered and killed.

In that life, I learned that loving somebody and having his child could result in the loss of both. It was dangerous to love someone and to have a child. It leads to death and agony and it also leads to 'a death of the soul', which is the same as not wanting to live. I understood that these interpretations had filtered through to my present life and had been holding me back, as I have indeed always felt unsafe in relationships. Having children never even came up. I was simply not going to have children.

I asked for these issues to be released in my best interests so that I would, going forward in this life and in future lives, be free to make decisions that were not dictated by fear.

I did not want to leave trance and so my guide, the blue man, took me to the spiritual realms. We were climbing the stairs of an amphitheatre overlooking a great stone hall. At the top of the amphitheatre we found a stone bench where we sat down. Suddenly, my guardian angel, wearing his usual white suit and pink tie was there with me. The blue man was gone. We chatted a while about my progress, about what I had seen in my last regression and about the fact that I was now free. He told me that I now had the information that I came for, but I still did not want to leave trance.

I asked him about an upcoming matter which was due to be heard in court soon and that had been weighing heavily on my mind. He told me that his energy would carry me through the experience.

My research informed me that Aberdeen is in Scotland. I did not know that.

Preparing for the upcoming court appearance was a breeze. I indeed felt energised while I was working. The appearance in court was an aggressive affair, but there was no doubt at the end of the day that my side had won the case. It was a really good feeling. I doubt that my guardian angel would have interfered with the outcome, but I do believe that I had a whole lot of extra energy to carry me through that potentially draining experience.

The 'dead' feeling I had encountered in the regression had in many ways always been part of my make-up. A part of me never believed that relationships and children were meant to be part of my life. These were the things that other people perceived as a normal part of life. In this, I have always been an outsider.

A few nights after this regression, my pervasive attitude about and belief that relationships are limiting prisons, was shown to me in a dream and during a follow up meditation I would be shown how I in this life had successfully used this mechanism to block relationships out of my life.

CHAPTER 19: Dream - 26 July 2013

On the morning of 26 July 2013, I had a vivid dream. When I woke up, my attention was diverted and I soon forgot about the dream. However, about half an hour later, as I was making breakfast, I started remembering the dream. It is unusual for me to have clear dream recall after not thinking about it at all when waking up. Usually, I barely remember the dream long enough to jot down a few notes.

Thinking it over afterwards, I realised that I might have been assisted in remembering the dream, as it was very necessary to bring my attention once more to a basic belief that I have had for a long time about relationships. In my defence, I have sat in my chambers listening to horror stories of betrayal and of people shamelessly using each other as meal tickets over many years of marriage. The abuse and power play within marriages and relationships that from the outside, or from the pictures on Facebook, appear to be very happy, are astounding. Most people never get to hear about the misery inside the marriages and relationships of other people, because no one likes to talk about it. And so society goes on to believe that many people are very happy in their relationships. The best one gets out of anyone is an admission that 'marriage is hard work'. It took my own failed marriage for me to become able to recognise the fine cracks in the marriages of others. I hasten to say that there are indeed many happy relationships and marriages; I have just not been exposed to all that many of them.

The reality is, however, that no matter how unsafe I think relationships are, they have a very definite purpose. They are designed to help us grow and to teach us the valuable lessons that our souls want us to learn. In my case, the problem is that my own bad experiences, in this life and previous lives, coupled with the many divorce cases I had to handle in my legal career, have perhaps exposed me to a little too much reality. I had totally lost the ability to trust that a relationship, when it comes my way, has a worthwhile purpose, even if it is painful. There are some happy relationships and there are some that are happy some of the time. I was just not in the mood to spend half of my energy on dealing with a relationship. I felt that there were many more interesting things to explore on this planet than something as unpredictable as a relationship that could easily lead to all kinds of hardship. The problem with this reasoning was that, in this way, one might indeed successfully avoid a whole lot of trouble, but it could also result in one missing a whole lot of learning, like I did in the case of the cyclist when I prematurely bolted from a friendship before the karmic balance between our souls could be restored. Sort of like skipping school I suppose.

In any event, my guide obviously felt that I needed a reminder of what I had discovered during my regression to the life of a young mother in Aberdeen five days earlier.

Dream 26 July 2013: I had moved from Cape Town to Johannesburg and after packing up and vacating my home *[presenting as a weird place that I was not familiar with]*, I moved in with a single female colleague *[who in real life was a married woman living in Cape Town]*. We shared her small, but stylish place in what could have been either Bryanston or Roodepoort. There were two beautiful swimming pools, one outside each bedroom. The views were fantastic and I knew I was going to be very happy there. Having settled in, we were walking around in bath robes and I was telling my colleague that she should keep an eye out for my high blood pressure pills, as I could not find them. I asked her to check regularly that I had taken my pills, because I had a tendency to forget to take them. I explained that I in fact have super high blood pressure, which meant that I absolutely cannot afford to forget to take my medication.

We went to visit some friends. I told them that I had moved to Johannesburg in order to facilitate a final break from my ex-husband *[though we had already been divorced for almost five years by this time]*. The scene moved to a restaurant where there was a clown act, a pirate act and a farm act, all three happening at the same time. I was telling the people at the table that I would never enter into a relationship again and they wanted to know whether I was referring to marriage only, or to relationships as well. I said I was talking about both as they were limiting and dangerous and I wanted no part of it and would never go back into that prison after taking years to break free.

The first thing I discovered after remembering the fragments of this dream, was that I had not been taking my blood pressure medication for three days. I cannot explain how this happened, as I know the risks. To make sure that I take my medication, I keep it in a pill container marked for each day of the week and I leave it next to the kettle in the kitchen, so that I would remember to take the medication when I make my early morning cup of tea. Our guides indeed do look after us when we do silly things. No wonder I was assisted in remembering the dream.

My resistance to relationships had now clearly been placed on the agenda and would have to be dealt with.

CHAPTER 20: Meditation - 26 July 2013

As the day progressed, my thoughts kept returning to the dream. I felt humbled by the trouble my guide was going to in order to protect me against my forgetfulness and in an effort to deal with my attitude on relationships, decided to follow up on the issue during a meditation that same night. I have to admit that I could feel some resistance during the meditation, but it was worth it as I was shown how I had been blocking relationships. Given the resistance I felt, I was clearly doing more than just blocking relationships; I was also still blocking the work I needed to do before I would stop blocking the relationships themselves. Shifting an attitude is not always an easy thing to do.

Meditation 26 July 2013: I was taken to the gazebo in the spirit world where I have previously met the master teachers. A female master was waiting for me. I had never seen her before. She presented to me as a grey haired, elderly, kindly, yet stern school teacher. My guide indicated that he would now leave us to talk about important matters.

She said that a happy relationship was the one thing I have always really, really wanted. I disagreed. She referred me to the dream I had had earlier in the day, where I had been shown a scene about how much I did *not* want a relationship. She said that I had always avoided relationships by believing that I was too ugly, or that no one wanted me, or that no one could love me or find me attractive, etc. Now, as I had been moving through my healing processes, my vibration was lifting and I was, as a result, no longer able to believe these things about myself and have started looking more favourably at myself. The minute that happened, I replaced the mechanism I had previously used to avoid relationships. I was now avoiding them by saying that relationships represent traps and are limiting and that they are therefore not good for me.

She took me to a place that looked like a theatre or an opera house and I knew I was supposed to watch a scene. I somehow managed to block the scene, as I suddenly wanted to get out of the meditation as soon as possible. I simply did not want to see what she wanted to show me.

I was very clearly and persistently being shown that more work was needed when it comes to relationships. I am afraid that I got more than I bargained for. When I started this journey, I had admittedly been curious about my relationship patterns, but I was not in the mood for a make-over. I knew I was blocking something, but I told myself it did not matter. It is just so much easier not to have to bother with the intricacies of relationships. I could not help remembering the cyclist again and how I had bolted from the friendship, just because I thought things might get uncomfortable.

I was now really starting to connect to my inner resources and enjoying the process tremendously. I had no need of a partner, as in my experience they mess things up, simply because it is harder to give one's full attention to important matters with a partner constantly derailing one's life. I have never had a partner who did anything but derail my life. Support was simply non-existent. I could not imagine having to deal with a partner's moods or inconsiderate behaviour while on a spiritual journey. This would certainly interfere with my ability to meditate, channel or do any self-regressions. I was beginning to see that I was living a magical life in a mystical world and I wanted no part of reality to spoil things for me. In my experience, relationships spoil everything and were not worth the tremendous trouble and sacrifice that go hand in hand with sharing one's life with another human being.

CHAPTER 21: Sixth Channelling - 29 July 2013

With my avoidance strategy now firmly in place, I decided to focus on the main irritation in my life, namely my case load. I had been struggling with a particular case and I had a bad feeling about the whole thing. I also suspected that the individuals involved were playing out an old and very dark karmic pattern. I just could not shake the feeling, but I did not want to interfere in other people's lives and needed to stay true to my professional principles and to do only what fell within the scope of my practice as my clients' legal representative.

Adding to my extensive list of questions for the next channelling, which as always included questions about my knees, I repeated the question about the tune that sometimes played in my mind. My question about this had been ignored during my second channelling.

Sixth Channelling 29 July 2013: *We are back at the beginning when you were despondent and tired and in need of a 'lift me up'. You harbour much resistance to our guidance. We have moved forward from this point before and we shall do so again.*

Coming to the tune playing in your mind, it has its origins in the bashful play you knew as a child. It is an effort to make you feel loved. It chimed in your mind when you needed to know that you are loved. You were about to face incredible pain and cruelty and we needed you to know that you are loved anyway. So when we play the chimes in your mind, you know that the love they remind you of, is ours. It was not a good day when you got married and it had nothing to do with how much you were loved, but our chimes do, and they will always remind you that you are loved, no matter what. Even if you think you are ugly, we think you are beautiful. We shall help you to see through the mist and you will eventually find your way to the light.

On the case you are working on, we have not much to offer, except to say that the matter has a pre-destined outcome for the sake of those involved, no matter what approach you take. Act at all times with integrity and you will find sure footing along the way and guidance when needed.

In respect of your knees, avoid drinking and eating what you feel guilty about and commit to light exercise. Straighten your back when you can and especially when you walk. But lose not hope, for the time will come when you will be free of this agony. Go forth in light and love until we meet again.

My guide, it seems, cannot be fooled. Nor does he miss much. I was obviously avoiding a particular issue and he had no hesitation in pointing out my stubborn streak in resisting good advice.

Once a channelling starts, I have to stay totally focused in order to pick up the waves of words I hear. It is not possible during the channelling to recall any of the questions I had asked beforehand, though I do always record the questions before I start. This time, my guide had answered all the questions on my list. I was especially intrigued by the explanation of the tune playing in my mind. Moving forward after this channelling, I was to discover that each and every time I felt really down or sad about just about anything, or even if I only felt really, really tired or stressed, the same tune would start playing in my mind. I used to hear it only while standing in front of my bathroom mirror, but it now no longer seemed to matter where I was in my home. I could hear it anywhere, even with my head bent down into the freezer looking for my dinner. The tune now had meaning and whenever I heard it I knew that it was my guide's way of letting me know that I am loved. On the next occasion when I was in tears and feeling very sad, the pain was softened when I suddenly heard the tune play in my mind. I smiled as I recalled my guide referring to the tune as 'chimes'. It reminded me that I was supported at all times. Someone was watching over me and I mattered. It was as if my guide was aware of my suffering and not only knew when to comfort me, but also wanted to do so. More than anything, this very personal connection with my guide removed the last bit of doubt I had that these channellings were real.

As for the case I had been working on, the next few months would sadly prove my guide right. My clients in fact never stood a chance. This reality was just not obvious to us in the beginning. Fortunately, before incurring serious costs, we made a discovery that literally meant that my clients had no case. As my guide had said, it was a foregone conclusion. It was just a matter of time before we, as well as the other side, would discover it. It was heart wrenching to see my clients try to come to terms with the unfairness that had been perpetrated against them and the fact that the law would not bring them the justice they sought.

On a deeper level I sense that the help we receive serves to support us through our life journeys to help us stay in line with the plan for our lives. The intention is not to limit us in any way or to interfere with our choices. We get to choose, as this is part of the deal. We in fact have to choose for ourselves. During this process, we will be nudged and given clues. If we ignore the information, the support remains and if we ask for help again, we will be assisted without fail. Some of us, however, seem to need reminders that it might be best to start accepting the guidance we receive. I believe that the reason my guide felt it necessary to keep pointing this out to me, was because I was moving outside of my life plan. Mistakes do not really matter and I have never felt that my guide judged me in any way, but he would always try to nudge me back to what was important in order to keep me in line with the plan for my life.

I would be free of the osteoarthritis in my knees in a little under a year from this channelling and it would only be during the writing of these pages that I would notice that my guide had told me that I would one day be free of the agony. But before that could happen, I had a whole lot of learning to do and I would not have strained to learn more about what was going on with me, had it not been for the pain I lived with every day.

CHAPTER 22: Seventh Channelling - 31 July 2013

Obviously, I wanted to succeed in whatever plans had been made for my life. It was time to go back to the place where I had run out on the female teacher guide who had planned to show me a particular scene. Ignoring guidance is one thing, but refusing to hear it in the first place is not only not very clever, but it also made me feel a little immature.

So, bravely declaring my willingness to face the music, having realised the error of my ways, I prepared for the channelling with the obvious protection in place. It was time to gain a little perspective and to work on creating a more balanced outlook on relationships. I detest the way society limits our thinking, feeding us acceptable programmes that we are doomed to live by, whether they tear our lives apart or not. So why was I now doing it to myself? What made me limit my thinking in respect of relationships? I could not blame society's limitations for my own limited thinking forever.

Seventh channelling: 31 July 2013: *Mistakes may occur in your general translation of what we give you, but be guided by your inner wisdom and accept that changes you make to your life because of channelling will always be beneficial to you, because we can talk to you, through you. It has immeasurable value to us if you assist us and help us communicate to you. It is incumbent upon you to keep track of what you are told. No other way of teaching is more powerful than this. Our assistance to you can bring about years of development in one day.*

With regard to the question of returning to the meditation you had blocked, when next you go into trance, ask forgiveness for refusing the lesson the last time and you will immediately be given access to what you need to see to help you move forward on the path to solve the puzzle relating to your relationships.

This was a very powerful channelling, but unfortunately there was a problem with the recording and I lost a big part of the content towards the latter half. I was unable to recall the intricate details of what I had been told. Sadly, it seems that one has one chance to get access to information at a particular time. It does not flow back later. From this experience I learned to be a little more careful about recording the material I channelled.

I was now able to channel more information, more accurately and faster. I did take note of the fact that my guide thought I got it wrong at times, which was not surprising. Especially in the beginning I often had difficulty putting the words in the correct grammatical order, because they came to me in waves.

CHAPTER 23: Meditation - 1 August 2013

I followed my guide's advice and the very next day I returned to the meditation that was interrupted when I did not want to view the scene in the theatre I was taken to by the female teacher guide. I asked forgiveness for refusing the lesson the first time as was suggested to me by my guide during the seventh channelling and indicated that I was now willing to view whatever it was that I needed to see.

Meditation 1 August 2013: I was shown a little girl of about eight or nine years old with dull brown plaited hair, wearing really thick glasses. She must have been almost blind. The girl was carrying a small soft toy. It was difficult to judge the era she lived in from her clothing, but it was probably somewhere in the mid or early nineteen hundreds. She was all alone somewhere in the woods. I could see tall, thin, white barked trees.

From what I gathered from the following scenes, she had been raped. I could see blood running down her legs. She had been threatened that if she ever told anybody about what had happened, all her loved ones would be killed. She had cleaned herself up and never did tell anyone about the incident. The little girl grew up to be a bitter, lonely woman who never got married. I observed her at a later time in that life, when she was somewhere in her fifties. She clearly did not spend much time caring for herself or her appearance. I did not see a death scene.

I knew as I watched the scene during the meditation that I had been the little girl in a previous life. I was shown that the experiences I had had in that life were the source of my almost total lack of attraction to most men. While many women are normally able to point to any number of men, or women for that matter, that they found attractive over their lifetimes, I can probably count on a few fingers the number of men I have found attractive in my entire life.

In my experience, one has to do more than just remember a past life to release the frozen energies. So during the meditation, I tried to release all the negative feelings and energy that I might have been carrying from that life, as I would have done had I accessed the scenes I had been shown in the meditation during a regression. Since I only observed the scenes as they were shown to me in the meditation, I did not feel any trauma as the session unfolded, as I at no point entered the child's body or engaged with the environment as I would have done during a regression. I also did not feel so connected to her as I normally do to a former personality during a regression to another life.

I did recognise some of the dark emotions I had felt in that unhappy life as emotions I had also felt in my current life. It was becoming clear to me that all these past lives each dealt with a facet of my complex view of relationships. This left me feeling tired. The journey I was on suddenly felt long and endless. And just a little less exciting. I have no doubt that the darkness of the life I had observed during the meditation carried over into my real time experience that day, as I found thoughts of the futility of trying to resolve all these issues entering my mind. Over the months of this particular journey I found that negative emotions, whether these were my own or another person's, had a debilitating effect on me. I learned to avoid certain people, because being in their presence or listening to anything they choose to discuss could literally punch holes in my energy body, causing my energy to leak out until I felt spent, with all my strength simply depleted.

CHAPTER 24: Eighth to Sixteenth Channellings – August 2013

A couple of days later, I felt better again. My energy levels were back to normal and I was ready to move forward on my journey. In the days that followed, I spent some more time channelling, mostly around the issues of my career and relationships. My guide remained helpful, even to the point of giving me a daily affirmation to use for purposes of releasing fear from the cells of my body.

> **Eighth channelling 3 August 2013:** *Standing in front of your mirror, say these words:* 'I understand where I am, I know my power and my purpose. Nothing can harm me while I walk my path diligently. I am doing well. I am free. I release all fear from every cell and organ in my body and from my mind. I am at peace.'

In the weeks that followed, I found a new sense of peace and it was easier to relax and to stop worrying, which was just as well as it was time to deal with a few serious court battles. My guide's constant reassurances that I was doing well on my path were uplifting and ensured that I was able to fully focus on work for a while. I was not lagging behind some deadline set for my spiritual journey, so it was safe just to allow what I had learned to settle into my life while I concerned myself with the work I was paid to do.

In between I continued practising to channel and found the experience helpful, though it did not take long to work out that I would probably never be making a living by doing channellings for other people. In hindsight I can see that learning to channel was necessary for me to truly connect with my guides and to satisfy the scientist in me that they were real. The channellings gave me immediate feedback and ways of connecting the dots that could never have been my imagination. This satisfied a part of me that still thought it at least possible that the images I see during meditation and regression work are all just figments of a powerful function of our brains that can help us heal by telling us the stories that we need to hear in order to do so. It is difficult to explain exactly how the channelling work shifted my perception of how things worked, but it definitely did cement the idea in my mind that there is a whole world or dimension, if you like, that we are not able to perceive in our everyday lives, but of which we are most certainly a part.

Every now and again my guide would drop hints that slowly, but surely started building my courage to eventually do the impossible, namely to follow my passion without any guarantee in place, something which I, with my analytical, organised, structured way of thinking, found deeply terrifying. My guide also knew how to work on my self-esteem. Although his efforts in this regard were always very nice to read when I typed up the channellings, it made me wonder each time if the channellings were 'pure' and if my human filter did not get carried away while receiving his words. In time I would learn to stop judging myself so harshly and to accept the ego strengthening words with gratitude, fervently hoping that they were all true.

Ninth channelling 4 August 2013: *Sometimes you face a matter that is simply intricate. That is why you carry the title and the burden on your shoulders and why you get paid the money that you do. But you understand this already. You also know how this affects your body and what you must do to release your fears and your* *stress. You do not need us to tell you this. Your choices are your own and you need only go where your heart tells you. You will find that absorbing yourself in anything you may choose to do, will reap the greatest rewards and bring the greatest joy. So follow your heart when you decide what you need and want to do with your life. Where you are is good; somewhere else might be better, but you will not know until you get there. Place yourself in a bubble of light and be wise, be kind and be gentle - always, even to those who choose to attack you. Your light shines through you and those who see you, trust you. They know you care, they know deep inside who you are, as you are a light bringer. The light shines through every part of your being. You can be rightly proud of your achievements in the field of energy and you will endure in a world of darkness, because of your light, your strength and your willingness to learn. We feel the time is right for you to seek what you have come to this earth to find: wisdom. It is what you have wanted above all else and ultimately you will find this at the end of your journey, just like your soul had planned. In all likelihood there will be more pleasant surprises in your future than unpleasant ones. May you go forward with great joy towards a brilliant future, shaped by your own decisions. Your joy in what you do will grow, whatever it may be you decide to do.*

I received a lot of support during the channellings to keep going in my profession, as it became harder and harder to suppress the voice that was telling me it was time for a change.   When I felt exhausted after long days of preparation, my guide would promise to help me sleep well in order to be fully rested when I walked into the court room the next day. He would promise that I would have the energy to get through the day. And he would never break that promise. The promised energy surge always arrived just in time. I was always ready when the day began. It was so much more than just adrenaline carrying me through, of that I was certain, because I did not feel hyped up; I felt utterly calm and in control.

One issue stood out in the teachings I received from my guide over a series of channellings, namely the importance of releasing fear. He never failed to bring it up and made a point of helping me to see how fear could stop me from living the life of my dreams.   How was I to know that he was preparing me? Fast forward a year into my future, I would sorely need every ounce of my courage to step into my dreams and there would be no room for fear. Having learned to eradicate fear from my thinking during the months that I learned to channel, turned out to be a very good investment, one that I would need to draw against quite heavily in order to eventually forge the life I wanted.

Eleventh channelling 7 August 2013: *What stands in your way, between you and your happiness, is fear. Continue to release it as you have been told and you will reap rich rewards in due course.   Stand still for a moment, accept your dreams for what they are and pretend that you are not afraid. Pretend that you hold out your hands and welcome your dreams into your world. They will come. Fearless you will stand in the* *midst of your dreams come true. Hold onto hope. Tread your path carefully, with dignity, honour and integrity. Sacrifice not your soul and never let go of what you believe is right.*

It was all so very interesting. Channelling became the highlight of my mundane life consisting of little else but work. I had by now completed eleven channellings. After the first channelling, lasting only a couple of minutes, I had a stiff right shoulder. It felt as if I had pulled a muscle. The discomfort was mild and I did not link this to the channelling, until after the second channelling a couple of days later when I encountered exactly the same problem, but more pronounced. The second channelling lasted a little longer. I finally made the link between the discomfort and the channelling and found a reference in the book on channelling explaining that people opening to channel often experience neck or shoulder pain. The third channelling lasted about ten minutes and did not lead to any discomfort, although I felt like air was popping out of one of my kidneys during the channelling. One month after my first channelling my life was somehow easier and I felt better. Each of the eleven channellings was powerful and each addressed in detail what I had asked about, as well as adding information that gave me more perspective on things without me having to ask for it.

The turmoil of the daily demands of my career kept derailing my personal life. I just did not have enough energy to fully live my own life after I had used up all my resources looking after my clients' cases. I was about to have my fiftieth birthday and I could not think of one good reason to arrange a get together to celebrate the day. I was simply too tired and the mere thought of preparing invitations and planning and arranging an event exhausted me. I decided instead to book myself on a Harley-Davidson motor bike ride to celebrate the day. I ended up doing this alone, a few days after my fiftieth birthday, as all my friends had rock solid excuses for not making the trip with me – yes, really. One of them had recently had a hip replacement and another had some years before almost lost her leg in an extremely traumatic accident, so they were not about to hop onto a motor bike anytime soon, even though they were exactly the type of friends who would have jumped at the opportunity, had their circumstances been different. The others already had other arrangements, because I had told them in advance that I would not be arranging anything for the day.

It is good to sometimes do things that are far removed from one's daily activities, even if one does them alone. The bike ride was awesome and for a couple of months I would dream of buying a shiny motor bike, picturing myself in leathers while cruising along the roads where I normally cycle. Work soon interfered and I never got around to buying the bike I had dreamed of for a while. I did not really have the time to cycle, ride a motor bike and fit in a wine tasting or coffee date with a friend over weekends when I mostly also had to allow ample time to work. There was no point in adding another activity to my already very busy schedule.

My work demanded my full attention. I was in the middle of four legal matters, with everything happening at the same time. I found the preparation tedious, as always, but it had to be done. The burden was becoming so heavy. As I realised that I would probably never be able to escape the reality of my day job, I felt the energy drain out of me. I lacked drive and motivation and perhaps the whole incident with the motor bike made me realise that life was passing me by while I spent all my time sorting out the mess other people had created in their lives. The reality was that I would never be able to work from eight to five if I stayed in practice. The flexibility that my career did allow, was not worth much, as my workload rarely provided me with enough time to be flexible. I spent all available flexible, free time trying to recover from pure exhaustion, instead of living. How was I going to keep doing this until retirement? Would I really have to face strife and disagreements every day for the rest of my working life? Was that all that I would have to look back on? I could not shake the absolutely authentic response to these questions in my gut. If the answers to these questions were yes, and they were, I would die feeling truly disappointed. I would feel that I had wasted my life, no matter how many people I had helped while practising law. I was never very good at lying to myself.

In all honesty, by now it should have been very clear to me that my guides had no intention of making the decision for me and whining about it in a channelling every night made little difference to my daily reality. I hated my job. It was killing me slowly, but surely, and knowing that I could not get out, from my prevailing perspective at the time, was the worst of all. My guides listened, encouraged me and gave me hope. But the decision would be mine and mine alone.

I would many months later listen to Les Brown's motivational speech on *Dream Blocks, Removing Yours*. His ability to powerfully motivate people from all walks of life is simply staggering. In the particular speech he says that life is a fight for territory and if you stop fighting for what you want, what you do *not* want will automatically take over. These words would eventually help me to understand with the benefit of hindsight that the frustrating last eighteen months of my legal career had been an opportunity for me to see what I did *not* want, so that I could start fighting for what I did want. These words would also help me to continue to fight for occupation of the territory of my dreams, even when my dreams appeared futile, to me and to those who cared about me. It is so deeply ingrained into the minds of some of us that one cannot always make a living out of what one loves to do, that even when it is all starting to come together one backs off and chooses to believe one's well-meaning, level headed critics, including that stern voice in one's mind calling for sanity to prevail before it is too late and one's very survival in 'the real world' is threatened. It is just crazy to follow equally crazy dreams and that is all there is to it.

But such insight would come later. For the moment, I was stuck in a very dark place. At least my guides seemed to understand what was happening and they urged me to learn to trust. They knew that I had not yet begun to fight for my dreams. They also knew it would not do to tell me that I should start fighting for my dreams. Some things, like finding the courage to choose a dream and then to manifest it into one's reality while risking everything that is safe, is akin to giving birth. What one gives birth to in these times, is character. A tremendous expansion of the soul takes place in the moments when one chooses to be authentic. It begins in one's mind, where it is safe to admit to having the dream, to play with it before one lets the baby dream grow up and run out into the outside world where it could break through one's carefully constructed fences and start to explore its freedom like a toddler allowed to run free without a parent in sight. That could be dangerous. Who knows where these dreams could end up? One has to dig really deep and listen intently to the whisperings of one's soul so that the dreams that one chooses to let out can grow into authentic adulthood, occupying the territory one had fought so hard to give them.

Thirteenth channelling 12 August 2013: *Trust that the events unfolding now will eventually help you to be free. Let things unfold without questioning the logic behind it all. You do not know the plan. From where you are now, you see only darkness and you have become stuck. The way forward will be easier if you surrender to the plan. Be present in all your moments. You have an interest in things outside of work, which is fine, but ultimately you will regret leaving behind what you have worked so hard to achieve if you let go before you are ready. Be strong and be mindful, present in each moment and everything else will be taken care of.*

This was the first direct reference to the plan that had slowly been forming in my mind. I wanted to leave my job and I had begun to dream that this might be possible, but the dream was still quite hopeless. My guide knew about my plan, although I had not yet fully admitted its existence to myself. But the time was not right and this he did not hesitate to communicate to me. Apart from my training in Reiki, I had no other healing qualifications. There was simply nothing yet to build a new career on. The difference at the time between my guide's approach and mine, was that he was saying 'not yet', while I was thinking 'forget about it, it is silly'. Even in these early stages he was already helping to prepare me for what I would eventually have the courage to do.

My fiftieth birthday fell on a Sunday. A very difficult week lay ahead with my various opposed matters growing tentacles by the day. I was concerned that I would have too little time and not enough energy to get everything done. I was beginning to realise that I would have to manage my health and my energy levels. My sedentary lifestyle, forced upon me by the myriad of shortened deadlines, often because of other people's incompetence or downright laziness, taking their time in doing their work and leaving counsel with a mess to sort out at the last minute, resulted in my fitness levels dropping and my weight increasing a little. Some attorneys would at times spend weeks sitting on a brief just to put things together and then drop my brief off at my chambers a day or so before the deadline, forcing me to work through the night to save a case I had been working on for months.

I was able to settle down for a channelling after having my birthday lunch with some of my close friends whom I could gather at short notice, given that they had all been told there would not be a celebration. My close family lived far away and after fourteen years in Cape Town, my wonderful friends had become my Cape Town family. My beloved godchild was in royal attendance, dressed up for the occasion in her fairy outfit and favourite tiara, wings and all. This was most appropriate, as she was not only personally acquainted with the fairies, she also had a godmother who had good contacts with the fairies. The fairies knew where her godmother lived and had instant access to her itinerary, so that they would always know when the little girl would be visiting her godmother in order to prepare a chocolate coin treasure hunt.

My guide was also especially nice to me on that day as the words of the fourteenth channelling flowed easily and strongly. I got the impression that my guides celebrated the fact that I had made it to the age of fifty. Instead of good wishes for my birthday, they assured me that I was at the beginning of a long and exciting journey during which I would be free to pursue my dreams. I was urged not to resist the good things when they came my way. There was an acknowledgement of the difficult times in my work life that lay ahead for the coming week, but my guides seemingly had endless faith in my ability to handle what I faced on a daily basis. They also urged me to be gentle with those who were giving me a hard time. They reminded me that earth matters are really irrelevant, as I had an important healing journey to undertake.

In a way, it almost felt like a birthday wish channelling. The message was especially interesting to read about eighteen months later, when so much had changed in my life and I had finally been able to leave the career I detested. There would be a different, happier path to walk and the healing journey would indeed be exciting. It is good to know that there is always a plan. Time would also teach me something that I had always known in my heart, namely that my time spent as a lawyer was the best preparation for ultimately travelling my soul path that I could ever have asked for. It was definitely not always as bad as I had experienced it towards the end. There were times that I loved my career, or at least I thought so. But how would I ever have ended up on my soul path if I loved my career so much that I would never consider leaving? I am sure that there are many lawyers who would never want to do anything else and who love all the things about the profession that I had come to hate. Thank goodness for that, because our society cannot function without a legal system and people who are prepared to take up arms on behalf of their clients, figuratively speaking.

I did not know it at the time, but I was to face a long period of utter frustration at work. It would take a lot for me to be 'irresponsible' enough to leave my career and I am pretty sure the universe knew this and was happy to provide the mechanism that would ultimately propel me forward. My matters became more and more acrimonious and my formerly reasonable colleagues were suddenly confrontational, aggressive and obstructive. They seemed totally obtuse, lacking insight and manners. I started thinking that I really, really did not belong in the profession. But this kind of misery is so necessary to make us move forward when we have become stuck. I for one would never leave a place where I was completely comfortable.

My guides, however, kept advising me to stay strong, to do my work with compassion, diligence and kindness and to respect the paths of those around me, no matter how difficult they were making my life. Most importantly, my guides endlessly asked me to release all forms of hidden fear and asked me to be patient as I was needed where I was at this point in time and was in any event not ready to get out. It was almost as if my guides wanted me to stay in the warzone until I was able to separate myself from the negativity while standing right in the middle of it and without leaving the space. Later I would realise that they needed me to learn to maintain my energy levels and peace of mind within the chaos, so that I would be able to find the calm strength we all have within, regardless of what was happening around me. This required me to learn to be patient and to accept the here and now for exactly what it is. In the end, I came to believe that I could do anything I set my mind to, no matter how tough things got. And this, I think, was the whole point.

I was at the time, however, getting really tired of hearing that I was in the right place and that I was making a difference. I still felt that I was helping people at my expense. I worked very, very hard and applied myself to each and every detail of each and every matter. This was exhausting beyond what I can describe and the harsh reality that many clients and attorneys are truly inconsiderate when it comes to payment, by either never paying, or by more often than not paying my bills very late, was not helping matters. There was something really wrong with fighting on the front lines and taking more strain than any of the other participants on one's own side of a case and then to have to beg and plead for payment after a resounding victory.

It was inevitable that I would make a mistake in circumstances where the pressure consistently increased. The day came that I missed something and I gave a client the wrong advice. Every lawyer fears this more than anything else in the world. I had over the years watched my colleagues and judges make mistakes all the time. We are all human and everybody lives with this reality. But somehow, when it was my turn to miss something, I experienced the fact that I had made a mistake as traumatic. It was not a serious mistake and did not cost my client any money, but it did waste time as I had to take some time to fix the problem. I was obviously going to have to inform the client and this in the end presented no problem, but the experience left me feeling incompetent, no matter who assured me that anyone could make a mistake. Given how my guide kept telling me to believe that I was good enough to do this job, that I was good at it and was making a difference, things like this happening made me want to say 'You see? I told you I hate this place'.

I had in fact reached breaking point. Fortunately, my journey through the desert, learning to be patient while I worked on releasing fear in circumstances that hardly supported the particular endeavour, was almost over. The hypnosis course that I had so been looking forward to and that had been cancelled in July, was due to start in a little over a week and it would steer my life into a new direction, providing all the excitement I could possibly have asked for, with a whole set of brand new tools to play with.

CHAPTER 25: Facilitated Regression - 7 September 2013

The formal start to my hypnosis training was the start of a new chapter in my life. Nothing prepares one better for hypnosis training, than having undergone hypnotherapy oneself. No instructor can teach a student of hypnosis the subtleties of what happens to the body and the mind when one enters the hypnotic state. The amazing benefits of hypnotherapy and regression work, whether it is regression to a past life, to early childhood or to any other event in the client's current life, can only really be fully comprehended if one has experienced it oneself.

Despite my by then considerable personal experience with hypnotherapy, self-hypnosis and facilitated as well as self-regression work, including regressions to events in both my current life and in my past lives, the formal hypnosis training would change me and my thinking forever. I did not merely learn new techniques and insight; everything in me shifted. On the day I started the course, the direction of my life changed irrevocably and nothing, but absolutely nothing would ever be the same after that experience. I had found my calling and I was prepared to do whatever was necessary to be able to spend all my time doing the work I loved from the very first moment.

Every morning, before starting his lecture, our instructor read a poem to us. On the first day, the poem he had chosen for us was beautiful and inspiring.

The Guest House

This being human is a guest house.

Every morning a new arrival.

A joy, a depression, a meanness,
some momentary awareness comes
as an unexpected visitor.

Welcome and entertain them all!
Even if they're a crowd of sorrows,
who violently sweep your house
empty of its furniture,
still, treat each guest honorably.
He may be clearing you out
for some new delight.

The dark thought, the shame, the malice,
meet them at the door laughing,
and invite them in.

Be grateful for whoever comes,
because each has been sent
as a guide from beyond.

Rumi

On the second day, the poem the instructor read to us really touched my heart. How did I go through life without realising how beautiful poetry can be? Perhaps it was simply the magic of beautiful words and like-minded people being together in one place with a single aim, namely to learn something that would lift our vibration, but everything somehow seemed brighter.

A Blessing for Equilibrium

Like the joy of the sea coming home to shore,
May the relief of laughter rinse through your soul.

As the wind loves to call things to dance,
May your gravity be lightened by grace.

Like the dignity of moonlight restoring the earth,
May your thoughts incline with reverence and respect.

As water takes whatever shape it is in,
So free may you be about who you become.

As silence smiles on the other side of what's said,
May your sense of irony bring perspective.

As time remains free of all that it frames,
May your mind stay clear of all it names.

May your prayer of listening deepen enough
to hear in the depths the laughter of god."
John O'Donohue (from 'To bless the space between us')

These words simply lifted me up into a magical space that I do not think I ever left again. It is not a bad idea to get stuck in a place such as this. There was something in the air. I felt like there was magic in every moment. The next day, the instructor was to demonstrate a past life regression to the group, using one of the group members as a subject. We all had to put our names into a hat and the owner of the venue was to draw the name of the lucky person who would be the subject. I somehow knew that I would be that person and afterwards the instructor told me that he too had had a feeling that it would be me.

On the first day of the course I walked into the room and heard a familiar voice, but when I turned and looked at the person speaking, it was a stranger staring back at me. However, the person was almost the splitting image of the one I was reminded of. The tone and accent were almost identical to that of the person I had known. I got to know and like the person on the course, who fortunately, apart from the voice and face, bore no other resemblance to the one I was reminded of and whom I had known as The Bishop. However, the individual's presence at the course had stirred something deep inside, from the very first day. The second member of The Triad had entered my journey.

On the day of the regression demonstration and before I knew that I would be the fortunate one to be the subject, the early morning poem read to us simply opened up the emotions that had been stirring since day one.

A Soul's Journey

There was a soul whose time had come to take a human birth, and so it went to the great cavern in the infinite void where all such souls went. In the cavern there were hundreds of thousands of souls, each manifesting as a small blue flame.

When it's time came, the soul stood up and said 'my time has come to take human incarnation, for I have work to do and many lessons to learn. In my life as a human I shall need family and loving friends to help me, to love me and to nurture me. Who will be my friends and family on earth?'

A ripple flickered across thousands of flames and shortly, a few stood forward and said 'we do not know you, we have not met before and are strangers, but being kind and giving love is a pleasant and easy task. We will be your friends and family on earth.'

The soul spoke again and said 'and on earth I shall need teachers, people to guide me, to correct me and to discipline me. Who will be my teachers?'

Again a ripple went round the assembled flames, and a group came forward and said, 'we have known you in other lives and we have grown to respect and like you. We will take on the task of being your teachers in this life.'

And a third time the soul spoke and said, 'and on earth, if I am to learn the greatest lessons of all, the lessons of humility, tolerance under provocation, and love to those who hate me, I shall need enemies. I need people to hate me, abuse me and do violence against me. Who will do this for me? Who will be my perpetrators on earth?'

There was a long pause in the cavern, until at last, a small group came forward and said, 'we are your soul group. We have known and loved you over aeons of time, and your growth and learning are as dear to us as our own. This is the most delicate and difficult of tasks, and if you are to be hurt and abused, it is better done by loving friends. *We will be your perpetrators on earth.*'

Author Unknown

I am very adept at controlling my emotions, but the tears simply started pouring out from the depths of my soul as I remembered the harsh treatment I had received at the hands of my ex-husband. But I also remembered how I had always believed there was a connection beyond our earthly, failed marriage. Although I had left him because of his cruelty, I had managed never to hold anything against him and eventually found peace in the great learning that flowed from that experience. I know without a doubt that he is a member of my soul group. Years after our divorce, the sincere grief and regret he had expressed at what he had done to me and his struggle to forgive himself for his actions, confirmed this to me. Today we are friends and we have an understanding that we will always help each other in times of need. He has on many occasions over the years extended a helping hand when needed, and I have done the same.

Everyone waited patiently for my tears to dry, as it seemed that we took turns in becoming emotional as the days went by. Our instructor explained that things often 'shake loose' in groups where trance work is involved.

The morning's teaching started off with a discussion about what we had learned the previous day and as we shared our experiences and insights, The Bishop's look-alike posed a question using an example that sent shivers up my spine. There was no way that this person or anyone else in that room could have known what I had suffered at the hands of The Triad. I wrote off the fact that the example used was an exact description of what had happened to me as a weird coincidence, but what was to come in the regression later that day, proved otherwise.

As I sat in silence contemplating the possibility that The Bishop who had caused me such pain might also be a soul I was closely linked to, like my former husband, I knew deep in my gut that the harm inflicted on me by him, was entirely different to the damage that my ex-husband had done. Compassion and understanding was part of the fall-out of the life lesson involving my ex-husband, while the results of The Bishop's actions were totally different and were also connected to the actions of The Pawn in this life. Earlier in these pages I referred to The Pawn, detailing the life we shared with the Samurai of Japan. Even after trauma counselling involving hypnosis during which I remembered some of The Bishop and The Pawn's deeds that I had blocked out for fifteen years, I never resonated with these souls on any level that is remotely connected to learning in the sense of our soul journeys. I felt that I had to learn to recognise and steer clear from the souls of these two people should I ever encounter them again, as they would always, if given the opportunity, bring me harm as they had done in other lives and in this life. I did not feel that they were 'my perpetrators' in the unique sense that the word is used in the poem above.

Needless to say, neither of these two people ever showed regret or remorse in any way at any time. I have always only been able to sense darkness when I tried to investigate my links to them, while the same energy healing process of dealing with other people who have also harmed or hurt me greatly, produced understanding and compassion for them and brought about a complete release for me. I did achieve a total release from these people years ago, but in the form of having disconnected from them and staying away from them, leaving all of it behind in the past. I am sure that if anyone would ask them for their version of events, they would still feel that their actions at the time had been justified. In fact, I doubt that they ever lost one night's sleep over their actions which had so drastically changed the course of my life.

By the time my name was pulled out of the hat that afternoon confirming that I would be the lucky one to be the demonstration subject, I was not surprised at all. Given my emotional response to that morning's poem and the presence at the course of someone who looked and sounded like The Bishop, the same person who just happened to casually mention the very thing that once tore my life apart as a result of the look-alike's actions, it felt like the most natural thing in the world that something in my life was up for discussion.

No one watching the demonstration that day had any inkling as to why I had been in tears that morning, nor did they know about the resemblance between one of the course participants and someone I had once known. They certainly knew nothing about the tragedy of my youth.

I was not expecting anything troubling to surface as I felt pretty sure that I had explored most of my lives that had any relevance to my present life and I was looking forward to having some fun. I had dealt with The Triad's actions years before during trauma counselling using hypnosis and that was all behind me.

The instructor used a physical bridge, instead of hypnosis, something I was not quite prepared for, as I at the time only knew about entering past lives using hypnosis. I found parts of the process quite frightening, despite my extensive experience as a subject in these matters. The physical reaction of my body was unexpected and it made the experience a little difficult. However, it also made me realise that what was happening, was authentic. Perhaps if I had known what to expect, I might have doubted the authenticity of my own body's reactions.

Facilitated regression 7 September 2013: I entered the life as a young child, playing outside at a small stream. My governess came looking for me and took me home where she locked me in a dark cellar, as I was not supposed to play outside. Many years later, when I was a teenager, I was still under her care. One day I stood looking out of the window. I could see a stage coach passing in the distance and I dreamt of being free.

Eventually, I was brave enough to leave home and I tried to get a ride on the stage coach as I knew this was my road to freedom. A friendly person did give me a ride, but unfortunately the coach overturned during the journey. I was thrown out and ended up pinned under one of the wheels. Everyone else was dead. I tried to dig myself out from under the wheel, tearing the flesh from my fingers in the process, but I failed. It took a long time for me to die.

The facilitator urged me to make peace with the governess and tried to assist me in doing this. *[I recognised the governess as The Bishop in my current life. I did not know the exact extent of The Bishop's involvement in the actions of The Triad at the time and only found out (admittedly via hearsay) about the more bizarre details of his involvement fifteen years after the event.]*

I was unable to make peace with the governess. When the facilitator questioned my subconscious mind about the advisability of holding on to negative feelings in this way, the ideomotor signalling response indicated some form of interference. It appeared that an entity was present in my aura and had settled in my chest area, blocking the release. The facilitator addressed the entity directly. She was a little girl by the name of Amelia. She was five years old at the time of her death by drowning. She said that she had no mother and that she was able to enter my aura, because I 'was weak'. When she was asked to go to her mother in the light, she became concerned and did not want to leave me. She wanted to know whether I would be okay without her. After receiving the facilitator's assurance that I would be fine, she went into the light. After Amelia's release I was able to make some reluctant peace with the governess, although I continued to resist the process. There was a coldness that remained between us and apart from a total disconnection from this soul, something that I had achieved during hypnotherapy a few years earlier, not much was achieved during this session.

A lot of work was done to free me from where I was pinned under the wheel of the coach, using energy healing methods and employing visualisation techniques to repair the damage and to return the strength to my legs and hands.

The session lasted a long time and afterwards I felt truly rattled, drained and utterly exhausted. When I got home, I went straight to bed. I woke up at about one o'clock in the morning, remembering that Amelia had drowned. I felt as if my hands were very large and floating somewhere above my body. Feeling weird, I decided to make myself a cup of tea before trying to go back to sleep. I could not stop thinking about Amelia's death and I settled down to do a search on the internet. I found no trace of any drownings involving a little girl named Amelia.

What I did find, however, proved far more interesting than I initially thought. There were a number of references to the drowning of hundreds of orphans off Danger Point at Cape Agulhas, many, many years ago. Amelia said she did not have a mother, which meant that she was probably an orphan too. The facts about the drownings made my hair stand on end as old memories started surfacing and things slowly clicked into place, like parts of a gigantic jigsaw puzzle.

A few months after my divorce, I was invited to the wedding of a colleague. As I did not have a plus one, I would have to attend the wedding alone, but that did not bother me much. I was lonelier during my marriage than at any other time in my life, so attending a wedding without a plus one was hardly something to be concerned about.

As it turned out, my colleague's wedding reception was held on the beach off Danger Point at Cape Agulhas, a few hundred metres from where hundreds of orphans had died in a storm many years before. I recall sitting in a marquee tent on the beach on a stormy night at a table of twenty one people. I was of course number twenty one. At some point, everyone was on the dance floor and I was sitting alone at the massive table. For some reason, I suddenly recalled The Triad and how their actions have affected my future in ways that I can only deeply regret. I had long since stopped feeling sorry for myself and in fact am deeply grateful that I was free of them, but in that moment, I felt very much like a failure, always somehow 'not good enough', as The Triad had tried so hard to make me believe. In other words, I was in victim mode, even if only for a few minutes, because I had momentarily forgotten that I had long ago worked out that it was envy that drove their actions. I suddenly felt something get stuck in my throat and I thought that I had breathed in a dust particle. It was a most uncomfortable experience. I had already been feeling miserable and breathing in goodness knows what, was just unnecessary.

I remember that moment so clearly, because I remained aware of that 'dust particle', as I thought of it, for months afterwards. It caused an ever present irritation in my lung and chest and I was not surprised when I had to work my way through a number of chest infections and bronchitis, which I struggled to shake during winter months. After this regression, however, the irritation in my chest would disappear and the chest infections would stop. It would no longer feel as if something was stuck in my chest.

Thinking about that night at Danger Point as I continued searching for information about drownings, I had the feeling that Amelia had entered my aura at the moment that I breathed in what I had thought was a dust particle. I was at that exact moment in time that I momentarily shifted into victim mode, sitting there all alone at the table, suddenly remembering a past that truly deserved to be forgotten. The memory of The Bishop and the actions of The Triad must have made me 'weak', in that it would have affected my energy body and therefore my defences, which would have given the searching and still earthbound Amelia the opening she needed and she settled in my chest area. So when the relationship with the governess, who was the very same soul as The Bishop in my current life, came up during the regression, Amelia probably blocked the resolution of the issue between us, as it was precisely my recollection of this same soul as known to me in my current life that had provided Amelia with an entry point into my current energy body. The memory of an old injustice had made me weak. If the issue with this soul in a previous incarnation as my governess were to be resolved as the facilitator had intended during the demonstration, Amelia might not have been able to retain her hold on my energy once the weakness had gone, and she was not about to allow that.

With the pieces of the puzzle now neatly arranged in my mind, presenting a very interesting mosaic of Google's historical facts and my own history, I still had doubts. Perhaps it was all my imagination.

The colleague whose wedding I had attended at Danger Point had after his wedding moved away from the floor of the building where we had both been practising. At the time of this regression I had not seen him, or had any contact with him, in about three years. On Monday, 9 September 2013, two days after the regression demonstration on the previous Saturday evening, I walked into my office to find a bottle of red wine standing on my desk with a periwinkle seashell sitting next to it. It had been delivered to my office the day before the regression, namely the Friday, obviously without my knowledge as I had been away attending the course. The periwinkle shell contained an invitation from that very same colleague whose wedding I had attended three years earlier. I was invited to the launch of his new wine, cultivated on a wine farm he had bought in an area just outside Danger Point, Cape Agulhas, where he had held his wedding. Coincidence? I seriously doubt it. If I ever needed any confirmation of the connection to Amelia and the fact that she had entered my aura on the night of the wedding near Danger Point, I could not have asked for anything more specific.

When my regression work entails any form of emotional release, or in this case a physical release, I always receive an almost immediate symbolic confirmation of my interpretation of these regressions and their impact on my health and life. Things seem to be intricately interwoven in a way I could never dream up, especially if one considers the events and coincidences leading up to this particular regression. It is the old saying of 'as above, so below'. When I deal with something on the energy planes, it releases in the physical world. The result is almost always some form of physical improvement that is measurable. Emotional healing is more subtle, but no less marked. It is also a little harder to prove to sceptics, yet this is a principle that had been firmly supported by both psychologists whom I had worked with in my own hypnotherapy. Their substantial experience had already proved this to them.

Interestingly, in my current life when I was a little older than the young woman who landed under the stage coach in an effort to get away from the governess, I was momentarily pinned under a horse resulting in a broken leg and substantial soft tissue trauma, all of which healed in time. Had I not at the time been wearing riding boots, my leg would have been crushed. The facilitator explained that we sometimes have injuries in our current lives, echoing more serious injuries we had suffered in other lives, which is why it is so important to release our frozen body memories during our current lifetimes.

The last day of our course was a culmination of a few days of extraordinary learning that would ripple out into my future, changing the course of my life forever. It was apt that the last morning's poem was a dedication to new beginnings.

For a New Beginning

In out-of-the-way places of the heart

Where your thoughts never think to wander,

This beginning has been quietly forming,

Waiting until you were ready to emerge.

For a long time it has watched your desire,

Feeling the emptiness growing inside you,

Noticing how you willed yourself on,
Still unable to leave what you had outgrown.

It watched you play with the seduction of safety
And the grey promises that sameness whispered,
Heard the waves of turmoil rise and relent,
Wondered would you always live like this.

Then the delight, when your courage kindled,
And out you stepped onto new ground,
Your eyes young again with energy and dream,
A path of plenitude opening before you.

Though your destination is not yet clear
You can trust the promise of this opening;
Unfurl yourself into the grace of beginning
That is at one with your life's desire.

Awaken your spirit to adventure;
Hold nothing back, learn to find ease in risk;
Soon you will be home in a new rhythm,
For your soul senses the world that awaits you.

John O'Donohue (from 'To bless the space between us')

It was as if the poet had taken a look into my heart and knew exactly what my soul was dreaming of. He managed to put into words what I was not yet able to express. I could only sense what was coming. Something was about to happen to me. I just knew it. My future had arrived. The baby dream had burst out into the world, not even noticing the fences trying to keep it safe.

CHAPTER 26: Seventeenth Channelling - 2 October 2013

I was still floating on a cloud, basking in the aftermath of connecting with my passion. What I took with me from my hypnosis course, was the certain knowledge that I now only wanted to follow my soul path. Nothing else would do. I had opened the door to an alternative healing practice, as I would after completing the compulsory case studies be qualified to work as a hypnosis practitioner. I had been practising Reiki for many years, but not on a formal basis. I realised that my alternative healing practice would have to be a part-time practice, but it would be better than not being able to do the work at all. And who knew? Perhaps I could look forward to being able to continue with the work after retiring from the legal profession one day, a day that seemed aeons away.

The time away from my legal practice had been bliss and returning to it was almost unbearable. I felt the environment I walked back into suck the life out of me and my newly replenished energy levels were soon dwindling again. I also started becoming aware that more and more people sought my counsel on their personal issues. It was as if my office had become a safe haven for people to share their deepest fears and hurt. It took a lot of my time, but I never thought of it as wasted time. I forged many strong bonds in those hours of sharing and just listening to anyone who knocked on my door while they were walking through a dark valley. Kind words of support cost nothing and these interactions made me feel as if I somehow mattered. It felt so good to make a difference on a human level. I knew that I also made a difference by handling my legal matters in a certain way, namely with compassion, but this somehow meant less to me, probably because of the very high personal cost to me. What I really wanted to do was to make a difference in the hearts of people. And that involved no personal cost to me.

The difference is that in a legal matter one's clients arrive at one's office with the facts and the evidence, or at least their version thereof. During consultation their problem then gets downloaded onto the advocate's shoulders, as it should be, given that the client is paying for a service one has chosen to render. By contrast, colleagues and staff asking advice on personal issues or simply using one as a sounding board, especially when they then actually do try and resolve their own stuff, do not actually download their problems onto the shoulders of the listener, nor does the listener need to pick up their burden. It was a far healthier way of serving humanity and it never exhausted me. It did eventually become slightly problematic though, as I had almost no time to work.

I often ended up working into the late hours of the night before I could go home, as I had spent half the day playing agony aunt. I was aware of this, but it did not matter too much. One learns an awful lot about people by simply listening to them. After a while, I became aware that I was listening with intent, because I was in fact studying the dynamics of the difficulties presented to me, without having to resolve the issue at hand. I would go home and think about someone's problem, making an analysis of the dynamics that led to the problem in the first place, thinking how it could be resolved.

Of course it would have been pretty pointless to share my analysis with those who had shared their pain with me, because I was in the role of listener, not therapist, and besides, I was certainly not qualified to give advice other than in the role of a friend. People in any event do not 'do as they are told', they follow their own paths and they heal when they are ready. I have so often seen people operate under the total misconception that they can dictate to others how things should be done.   They do not even notice that they are being ignored. No one follows another person's advice, even if such advice had been solicited, if it does not resonate with them or if they are not ready to hear it. We should also be very, very careful before we judge people who appear not to be making progress in our opinion.   This is because we know absolutely nothing about the plan for their lives. We do not even know all that much about the plan for our own lives, let alone another's. It is therefore best to devote all of our time to working on our own paths, sharing what we can, teaching and giving advice only when appropriate and solicited.   As it is, it takes a lifetime to move through one's own life plan; there is no time to interfere in the life plan of another.   Our interference will simply be ignored anyway. Every minute we spend trying to correct others from our very limited perspective, is a minute wasted, which could have been spent on unearthing our own hidden blocks.

I am grateful that I understood at the time that people sometimes just need to talk things over in their process of trying to make sense of what they are going through. I also became aware of how many people were, like me, battling with repetitive patterns, being held back by fear and a myriad of other things, not knowing what to do about their situations, except to keep straining against their invisible chains.   As my research into and studies of hypnosis progressed, I would come to see that nothing works better than hypnosis when it comes to breaking the chains that we can feel, but that we cannot see. And so it was that my last months in the legal profession, though I was at the time not aware that my career was coming to an end, provided me with the exact type of training ground that I needed to get into a space where I could really hear what a client is trying to convey to me.

My knees were once more acting up. Oddly enough, for a couple of weeks after the hypnosis course, the condition of my knees had improved drastically and I thought that perhaps dealing with the old issues during the regression had caused me to become unstuck, resulting in the improvement. However, the problem soon returned and I was frankly starting to get really worried. On top of it, my energy levels were lower than ever.

The hypnosis course had rocked my cage where after I had been thrust back into my stressful reality, leaving me feeling more than a little unsettled. I started feeling confused about the direction I wanted my life to take and I felt as if I was being pulled in many different directions at the same time. I was really looking forward to a life between lives spiritual regression that I was soon to have and which I had already booked some time before after fulfilling the facilitator's requirement that I should first have a formal past life regression session with another regression therapist. This I had done during June 2013 and in the process had met Marcus the merchant and the Egyptian architect who had eventually died as a slave. The spiritual regression session was still a few weeks away, however, and I needed more immediate help.

I need not have worried, as my guide was waiting to give me all the help and support I needed. In a long channelling he urged me to continue looking for the sources of my difficulties and to support and comfort myself using the messages he promised I would find by turning in. My involvement in other people's lives, playing the role of listener, appeared to carry his approval and he explained that assisting others in this way was an invaluable source of light on the planet. Oddly, he urged me to let go of the things of the past and not to hold on to them. I was not aware that I was still holding on to anything from my past. Besides, had I not been in the middle of a process of doing exactly that, letting go? I suppose we seldom consciously hold on to our baggage, as nowadays most people understand that letting go is the best way to move forward. I decided that I would keep digging, because my guide would not have mentioned the matter if it was not relevant. I liked the way he ended his message to me, as set out below. Somehow, he always knew exactly what to say to lift me up.

Seventeenth channelling 2 October 2013: *Ultimately there is nothing more you can do than live your life as best you know how, finding your lessons along the way. Be patient and live your life in kindness. Learn to hold the gentleness of the universe in your heart. You are right to worry about things like arrogance and the need to curb your tongue. At times your words can be sharp, unnecessarily so, and you have learned the unkindness of this. In gentleness go forward every day of your life. It is not always easy. Hold on to the hope of a good future. All things will come to you as you may need them.*

I needed the support I received in this channelling. There was hope. Something in the words made me feel very optimistic and this feeling would carry me for a while. It seems that my guide was always watching. He even knew about the fact that as a lawyer, I tended to have a sharp edge without which I doubt that I would have survived, at least not in a litigation practice. The various role players tended to push hard for what they wanted and every now and again it would be necessary to stand one's ground against a bully who had never heard of the fact that one's professional opponent need not be one's enemy. I believe that it is perfectly in order to be civil with one another while still handling ones' respective cases objectively, but many of my colleagues interpreted the whole issue of opposing each other in our adversarial legal system to mean that court cases should be dramas fit for the arenas of the Roman Empire. Who knows? Perhaps some of them might be acting out of experience!

I am a kind soul ninety nine point nine percent of the time, but if you push me too hard and press that button, the other zero point one percent of me is at hand, ready to push back and when that part takes over, my words are not chosen with care and tend to be sharp. Frankly, I should know better and my guide was right. The button would have to go.

CHAPTER 27: Life Between Lives Facilitated Spiritual Regression – 24 October 2013

It was finally time to see the life between lives spiritual regression therapist and I started counting the days to my appointment.

It is odd how your mind starts racing when you know that you are about to be given an extraordinary opportunity to ask questions about things that you have struggled with all your life. I tried to identify the key areas I was concerned about, but in the end I decided that it might just be best to go with the flow and see what comes up at the time.

The session was to take place over two full days, with two past life regressions to be conducted on the first day. On the second day, one is taken through childhood into the womb experience and from there into the life immediately preceding the current life and into the death scene of that life. Thereafter one is taken to the gateway to the spirit world and finally into the spirit world itself. Here one could meet one's guides, teachers, soul friends, soulmates and soul groups. One could visit the Council of Elders overseeing one's life plan and go to the life selection room where a body is chosen for the next incarnation. I was already more than familiar with this information and the general structure of a life between lives spiritual regression session, because I had been reading up on the process and had read Dr Newton's books more than once over the years.

I was ready. At least so I thought. It is important to remember that when we embark on these journeys, we do so while we are in the middle of current life dramas. We may still have to execute spiritual contracts with other souls and most certainly we might be knee deep in trying to resolve old karmic patterns. I could easily go into and hold trance unassisted and so I made the mistake of assuming that my life between lives spiritual regression session would be smooth sailing, because I was very excited about the process and already had a working knowledge of and plenty of experience with hypnosis and working within the spiritual realms.

My session would, initially at least, turn out to be very disappointing to me in many ways, though I hasten to say that this is not any reflection on the experienced therapist's competency. I would not get to meet my soul group, nor would I receive any answers to the questions I ended up asking. I would see things that I did not find surprising, given the work I had already done myself. There would be a little bit of information disclosed to me about the energy healing processes upon entering the spirit world, but all in all, I would end up feeling heavy and slightly shaken by the experience. Parts of it would frighten me, because I simply would not be able to make sense of the way I would be blocked from seeing information that other people get to see all the time in their life between lives sessions. It would take months of processing to finally figure out what it had all been about. Nature takes time to forge priceless diamonds in the depths of the earth, why would the treasures of our souls be created any differently?

Fortunately, our futures are shrouded in mystery and so, as I prepared for my session I was barely able to contain my excitement, not knowing what was to come. I had finally managed to prepare three questions to be addressed once I get to a place in the spirit world where I could ask them. Firstly, although I seemed to have resolved my anger issues and had been downloading a lot of information that went a long way to address the issues that caused the anger in the first place, I thought that it might not be a bad idea to investigate the issue of my perception of the Creator. My rigid beliefs that had caused my anger were now gone, but I did not yet have anything to replace them with. Surely one has to have some sort of belief system?

Secondly, my equally rigid attitude and fixed beliefs about relationships did not 'feel' right. I was by now also more than aware that I was prone to resist the learning when it comes to relationships. The words 'rigid' and 'fixed' hardly indicate the presence of a state within which anyone can expand themselves and learn, never mind move forward. Apart from my less than ideal attitude, I actually also felt a lot of confusion about relationships. I am a logical person and I will always try to build boxes to sort things into. I am a very slow learner when it comes to this habit of putting things into boxes. It never works, but it is always the first technique I try to apply to any confusing situation. Relationships were no exception. To me, relationships were limiting, albeit for purposes of learning or resolving karmic issues. There was nothing special about them. Yet, when I am outside of a relationship, I sometimes wonder if I am not perhaps missing out on something good. I had only really known loneliness within my relationships, instead of outside of them. So why was I sometimes still hoping to find a special relationship, even if only fleetingly? Perhaps a direct chat to someone in the spirit world who might be in the know, might help to sort out the confusion I felt about relationships.

Of course, for my third question, I could not resist to once more try to find someone who would listen when I say I really, really hated my job. I was convinced that I might in the spirit world find a sympathetic ear and that I would be able to find clearer direction on this issue. Something along the lines of 'you were born to do healing work', would have given me the necessary ammunition I would need down here on planet earth to ditch my court robes and send my legal clients to therapy or to counsel next door.

And so we started on the first day, visiting two past lives. There would be time to deal with my three questions on the second day.

Life between lives facilitated spiritual regression 24 October 2013:

Day 1: *First life*

I was a Native American male in my late twenties. I was in the woods, hunting rabbits during a humid summer and wore dark brown moccasins, red skin pants and a dark brown waist coat. An amulet made with brown beads on a string was tied around my neck. I had a brown leather band around my head keeping my long, black hair in place. I usually set traps for the rabbits, but I also had a small axe with me that day. I had sort of given up on finding rabbits for the day, because it was so hot. The rabbits were unlikely to be running around and were probably hiding somewhere in the shade. When I reached the edge of the forest, I saw some soldiers camping down in the meadows. There were about a hundred tents. I suddenly understood where all the rabbits had gone. There were so many people to be fed, they had probably killed off all the animals in the area. The soldiers could only mean trouble.

I had to get back to the village before someone spotted me. The soldiers had horses and I was on foot. I moved back towards my village through the pine forest, trying not to make too much noise, because the soldiers might have put out scouts. I hoped that they had not spotted me, because I was alone and I did not have my full weaponry with me. This encounter was unexpected.

I was about an hour away from my village. I hoped that I might be lucky enough to get away without them seeing me, because it was hot and they might have been lazy, hopefully causing them to stay at the camp. I reached a valley. My small village was just over the hill. The children were playing and people were cooking as some of the other hunters had brought back guinea fowl. There was a four year old little boy – he was my son. He was happy to see me and showed me a clay animal he had made during the day while I had been away. I told him that I was impressed with the toy that he had made for himself.

The little boy had a round face with huge brown eyes and a button nose. He did not resemble me. His name was Akathan. [*The soul of the little boy is in this life known to me as Jovann, my nephew.*] The soldiers appeared and attacked us. They must have followed me. It was chaos. Two soldiers dragged me away from my wife and my child. They were being taken away. My son was screaming. The other men of the village were fighting back, but there were so few of us. We were totally outnumbered.

The soldiers shot me in the chest. It was a fatal wound. It did not take me very long to die. I could no longer see my family; they were gone. My last thought as I died was 'I did this'. I felt responsible for the death and destruction. My carelessness had brought the soldiers to our village. As I floated out of my body looking down at it, I saw that the soldiers had just left our bodies out in the open. They had taken the amulet around my neck.

As I looked down at the body I saw that I had a pointy nose and chin. I did not have a good skin and I had been of average height. My body had been healthy and strong. All the men were dead and all the women and children had been taken to the soldiers' camp where they were tied to trees while the soldiers decided what to do with them. Akathan would not stop crying as he was very frightened. One of the soldiers hit him with the back of a gun, because he would not stop crying.

Akathan's mother was also tied to a tree. She wore her hair in a ponytail in her neck. Her face was oval and she wore a string of white beads around her neck. She was almost as tall as I had been. I had made the string of white beads for her. Her name was Nelan. She was eventually made to work for the soldiers, doing their cooking. She and Akathan were later taken to a reservation.

Akathan grew up to be very angry. He had lost his culture and he never forgot what had happened to me and to our village. As time went by he became westernised, while Nelan stayed a servant and had to work to survive. Nelan was concerned about our son's anger, but she herself never became bitter or angry. She had accepted her fate. Nelan never married again.

After the massacre, a traveller came by the village and saw what had happened to us. He put our bodies together and gave us a good burial, by burning us all according to our tradition. Zooming out after my death, I could see that we were in Central North America.

My name was Mo'an, meaning little bear. As a child, when I was playing and even as a baby, I reminded my father of a bear cub. Both my parents had already passed on by the time of my death.

One of the happiest memories of my life as Mo'an was teaching my only child, my son Akathan, to ride. He was a natural rider.

The most significant event of that life was when I got married. It was the happiest day of my life. It was not an arranged marriage and Nelan and I loved each other. On the day, I had been elaborately dressed, wearing lots of beads. Everybody was very happy, because they knew that Nelan and I were soulmates who had found each other. Our families approved of the union and a leather band was used to tie her right hand and my left hand together. The knot was folded across in the form of a figure of eight. It was symbolic of connecting interwoven lives.

We received a blessing from my uncle, who was our chief. I could not get his name, but it started with an 'A'. He gave us his blessing by waving a burning bush of tied herbs around our heads, which gave off a pleasant fragrance. We then drank herbal tea from a calabash. I drank first where after Nelan had to drink from the same calabash. The tea drinking ceremony symbolised the fact that, as we had now been tied together, we would from then onwards share everything that we were given. I felt as if the ceremony was both a culmination and a celebration. Life could now begin and we could move forward. After this, there was a lot of dancing while Nelan and I watched. At some point, the ties were undone so that we could take part in the festivities that lasted most of the night.

The most important lesson in that life was to be more vigilant and not to assume everything was okay, just because it was easy. Danger lurked everywhere.

I would later have time to mull over the contents of this past life regression. My very strong connection to my beloved nephew did not surprise me and it was something that pleased me greatly. I do not have my own children, but I have always felt that Jovann and my goddaughter were somehow part of me. Each of them, very early in their young lives, lived through a traumatic event. Jovann spent seven weeks in the intensive care unit after his birth, while Samantha almost lost her mother in a car accident five weeks after her birth. Both these little people were very fortunate in having wonderful parents and family members who loved and supported them, but I had the chance to be involved in their care to some extent during these turbulent times in their young lives, which I believe cemented the bond I feel with these two truly special children.

I immediately recognised Mo'an's view as formed at the time of his death, as it is one I shared with him for most of my current life. Danger indeed lurks everywhere. I have always been a very careful individual and somewhat mistrustful of strange places and strangers. Forests in general feel like places where dark things hide. I am almost always nervous in a forest, unless I am in the company of a number of people.

After taking a short break the facilitator and I were ready for the next round.

Day 1: *Second life*

It was late at night and I was walking along a sidewalk. The city streets were deserted. It was a clear night. I was wearing a trench coat with a hat and thick, black rimmed glasses. My black leather gloved hands were in my pockets. I was well-dressed, wearing dark leather shoes. I was nervous and did not want to be seen. I was on my way to meet someone in secret and I was trying to look inconspicuous, so I was just walking at a normal pace, because there was actually no real reason why anyone would be walking around in the particular area at that time of night.

I went into a smoky bar. It was a seedy place. There were about seven or eight people inside, all smoking cigars. I headed towards a table in the corner where an old, wrinkled gangster was sitting. His grey hair was cut short in a spikey brush cut. He was a hardened criminal; a cruel man with lifeless blue eyes. I would not have wanted to mess with him. He was drinking and smoking. I did not sit down and was standing next to the table, because I had to wait until he was ready to speak to me. He finally asked me if I had what he wanted. I was very uncomfortable, because I was supposed to get a document for him, but I was having difficulty getting hold of it. I had arrived without it, as I had been unable to find it. The gangster was blackmailing me. He had threatened that, if I did not get him the information he wanted, he would hurt my father. My father was a diamond jeweller.

The document related to where the precious gems and diamonds were kept at my father's place of work and the gangster needed it for purposes of planning a future robbery. The old gangster asked me how many more chances I wanted and I assured him that I needed just one more, as I was close to getting the information he needed. I was not armed and I knew that the gangster needed no weapon to harm me.

I left the bar, but I did not get very far. He sent his thugs after me, because he had lost patience with me. He felt that he had given me one chance too many and so he told them to get rid of me. They beat me up and left me for dead behind some dustbins left out on the street, but I survived and eventually managed to crawl out into the street to try to get some help, but I was run over by a car and died.

Looking down at my body, I saw that I had blonde hair with blue eyes. I did not have a lot of body hair and I had white eyebrows and eyelashes. I was an insignificant, pale type of person with an angular jaw. Not unpleasant looking, just insignificant. I was between twenty eight and thirty five years old. My name was Andrew.

Looking back over that life, I saw that the gangster had me kidnapped on the street one evening as I left work. I was a journalist for a small newspaper. Two men had jumped out of the darkness and put a bag over my head. I was taken to the gangster who told me what he wanted. He said that I needed to search through my father's documents to find the one he needed. The document was at my father's workplace, where I often went. My father and I spent a lot of time together. The gangster wanted the combination to a safe and the date when the next consignment of gems was due to come in. They wanted to be ready with the combination when the consignment arrived. They did not want to compromise my father by getting the combination to the safe from him, as he would be the key to get the future information about when the consignment was due. The plan was to get the information about the combination from me, so that they could also have my father's life as leverage. If they had taken my father to force him to give them the combination to the safe, they would have had to kill him and then they would have had no way of knowing when the consignment was due to arrive. But if they took me in his stead, they would have leverage and access to both sets of information when they needed it.

As Andrew I had lived in Boston. I had been born there and I had grown up in my father's workshop. My mother had died when I was five and my father, whose name was Adrian, had raised me on his own. Adrian was the same soul who is my father in my current life. He was a private jeweller, but when he got older, a rich man had bought his business and expanded it. He was happy to stay on and work for the new owner. He was not a very good businessman, but he was an honest man and an excellent artist and craftsman. He was especially good at designing and making diamond rings. He called me Andy.

I was a good son to my father and I had saved his life by protecting him from the gangsters. I never married and had no children. My greatest challenge was growing up without a mother, though my grandmother on my father's side had helped to raise me. I had a good life with a good education and after I had finished school, I worked my way up at the community newspaper. I wrote articles telling the stories of the people in the community. I did not have a lot of ambition. Life was simple and I liked it that way. I believed that 'you find something you like to do, and you just keep doing it'.

Of all the events that occurred in that life, my mother's funeral had had the most profound impact on my life. It had sealed my fate. She had been coughing a lot. My father had been the most important person in my life. He was good and kind and at peace with himself.

The police informed my father of my death. He never knew of the gangster's involvement. He was told that I had been killed in a hit and run accident. He was distraught, but he was used to death taking what was important from him.

My most important lesson in that life was that if you risk nothing, you gain nothing. My life had been bland, because I had never tried to reach out, or to reach up, or to reach inside. I had just existed.

The one thing I regretted most at the time of my death, was the fact that there was no one to teach me how to live. After my mother died, I just carried on breathing and merely existed. I did not know I was supposed to live. I died in 1941.

Looking back over Andrew's life, I could see the similarities of his life compared to my current life. In my current life I have always lagged behind everyone, in everything. I eventually reach the milestones society expects one to reach, but usually long after my peers. I am a late starter in almost all areas of my life. I went through the initial part of my life totally uninformed and unprepared for the reality of life outside of the protective cocoon I had been raised in. It is also as if there was a deliberate concealment of information in my current life. I had to struggle for a long time before I finally found the information I needed to move forward and a lot of time was lost in this process. My opportunities were limited and I mostly had to create them before I could use them.

Since Andrew's life, my soul has grown and looking back over his life and my current life, I could see that in my current life I faced many more challenges that 'broke me open' at an early stage. As Andrew I never reached the point where I could break open. I just stayed hidden. In this life, I had been in the same cocoon, but I got out, because life came to find me there, literally tearing open my cocoon and hauling me out into darkness from which I had to fight my way back to the light. I did not bring any gifts from Andrew's life into my current life. I learned nothing worthwhile in that life and made little progress as a soul. I was like a ghost and left no imprint anywhere. Andrew was good, but insignificant.

If Andrew could give a deathbed message to me today, he would say 'Do not wait for life to come to you. Go out and meet it.' I have been trying to do just that, especially in the latter part of my current life, but I shall probably always regret all the wasted years that I had spent being the good girl, doing the right thing and following the rules that had prescribed how I should live and how I should do things. And especially what I should believe.

It had been a very long day and I was really tired. The life of Andrew was hardly inspiring, but it did not matter too much, as the main point of the planned sessions was to enter the spirit world, a journey planned for the second session booked for a couple of days later.

CHAPTER 28: Life Between Lives Facilitated Spiritual Regression – 26 October 2013

The second day of my spiritual regression session did not start off well. I did not enjoy the trip down the memory lane of my current life, going back into my childhood. This current life exploration is apparently part of the journey into the spirit world as prescribed by Dr Newton and taught to the life between lives therapists he trains in his spiritual regression technique. I am sure there are good reasons for this and that it works out well in most cases, but in my case it served to seriously spoil my mood. So let us just skip this part of the journey, as try as I might, I shall not be able to give a positive account of it.

Once we had left my childhood and entered the womb, things got no better. In fact, they became much, much worse. My distress in the womb was significant, for reasons that I would only fully understand almost two years later and that had absolutely nothing to do with my mother or her emotions at the time. What follows is the full transcript of my experience in the womb, directly after the equally distressing trip through my childhood. I include the basic questions asked, as the text would otherwise not make much sense. Given what is explained above, it is easy to see where things became difficult.

Life between lives facilitated spiritual regression 26 October 2013:

Day 2: *Journey into the womb*

I am floating in the foetal position. *Is your head up or down?* My head is up. *Are you on your back or your* *tummy?* It feels like I am lying on my back. *And your arms and legs?* I am studying my arms and legs. *Listen to your mother's heartbeat.* My mother's heartbeat has an echo after every beat. It is almost like it reverberates all around. A beat and an offbeat. *What is mom feeling?* Mom is very stressed and angry, not happy. *With your all expanded all-knowing soul state awareness, are you able to influence your mother's emotions from where you are?* No, I am separate. *From her?* Yes. *What is the reason?* Not sure I should be here. *Does mom speak to you, or communicate?* I don't connect to her. *While in the womb when mom is stressed and angry, how does this affect you?* This is not a good experience for me (becoming agitated). *How does her stress affect you in the womb?* I feel lost. I don't know where I am. *I want to ask you a few questions?* Hm. *You're a beautiful spirit and you have entered this little feminine body. Now that you've been in this body for a while, why did you choose a feminine body for this life?* I didn't want to come here (very emotional). I just hate being here. *If you don't want to be here this time, what is the purpose with which you've come?* Just tap into your all-knowing soul state awareness and get a sense of with what purpose did you come?* I am so angry. *Tap into that anger, what is it about?* I can't handle this being here (very emotional). *Did you have a choice? Does it feel as if you were forced to be here?* I didn't have a choice, it wasn't voluntary.

Tap into your soul knowledge and if your soul didn't want to be here, what was your soul thinking when it chose this body? I can't say. *How does your body's character differ from your soul's character? Get a sense of the difference and describe the differences or the similarities.* It's blocked. *Take a moment and go deeper into those primal safe waters inside the womb where you are safe and just allow yourself to relax completely.* It's *not* safe here! (getting agitated and very emotional). *Did you survive the birthing and grow up to be an intelligent woman?* I landed on earth (upset). *So just reconnect with those primal waters.* I feel like I'm locked out (crying). *Locked out from what?* From where I wanted to be. *Where does it feel like you wanted to be?* I don't know, I just don't want to be here. It's like I have been put here and the door is locked. I can't leave. *Maybe a door will open for you. Maybe on this journey or shortly after this journey a door might open for you. I want you to relax and I'm going to ask one or two more questions and then we can move further back and it will become much more pleasant for you. Scan back and tell me at which month did you, as a soul, enter that baby body.* Eight months. *Move back to that moment. I want you to find yourself hovering outside your mother's body. Describe to me how you enter the mother's body and how you enter the baby body with as much detail as you can. Take me through the mechanics of this exercise.* I can't do this.

Rise up above into the corridor of time. We are going to move away from the womb.

Therapists can unfortunately not see what their clients see. In this particular case, when I said 'I can't do this', the therapist reasonably assumed that I could not continue with the session at that point, as I was already really distressed after travelling back through my childhood. She moved away from the experience and aborted the effort of trying to get me to describe the process of entering the body. I was too deep in trance to communicate the misunderstanding to her. People in trance only respond to questions, they do not elaborate. In reality, when I was hanging above the baby body, before my incarnation, there were two 'aspects' of me. The one I felt was the soul energy about to enter the body, presenting very much like an abandoned 'orphan' energy. The other energy was an aspect of the same soul, my soul, but which was unemotional and in fact cold. It was as if one aspect of my soul took another aspect of my soul to a place where the 'incarnating' aspect clearly did not want to go. That was when I said 'I can't do this'. The 'I' that I was referring to, was the soul waiting to incarnate, not the 'I' sitting in the therapist's chair, but the therapist could not have known that.

During the intake interview, the therapist had explained that a spiritual regression is never a bad experience. The therapist was understandably not expecting that I, as a soul, would feel unable to enter a body. Who would want to miss such a wondrous occasion? After all, souls jump at the opportunity of taking a body, as it is regarded as an enormous privilege if one considers the accounts of Dr Newton's case studies.

In our discussion afterwards, the therapist explained that no soul is ever forced to come to earth. I am aware of this as I have come to the same conclusion after reading Dr Newton's books, but unfortunately, that knowledge did not help me very much during the session, because the fear and misery I felt while hanging over my body and the anger I felt whilst floating in the womb, were real. My soul felt unable to enter the baby body and was in fact in a very, very dark place, feeling utterly abandoned before incarnation into my current life.

At the time I thought that if I had been able to communicate the misunderstanding to the therapist and we had managed to stay with the experience, despite my distress, we might have been able to get to the heart of the single biggest issue I had faced in my life, namely my deep, dark anger about having been created. If I had been able to find out what had caused the severe distress of my soul before entry into my current body, I might have been able to more fully understand all the reasons why I eventually needed my teacher guide to lift the anger for me. Nevertheless, I firmly believed, and I still do, that spiritual regressions are always being watched over and no mistakes occur. I thought that perhaps I was not supposed to find out what had caused my soul's distress at that point. I could not have known how right I was. The regression was in fact a huge success, but neither I nor the therapist could have known that on the day.

Despite not having been given all the details, I knew without a doubt that my guide had a very good reason for helping me to the extent that he did when he lifted my anger. He knew about the darkness. He knew what had happened to terrify me so much before my incarnation and he knew that I did not stand a chance of moving that mountain myself. That must be why there was an exception to the rule that one first has to do the work before the help arrives. He helped me to remove the stumbling block first and then also helped me to do the work that would originally have been required to remove the stumbling block in the first place. All this I would only put together much later, though, during the process of working through what had happened.

After the traumatic womb experience and aborted questioning on this aspect, I was not feeling well. I was emotionally drained and tired. But, I had come a long way and so I needed to go back into trance for the journey to the spirit world.

During the last stretch of the journey I was to enter the last life I had before my present life. On this point, I have often wondered whether our souls, living in a timeless space, can enter lives on the timeline haphazardly. For instance, can I go to a life in ancient Egypt and then enter one in say, the twentieth century, before returning to a life in medieval England? I recall a Physics professor explaining to us during my second year at university that time is a line within eternity that can be entered at any point. The way I see past lives, is that time is like a field trip for souls. We go into time at any point where we wish to learn. And perhaps after entering a life in Egypt, one would return to the spirit world and prepare for a life in the twentieth century and then return home again to prepare for a life in medieval England. For purposes of my session, the next life I entered was a life in Arizona during a time period long before Andrew the journalist would live in Boston, which would mean I prepared for my current life after the life in Arizona, not after Andrew's life. This would indeed have required me to move around on the timeline.   I am of course only speculating about this.

Day 2: *Life directly before present incarnation*

I was a white male in my late thirties. I was quite dirty and was riding a saddled, chestnut brown horse. It was a slow ride through the Arizona desert. I looked a little like a bank robber. I was wearing a jacket and had a lot of bullets tucked into the gun belt tied across my shoulders. I had a gun in a holster on my hip and a rifle in the saddle, as well as a rope, a water bottle and a blanket. I was already two days' ride away from the nearest town. It was Indian country. I had travelled from Mexico where I had bought cattle from a rancher. I had left the cattle in Mexico and was now on my way to the man who had sent me. Some cowboys would be returning with me to drive the cattle to their new owner's ranch in Arizona. I wanted to get to the railway station and make the rest of the journey by train and I was upset to find that they were still busy building the railroad.   I ended up continuing the journey on horseback.

I was always travelling and did not really have one place to stay.   I did long distance contract negotiations for people who did not want to take so much time to travel somewhere, so I did their business for them.   I was a loner. I did not mess with other people and I expected them not to mess with me.   Nothing much upset me and I was never overly concerned about anything. I just took each day as it came. It took me three months to reach the rancher who had sent me to buy the cattle. He was living in a sprawling house on a cattle ranch. He had lots of animals and horses and a number of Mexicans were working for him. I had in fact purchased the cattle in Mexico from a family member of the rancher's chief farm hand. It was a good contact to have. The old rancher, named Hunt, came to greet me when I arrived on the ranch. He was in his late sixties, but he looked much older. His medium length hair was white grey and curly. He was bow-legged and wore a big belt buckle with a bull engraved on it, an off white shirt, tan coloured breeches and cowboy boots. Hunt had a big nose and dark brown eyes and I thought that he probably had Mexican blood. *[I think he is someone I know in my current life, but I could not place him.]* He had not expected me to be back so soon. It was clear that we had a good relationship. He welcomed me by patting me on the back and called me Al. We had lunch, which consisted of beans, homemade bread and potatoes served with fried onion, beef and tomato stew. I would rest for a few days and then I would join the cowboys going down to Mexico to fetch the cattle I had purchased for Hunt.

[Moving to the most significant event in the life.] We were driving the cattle from Mexico back to Arizona. Our leader was a ranch hand named Anthony. He was

very good at driving cattle. My role was to accompany the farm hands to Mexico and to then guide them back to the ranch along the safest route, because I knew the land really well. I was a good rider and I knew all about cattle, so I helped the men to handle the herd and took part in the cattle drive. I knew where to go, because I had done this many times. It was how I earned a living. I knew the mountain ranges like the back of my hand. I got to know where the rivers and the streams were. As time went by, people started building small towns, as well as the rail road, which made things easier.

During the drive, there was a bit of a tussle and some of the animals got bunched up as they pushed out to the side of the herd. The animal on the far side of the herd unexpectedly tossed its head out and its horn got hooked in my stirrup, snapping it off. I lost my balance and fell to the ground when the stirrup snapped, as I had actually been galloping at the time to try to drive the herd back. I was trampled to death.

Looking down at Al's body, I saw that Anthony got to my body first. He closed my eyes and took off his hat, saying a prayer. He was a hardened cowboy, living off the land. We were so much alike. He knew that I would not particularly mind how I had died, or that I had died. It was obviously a messy scene, but the cowboys were used to this kind of thing. It happened all the time and was just part of the risk farm hands faced. Obviously, it left them with a bit of a problem, because I had been their navigator. They sort of straightened my body out, because my legs had been twisted and broken during the trampling. They buried me near a tree on a rocky outcrop. They took some time and trouble to cut a few nice white rocks and put them in a pile on top of my grave to protect my body from the animals. They also made a rough, unmarked wooden cross and put my dirty, sweaty, dusty hat on top of it.

Before crossing over, looking back over Al's life, I saw that Al had been an orphan. He had been born on Hunt's farm. His father, who had died at quite a young age, had been a ranch hand there. Al's mother had died at birth. Hunt raised him after his father's death. There was no one my soul needed to say goodbye to before going to the spirit world. I knew that Hunt would understand that this is just how it is.

What follows is the direct transcript of the answers elicited by the facilitator during my journey into the spirit realm, with only some of the questions included for purposes of clarity.

Journey into the spirit realm

I move away, not too fast and straight up. I can see everything getting smaller. It's nice to actually see from up there. The space around me stays the same really. I am in the clouds. There's somebody there, in the clouds. It's a male. It's a teacher that I've seen so many times before. He always wears what looks like a Greek or Roman robe – it's just a robe, it's not elaborate or anything. He has grey semi-curly hair, shoulder length. Old and wise with blue eyes. He waits for me - I have to go to him. I join him there. I feel like I've been away and I'm getting back after a long trip. He is here to welcome me. He is called Akaron. There's a hill. We're walking up a hill now. He's on my right hand side. He has his hand on my shoulder and I can see I'm gesturing and explaining.   I'm telling him about how I got trampled. He's nodding his head. We get to the top of the hill and there is … it's like a huge stone city in the valley. I don't know what this place is. I can't really … it looks … I don't understand what's happening now. There's nowhere to go.   There's just this place, but it doesn't seem to be a real place. I don't think we're going to go down there. I think Akaron is reminding me of another life. And … this place is a reminder … a key … an ancient life I had … I think in that life I was a young man and I think in that life I died and there were some white rocks involved. I got crushed by those rocks. He is showing me the similarity in the two deaths. Oddly enough, Al's grave was marked with rocks that looked like the rocks that killed me in the ancient life. He is trying to show me something … it has something to do … with being crushed. He's showing me a pattern and that it doesn't always need to be like that.

We're now walking again and it looks like we're walking on a pathway running along the top of a range of hills and there are all these deep valleys on the side of the pathway. We walk in between these valleys ... they are my lives. It's like ... if you should go down into the valley you would walk into an amphitheatre from where a life can be observed. But we're not going to go to all ... or any of them. We can, but it is not necessary. So I think we're just walking through them. It seems like I've had quite a few and some of these valleys have nothing in them so ... that means that it is done and closed and there is nothing more that I could learn from them or need to be reminded of. Akaron and I talk as we walk, but it's like a general discussion ... it's a 'we'll talk more later' scenario ... It's almost like ... I'm excited to share something that I am over eager or over enthusiastic about. It feels like when you've just been through an obstacle course and you've cleared some hair raising hurdles and survived them all and you just want to tell somebody about it. I'm obviously happy with myself. I'm watching from the outside. I'm not really part of the discussion. I am not sure where I am watching from.

We've arrived somewhere else now. It's a portal, a round hole with light shining through it. We're in the dark now, it looks like the inside of a cave, but we're actually outside. So the darkness of the cave is outside, it is inverted. I'm supposed to go through the portal. It doesn't look like Akaron is coming with me. He says 'I

---

can't come with you this time, but you will be alright'. I find it strange, because he always goes with me. It's a weird place. It doesn't look ... ah ... there's a Japanese garden ... there's a Japanese master coming towards me. He has a long, grey beard and he's wearing a pointy hat with a tassel at the top. His moustache is also long and pointy and he wears ... loose fitting garments ... dark, more navy, with sort of puffy sleeves. The bottom part ... the pants ... they're cream and also puffy and taken in around the ankles, with white socks and the same dark navy ... slipper-like soft shoes. His tassel represents the fact that he is a master. He works with energy. He says I need some healing. He meets me halfway. We meet at a pink cherry blossom tree and there's a lovely pond and clear water and some rocks. He invites me to sit down with him ... on a stone bench. He says I need to leave the old and injured body behind, as I'm still carrying the essence of that body with me. I think he's right. He will help me. He is making a ball between his hands. It looks like light and water mixed. And he asks me to stand in the middle of the pond. He reaches up and puts the ball above my head and it just sort of ... stays there. I'm already feeling so much better and I know that this will be an energy rinsing so it's clearing it all away. He's making me do it myself. He has put the ball there, but he says I have to learn to do this and I have to reach up and in and connect with the ball and only then can the energy be released, once I've reconnected with my essence. I reach up into the ball

205

with my mind. I just … it's like a deep meditative state. And then the ball just lights up and expands … grows larger and larger and lighter and lighter and becomes pure white and then the energy starts pouring out from under it and over me. It's gentle … but I'm still … I can't feel anything. I'm watching. The master is Li Mang. He seems to know me very well. He is very familiar. I don't know that I know him. I just recognised him without … it's like it wasn't a surprise to see him. I don't know who he is, but I think he always does my healing. [*During the writing of these pages I realised that I had met Li Mang for the first time in a dream three months before this session.*] I can't find my name. [*In response to a question regarding the name Li Mang uses to address me.*] I don't know what it is. I feel my soul now … It's like I have left the other identity behind. I think the ball is done now. We start walking. We're on our way somewhere again, in a different direction to the one I had come from. There are again just these flowing, rolling, green, grassy hills. We're talking about the mechanics of energy. He shares with me the importance of energy healing. He says it will be better if I can connect to the ability to heal myself when I'm in a body. He says that I will be reminded of the energy ball next time [*current life*], and of how I can make it between my hands and then tap into it. I am already working with energy as a soul, I just didn't focus on that this time round [*in the life of Al*] and … there was something else I was supposed to do, so energy work wasn't the focus of that life. But energy ... as a soul ... is very important to me. Li Mang says that, in a way my connection with energy can be triggered by the Eastern ways, because I associate the energy work and energy healing with the teachings of the East. This will trigger my interest in Reiki in my next [*current*] life because it is Eastern in origin so next time when I need it, it will come in a form that I will recognise. Li Mang says my current life is all about energy. He's smiling. It is my life's work. Energy is everything. Understanding it can be everything and it doesn't matter what you do, if your trade is energy, then you can work anywhere, in any space and at any time. You just need to focus on what resonates with your soul and if where you are interferes with the resonance, you have to remove yourself. You have to let your experience of what resonates with you, guide you. [*In response to a question about whether I need to give up my career to embrace healing and energy work.*] He says I'm a good student of energy with a lot to learn and a long way to go, but he's very pleased with my progress. In the short term I should focus on healing. I get the sense that he doesn't want to be more specific. He has brought me to the next place that I have to be at. There's a stone wall with a wooden door, a lime-washed wooden door ... and there's a knob with two stone steps going up and there are flowers growing on the side. Li Mang is now saying goodbye and walking back. I must go through this door now. There's a passage beyond the door and there's a light at the end of the tunnel. I get out of the tunnel … and there's a little bridge over a stream and it's tropical … like a forest. There's someone waiting, sitting on a rock. It looks almost like a fairy … elf-like person … she looks a little like Tinkerbelle, well, a big Tinkerbelle really – she is the same size as a normal human being. She is here to address the more feminine aspects of me. I get the feeling that I am on my way somewhere and that along the journey every time there'll be somebody, and this is her stretch with me and we're going to go through this jungle together. It is in fact like 'a classroom' and she is not really a fairy, she just presents herself like that. I get the impression that she has been patiently waiting for me, she is very friendly and happy to see me, eager for us to continue. I am supposed to reconnect … with my feminine aspect. This is the purpose of the jungle, because being close to nature and just absorbing nature, like I used to know it on earth, will reconnect me. It is the power of water, the power of being outside in a lush green garden … because the space is grounded and the space is … it's almost like the heart of the universe … it's where things grow and where things start and where life begins. (Sigh) I still don't feel much … I still feel disconnected in a way … I see things happening and it's almost like intellectually I know what's happening, but I'm not there. I feel something's lost … like a … it's like a … a disconnected aspect. (Sigh) … I don't … I don't even know if anybody knows it's gone, because it's isolated and I can't get there and they don't know about me … so I just follow. [*Therapist asks if healing/EMF balancing from her would help me reconnect.*] I seem to hear 'yes', but I can't say where it comes from. [*Healing given − with assistance of female guide accompanying my soul through the forest.*] I feel okay now, I think it's okay. And I must go on now. There's a pathway and I walk up it. There's a blue light at the end of the pathway, shining out of another portal for me to go through. I'm alone now, but somebody will come for me now. My guide [*the blue man*] is now waiting there for me. He asks if I'm ready and I say 'Of course, always'. He has a sense of humour. Whenever he's around, I'm always happy, smiling. He is the guide that is always with me when I do regressions. It looks like he is wearing a Spiderman-like suit, made of blue crystals. I can't see his face, but I can sense his emotions when he communicates telepathically. He has a huge yellow crystal on his chest, which is almost like a heart. It has five points and it symbolises healing − to me at least. He's just always present, wherever I need to go, he comes to help. He's never wanted to reveal a name to me. I just call him the blue man. The five points of the crystal on his chest represent love, light, happiness, kindness and grace. We have to go through this portal now into the blue light.

I'm now sitting on the outside of a cave on a rock. I'm just watching the valley below. It's huge. I seem to think it is the spirit world. Oh ... it's hard to concentrate on this. The blue man is asking me what I want to see. I say that I thought he was going to take me where I need to be. He says he doesn't always have to make things easy for me, although he tries, but it is not really his job. It's so typical of him. I just know he's laughing, even though I can't see his face behind the mask. Hmm, I'm missing something, clearly. He's asking me what I have come to do. I've come to reach up. I'm reaching up and ... and in a way ... it takes a lot of trust to reach up and if I don't somehow connect to anything that propels me forward it is going to be very hard to go back and carry on. He wants to know if I don't think that the whole process of reaching up can in itself sometimes be sufficient. I don't agree. I want answers. I'm tired of reaching up all the time and getting a droplet of information each time. It's taking too long. He says I'm being true to myself, impatient as always. (Sigh). So now it seems I can decide and choose where I want to go. And that will then be evaluated to see if it can be done. So now I don't know. *Where would you like to go?* Well, this is the first thing that comes up now, but I didn't think it was important at all, yet in this moment I seem to want to know ... why I have to live without my soulmate present this time around, because I think it is for the whole life, I don't think it will change and I seem to think there is a reason for it, but I need to understand that. I think I know what it is anyway, but I just … *Maybe we can expand the question and ask the blue man – am I going to meet my soulmate in this life or am I going to be alone in this life and what is the reason?* I have a feeling that I can't ask that. *Are you limited in what you may ask?* No, it … I think I'm … the issue of meeting my primary soulmate or not, has not yet been decided … it's in a sense something that I still need to choose, or not. *Can you accept that?* Yes, but … (sigh) … it's the kind of thing that frustrates me, because I know there are choices, but I don't know which one is best. Both can have value, I just don't know which choice would be best for the path. (Sigh). I don't want to choose something that slows me down again. (Sigh.) The blue man is now very silent. I'm feeling a bit stuck now … there's suddenly just nothing. And I'm not there anymore. [*Therapist asks Akaron to come and help me move along to where I need to go, or to a place where I can get answers.*] (Deep breath and release.) Okay, my teacher guide is now back. And … it's a place I've been to before … it's a … there's a stone bench in an amphitheatre and again the rolling green hills everywhere … and there's a temple (deep sigh). I'm outside in the amphitheatre on the stone bench. There is somebody else. The blue man is no longer here. It's just my teacher guide and there's … I'm not sure … I've seen … this guide before … but I'm not sure if it is a guide or an angel actually … he presents as … he looks like an angel with the typical perfect golden hair and blue eyes and white suit with a pink satin tie. But I know it is just a presentation it's not ... really what he looks like. Ah! He says my soul is torn. (Upset, crying) It's just that old familiar horrible pain ... it's just this endless, endless, endless source of pain ... it never, ever stops ... I'm tired of trying to heal it. It is just never possible. It blocks me from everything. I can't grow. I can't progress. I can't heal. I can't get better. I can't connect. I can't be free. (Very, very upset.) *So why is he showing you this now? What can you benefit from him showing you this?* Because this is the source. *And what can you do about this pain? Connect with the angel and ask him to show you how you can start healing this pain and disconnect from it. How can you put this pain behind you?* You have no ... idea ... how ... much resistance I'm feeling ... now (Struggling to speak, throat constricted – holding in emotion). *Would you like to take a break?* It won't help. *Okay. This resistance you are feeling, can you describe it? What is it resisting against?* (Difficulty speaking – jaw clenched). Against getting better. Against healing. It's always like that. (Difficulty breathing, holding in emotion.) *For how many lives have you felt this pain?* Forever. It's so thick and deep and dark ... it's endless ... endless. Like a black hole in my soul. It just pours out. *Good, I want you to move away from the pain.* (Struggling – holding in emotion). My throat is closing up. *And as you feel my hand on your shoulder, just rise above that and I'm going to ask your guide to take you away from this and possibly visit the Council of Elders or possibly your soul group. Where would you like to go?* Ahh, I'm feeling so dejected (crying). [*Therapist takes several minutes to calm me down.*] *Tell me where your guide takes you next.* I don't see anything. *I'm going to ask you a question: would you like to visit the Council of Elders or would you like to visit your soul group?* I don't know, something's wrong. [*Taking a break.*]

We tried one more time, but the session had to be aborted. Upon entering trance again, I continued to feel 'cut off', from the spirit world itself I suspect and I experienced unbelievable emotional pain and could not stop crying. It was pointless to continue. The moment the therapist expanded on my original question about the reason why my primary soulmate and I had apparently decided not to incarnate together and asked whether we were actually going to meet, I could literally feel the connecting energy shut down. I felt that I had been kicked out of the spirit world. Akaron did come to help when the therapist asked him to help me move along to where I needed to go or to take me to a place where I could get answers, but by then I had already left the place in the spirit world where I had been waiting to go further. Akaron took me to a place that I often visit during my meditations. My guardian angel was also present and he was the one who told me that my soul was torn. That was the source of the pain.

In the discussion that followed, we tried to make sense of what had happened, but I was now drained and in the grips of the awful emotion that seemed to reach into my bones. In those moments I felt as if I do not have a soul group, something which I know not to be true. I was feeling like a lost soul, trapped in a very dark and lonely place, with no way out of a loop in time. I remembered how the one aspect of me seemed to go through the reconnection to my feminine aspect in the jungle, while another part seemed to follow unnoticed. It was the orphaned part of my soul, the part that no one even seemed to know was missing, the one that felt sheer terror at having to incarnate. Is this why my guardian angel looked so serious when he told me that my soul was torn? It certainly made sense. Nothing else could possibly have caused the pain I was feeling.

Something inside of me obviously had great expectations for this day, but I was so tired and this probably added to the dark mood that followed me into the evening of that day. A part of me was losing hope, although I could not say precisely in respect of what I was losing hope. I felt despondent and unloved, in the divine sense, as I indeed come from a very close knit and loving family. In fact, I could feel nothing. There was a deadness in my bones, almost as if the only emotion I was capable of, was pain. So I could either feel dead, or I could feel pain.

Slowly but surely the darker years of my life came back into my memory. If this is the space my soul is in, then it makes complete sense that I in this life seldom managed to go through a single day without feeling a deep, deep sadness. It is no wonder that I have never resonated with life, as if I was not really a part of it. I have always been completely incapable of understanding people's joy and love of life. To me, they appeared uninformed, shallow and silly. I began to realise, however, that I might have been exposed to a form of darkness that had destroyed my ability to love life, before I was even born, as whatever it was, had also resulted in my soul being torn. Perhaps most people are not exposed to this kind of darkness before incarnation and perhaps that is why people in general see life as a wonderful gift, while I could not.

The odd thing is, I have no idea how my soul got torn and how I ended up in the darkness. I do believe that whatever happened, had happened before my incarnation. If my soul was torn, I would never, ever have been sent into an incarnation, leaving the spirit world without the basic requirement, namely a soul that is well prepared and ready for the journey. Of that, I am very sure. Of all we know of the spirit world, thanks to the brilliant work of people like Dr Newton, the process certainly does not include abandoning a soul or sending it to a place where it will not cope due to its condition. So I either chose the disconnected circumstances of my present incarnation or something happened somewhere between my soul leaving the spirit world to take a body and actually hovering over my body. There was a missing piece of the puzzle.

I did not get very deep into the spirit world and only managed to skirt around the areas of healing that most souls are taken to after crossing over before entering the spirit world to continue their work there. As a result, I actually have no idea what my life plan is or who my soul group members are. I did not get to find out why my primary soulmate and I had apparently chosen not to incarnate together this time. I would also have liked to know why I had experienced such resistance upon entering my current body. The reasons for the resistance I felt when I was called upon by the blue man to decide which part of the spirit world I wanted to visit also remained a mystery.

The therapist and I spent some time discussing the possibility that my soul had been disconnected from the soul matrix. I was not quite sure what this really meant and the idea did not really resonate with me. I was exhausted and battling to cope with the wave of negativity that seemed to hit me in the aftermath of this session. It would take months for me to come to terms with the conclusions I could put together from the facts of the session. It was not easy to recognise the familiar underlying emotion I had carried with me every day of my life for over four decades in its raw form. This was without a doubt the source of my inability to connect to happy feelings or even to remember happy moments, despite the fact that loving parents had raised me. When I did feel a measure of happiness, the feeling was fleeting and not sustainable. It certainly explained the miserable journey through my childhood into the womb on the first day of the spiritual regression sessions. No happy memory can survive a pain so deep that it is ingrained into one's very bones, filtering through to every cell of one's being.

I started seeing why I felt so different from everyone else. Everyone seemed to accept and to be grateful for the human condition, operating within their different religions or belief systems, happy to be human. I, on the other hand, found myself seriously rebelling against the very existence of the human condition. On more difficult days after this session, I would wonder if I had not simply been cast out of the spirit world. Odd how one's own conditioning takes over in moments when one feels down, especially if feeling like a victim and acting like one has been part of one's make up for a very long time. I certainly never experienced my Creator as loving and kind, quite the opposite in fact. Whatever I prayed for, I could be very sure that I would get the opposite in its worst form. So I had almost fifteen years earlier, after thirty five years of unanswered prayers, finally given up on praying. Thinking back over those years, I was beginning to think that perhaps there was such a thing as being disconnected from something, whether it was from God, the spirit world or the soul matrix, whatever the latter might be.

Connecting with the dark pain was like discovering that my soul is sick. I felt like I had lived a million lives and that all the pain of those lives had been collected into one pool. And I was drowning in it. Sadly, this had come up once before, during trauma counselling. I thought then that I had handled it, but it was because I had thought at the time that the source of that pain was seated in this life and caused by the vicious actions of The Triad. Maybe it was the distortions created in my energy body by the fact that my soul was torn that had drawn individuals into my life who had the power to almost destroy my sanity through their cruelty. What if an ancient or a pre-incarnation trauma was the reason why such people could enter my reality? I was going to have to look more closely at my soul's condition.

As I said at the beginning of these pages, I had made my peace with my anger and had buried it, not allowing my arguments justifying my anger to control my life. Whether I belonged here or not and whether I liked it or not, it was no use fighting a system one cannot escape from. I could hardly move to another universe because I did not like the present one. So my motto was 'work with what you have'. I was just really disappointed when I ran into a wall in the spirit world. I had had such an amazing journey since the day my guide had lifted my anger and I had truly started connecting with life itself. I really did hope that all of that would culminate in a good experience in my spiritual regression.

I have lived my life as best I could, because I had no choice but to continue breathing. One cannot just sit around waiting to die. It simply does not work that way. Besides, sitting around all day, feeling like a victim and pondering all that is wrong with the world, has got to be the most boring thing to do. I had years ago learned that things got much easier when one got up and moved on. Therefore, although the life between lives session had plunged me into a bit of a downward spiral for a short while, my enthusiasm about my new found passion for hypnosis soon took over again and as I continued to work on my course case studies, my subconscious mind was left to ponder the mystery of what could have happened to my soul.

Eventually, allowing my subconscious mind the time it needed to process the information, I made sense of the experience for myself by accepting the fact that my soul worked with energy dynamics in the spirit world. At least that much had been revealed to me and as that was very positive, I decided to work with that. My soul's interest in energy did not surprise me in the least. As a child, I just loved figuring out how things worked and one of the best gifts I ever received was a microscope. My interest in the sciences propelled me into studying Mathematics, Physics and Chemistry and, some years later, doing an additional course in Astro-Physics, which would change my thinking forever. Certain kinds of knowledge or information have the power to shift one's thinking. Astro-Physics did that for me. I was like a sponge and where I had struggled with Physics, Astro-Physics felt like second nature to me and I excelled at it. This resulted in me being offered a position to work at an observatory.

Tragically, I did not continue with my plans to continue my post-graduate studies in Astro-Physics. Instead, The Triad entered my world. The particular experience was a necessary part of my growth in this life, but I often wonder how things would have turned out had I continued my studies in the mesmerising field of Astro-Physics. Unfortunately, by the time I had paid the price for the poor decision to allow The Triad into my space, my health and my peace of mind had been severely affected and I would not be in a space to study anything for a number of years to come.

When I did study again, my soul steered me towards the legal profession. There I learned about the power of the analytical mind. I also learned everything there is to know about the dynamics of human relationships when observed during times of strife. It gave me the insight and intuition I would need to be a good hypnosis practitioner in years to come. Somehow, the knowledge I had gained in Astro-Physics, or rather the mind-blowing insight that it gave me, combined with what I saw happening in human relationship dynamics, allowed me to begin playing around with the use of words to steer a legal matter in the direction that I needed it to go. I learned that words have energy and that I could tap into that to create the outcome that I wanted. Everything is indeed energy. I came to exactly the conclusion that Li Mang would confirm years later during my life between lives session, namely that 'Energy is everything. Understanding it can be everything.' I have for years believed that if you understand energy and how it works, you understand dynamics, including the dynamics between people in all kinds of relationships. And this gives you all you need to create the life you want.

I tried to make sense of the life between lives session from the angle that my soul loved playing around with energy. I remember how excited my soul was about discussing the mechanics of Al's death when he was trampled by a stampeding herd of cattle, with my teacher guide. I began to think that if there was some kind of disconnection, especially given that there was an aspect of my soul that stood watching as I was about to enter my current body as a soul, and an orphaned aspect that seemed to feel invisible and disconnected after my soul returned from my life as Al, then perhaps my soul intended for this disconnection to be an experiment. Perhaps the idea was to disconnect from the soul matrix to see what it would take to re-connect.

The idea that my current life was perhaps an experiment, resonated with me. The therapist at the time suggested that there might be one other possibility, namely that my soul had been the victim of a soul snatching or abduction, which takes place somewhere between the soul leaving the spirit world and entering the human baby body. Apparently, according to her information, when these souls are captured, they endure horrendous pain at the hands of the dark forces responsible for this abduction. When they are returned to the womb before birth, they remember only the pain, not the abduction. I have to admit that this possibility frightened me too much to even try to determine whether this could be true. I recalled the serious atmosphere during the discussion with Akaron and my guardian angel during the spiritual regression after I was not able to continue onwards in the spirit world and when I was informed that my soul had been torn. I saw the grave concern on my guardian angel's face. This certainly would fit the version of an abduction, but the idea still did not resonate with me.

I did not have all the answers. Perhaps my soul is an over eager, over enthusiastic energy dynamics expert who will do anything to test a theory, or perhaps my soul has seen darkness too deep to even begin to remember. Maybe the orphaned aspect of my soul resulted from the fact that my soul was torn at some unknown point. All I knew for certain was that I was supported and assisted on this journey. In that, I was just like everyone else on this planet. I had not been abandoned and whether I was fixing a torn soul or re-connecting to a soul matrix, the process was the same. With that decision, I was able to make some peace. Hopefully, during my next spiritual regression I would be ready for more information. As the months went by, I would eventually see that I still had so much to work on, that disclosing much more to me during the life between lives session would only have interfered with my journey and the work I had to do in this incarnation.

Where the session was a disappointment initially, I found that in typing out the details of the session more than a year later, I was able to find valuable snippets and phrases spoken by those guides and teachers I was allowed to meet, that changed my attitude about a lot of things. I also realised that the session ultimately gave me the courage to make a massive shift in my life. On some level I had always known who I truly was and what I was actually supposed to do with my life, but in many ways these private thoughts sounded arrogant to my human ears, holding me back from even attempting to walk the path that called to me. The spiritual regression eventually helped me to allow myself to acknowledge my destiny, while feeling less arrogant and more daring. It gave me the strength to just jump into the void and to do what I absolutely knew to be the right thing.

Had I not experienced that life between lives spiritual regression, I would probably have remained stuck forever, despite my other efforts to clear certain issues and follow my soul path. How could I follow a soul path I could not see?

In the interest of a proper perspective, the spiritual regression experience was most uncomfortable in my case, but in the end, is it not best to know the state that one's soul is in, even if it is not easy to watch its suffering? Despite the discomfort, the session was of tremendous value to me.

Eighteen months after the life between lives session, I would listen to the recording of that session again. What in hindsight jumped out at me was the fact that, when Li Mang had been asked whether I needed to give up my career to embrace healing and energy work, he became quite vague. His reply was that my current life was all about energy and that it was my life's work. He continued to say that 'Energy is everything. Understanding it can be everything and it doesn't matter what you do, if your trade is energy, then you can work anywhere, in any space and at any time. You just need to focus on what resonates with your soul and if where you are interferes with the resonance, you have to remove yourself. You have to let your experience of what resonates with you, guide you.' For the longest time I had stuck to my day job, because I felt it was the responsible thing to do. I also tried to sell Li Mang's advice to myself, by trying very hard to accept that one can work with energy anywhere and that I thus had no excuse to leave my practice. I had completely forgotten about the rider Li Mang had added, namely that I needed to focus on what resonated with my soul and if where I find myself interfered with the resonance, I had to remove myself. I am quite happy with the fact that despite completely forgetting about this part of what he shared with me that day, I ended up doing just that anyway. My work was making me sick. It attacked my body and upset my well-being, in other words, it no longer resonated with me. This would be why I felt I had no choice but to leave it behind, no matter how many people kept telling me that I was very good at my job and that I was 'needed' in the legal profession.

So why did I forget about the rider? The answer is simple. I know now that I went to the life between lives session, hoping that I would be given permission to quit my career. It would simply take too much courage otherwise. And I did not have that kind of courage at the time. When I then received an answer that ensured it would remain my decision whether I wanted to stay or go, and on top of it telling me that there would be no real reason why I could not stay in the legal profession, apart from the rider, I felt deep disappointment. I was, however, at the time so overwhelmed by having been in contact with the darker recesses of my pain, that I did not immediately recognise the disappointment that I had felt in this regard somewhere in the turmoil of emotions stirred up that day. Besides, by then I had been in the legal profession for over fourteen years and on some level I did not really think I would ever escape from it. And so the rider was shoved into a file. Thank goodness for recordings.

CHAPTER 29: Eighteenth Channelling – 9 January 2014

In the two months that followed my spiritual regression, I had to focus on other people's healing journeys for a while, specifically the case studies I had to complete for purposes of my hypnosis training. I loved every minute of it. I could not wait to get home after work each day to follow up on a case study client or to type up the feedback I had received about their progress. For the first time in my life I was truly and deeply excited about what I was doing. Everything inside me lights up when I am involved with hypnosis, whether I am working on a client, talking about the effects of hypnosis with other therapists or students or merely reading about the results of hypnosis or regression work as published in the many publications available.

However, a few days after handing in the last of my case studies three months before the deadline, I seemed to be losing energy again. It felt as if my energy was simply pouring out of me. It was the beginning of a new year and all I had to look forward to was a heavy case load. The usual stress, deadlines, non-paying attorneys and clients and the never ending requests for assistance from junior colleagues would also be part of my daily life. I knew that I would once again have to fight to have a little spare time to work on my passion and even if I could find the time, it did not necessarily mean that I would have the energy.

I started needing more and more sleep. As I have repeatedly stated, I accept that relationships are crucial to our souls' learning and that they appear in our lives when they are needed. The rest of the time is best spent working on ourselves. Yet whenever I get tired and my resources start to dwindle, a familiar dichotomy regarding relationships pushes forward to be heard. On the one hand I would think about how nice it would be to be in a happy relationship, only to remember how bad relationships can be, before switching over to thinking how fortunate I was to be single and then to remember that good relationships do in fact exist. It is a really tiring argument to have play in one's mind, like a perpetually swinging pendulum in space. Could I not just pick one of the two arguments and stick with it? I think it is built into our genes to want to have a partner; yet logic and fear dictated that I should stay single. I knew that I would somehow have to get my genes and my logic onto the same page, although I had little doubt that fear would not be able to earn itself a legitimate place on that same page. The fear would have to be released and perhaps then I could find a way to mediate a truce between the logic of wanting to stay single with no one making my life difficult, and my genes programmed to believe it natural to have a partner who would naturally be limiting me at least to some extent even in a happy relationship.

And so, feeling a little lost at sea, again, I decided to do another channelling, something which I had not had time for in a while. I also still had a lot of processing to do about my life between lives session. I had not forgotten that the reason my spiritual regression ultimately failed, was because the issue of my primary soulmate had come up. I still had a residual feeling of having been kicked out of the spirit world because of the question about it and this did not make me feel any better about the whole relationship business.

Eighteenth channelling 9 January 2014: *Only one thing really matters and that is the ability to move forward. Your lack of energy is not a matter of consequence and* *it will soon change again. You just need to adapt your programme to your biorhythms and take the supplements that you need. But as you know this, we will not spend any more time on it.*

Unlikely as it may seem, you will find love eventually in the strangest place where you have come not to expect it. It is time for you to lift the burden off your shoulders and put it down. You can't carry on needing the world to change when it cannot. It can only show you and bring you what you ask. Change your way of thinking and you'll change the operation of your soul's creative mechanism. It is the umpteenth time that you are battling the same demon. Over and over again you have come to this point and each time you take the same road. Pick up your shovel and dig away at the dirt of the past and what fogs your mind, so that you can see - it is there for you to see, but buried. Let go of things no longer needed and you'll find what you are looking for when you are ready. See what has to change and get to it. Don't concern yourself with financial worries. If your funds are depleted, it will be filled back up again – it is the pattern. Trust and have faith in that in which you do not believe and it might surprise you yet.

I found the message inspiring and uplifting. And so I stocked up on supplements, forged ahead and tackled the new year believing that this year perhaps the tides would turn. Interestingly, my guide in this channelling told me that it was time to take the burden off my shoulders. He did not say which burden. It would indeed be a year in which a great burden would be lifted off my shoulders. In fact, I would choose to put that burden down. In every channelling the same three issues that were fast becoming thorns in my flesh were touched upon even if not outright dealt with. These were relationships, finances and my career.

CHAPTER 30: Nineteenth Channelling – 2 February 2014

The odd thing about being stuck is that we return to the same point over and over again without actually realising it. I noticed that events in my world and people I would either meet for the first time or would run into unexpectedly, dictated which of the three thorns in my flesh would burn the most.

There were times when difficult cases or colleagues drove me up the wall, reminding me of how draining I experienced my work to be. Then there would be days where I would see things and people going about their business, suddenly reminding me that I was solely responsible for my entire life and that I did not have the support of a partner. When I was sick, I had to find a way to get myself to the doctor and get the prescription filled, whether I felt well enough to do so or not. At least once a month there would be the inevitable begging for payment of well-earned fees that were long overdue. The empty promises from attorneys made me feel so disappointed about the state of the human condition. People shamelessly used others and avoided responsibility with almost monotonous predictability. My guide was right when he said in my previous channelling that the world could not change because I wanted it to and that it could only show me what I ask.

This particular month end saw all three of my thorns starting to burn my flesh and it was time to turn in to see where I was missing the point. Again, all I could ask was 'what am I not seeing', as if asking it for the hundredth time would elicit a better answer than it did the previous ninety nine times. It was no wonder my guide became so fond of the word 'umpteenth'.

Nineteenth channelling 2 February 2014: *You're lost and you don't know where you are, but just keep going for you'll be able to see the wood for the trees as you carry on towards the light. Do what you always do. Stay true to your soul and to yourself and you'll be just fine. Hold on to your faith in what is right and good. You are a favourite of the light, a kind and gentle soul. Kind to others, but oh, so human, fallible and flawed, yet gently you tread the earth and bring light wherever you go. Your kindness and gentle heart will carry you forth until your last day. In anger you could not live and you found a way out. If you could do that, you could find your way back to love too. It might come to you on the morning breeze, it might sail to you from the corners of the earth. You never know when you will find love. One day, it is just there. Spread your kindness and gentleness as far as you can. It is so sorely needed in this world and it will bring your kindred spirit close, it will draw him in, it will draw him near.*

This was another uplifting, heart-warming channelling that filled me with hope of a better tomorrow. I would go to sleep and try again in the morning, even if it meant facing the same demons, asking the same questions, forging ahead in the same rut as before. Yet, despite my guide's beautiful, hopeful words, deep in my heart I knew that I did not believe a single word he said when it comes to my kindred spirit. Perhaps Akaron was a romantic at heart, but I had certainly lost the ability to believe in happy endings of the romantic kind, many moons ago. There was magic in the world outside of relationships; and in that space I could live a full and happy life without fearing when my partner would stick a knife in my back. Experience had taught me that this is what partners do.

CHAPTER 31: Meditation – 16 March 2014

It finally dawned on me that my guide, as supportive as he is, could not help me more than he already had. The hard work to be done was mine and mine alone. I remembered what he had said in the last channelling: 'In anger you could not live and you found a way out. If you could do that, you could find your way back to love too.' So I asked my guide to show me the problem in a way that I could understand it, as it seemed that it would be up to me to find a solution, yet I could not do this if I did not know what the problem was. I had been whining about the same issue for a long time and continued asking my guide's advice, but I had not up to that point taken it upon myself to work on the issue.

A day or so after this request to Akaron I had lunch with a friend. She is one of those lovely women that people stare at, because they just cannot help it. Needless to say, I always feel quite invisible walking next to her. As we entered the restaurant, I felt underdressed and plain beside my beautiful friend. Heads were turning as we walked along. As I spent a fleeting moment thinking that I should start paying a little more attention to how I dress, I realised almost immediately that it would make no difference. I always pay attention to what I wear and although I tended to dress a tad formally due to the environment I was functioning in, I was hardly a slob. What I was, was invisible. It had nothing to do with what I was wearing.

The same friend and I went for a walk along the beach a few days later and we talked about how invisible I felt. Underneath this feeling was a firm conviction that no man could possibly find me attractive. So we spoke about what this obvious block felt like. If I had to describe it, I would have to say that it had the shape of a steel pole driven through the centre of my being, almost skewering my soul. When my friend asked if I wanted the block removed, tears welled up in my eyes. I could not answer the question. I felt guilty even to think about the possibility that someone could be attracted to me. It was as if a vicious, angry voice whispered in my head 'How dare you think that?' My friend advised me to learn to flirt. Well, that was so not going to happen. Besides, if I even bothered to try, the voice would most certainly ask 'Are you insane?'

I was beginning to regret asking my guide to help me see what the problem is. I should have known by now that Akaron pays very close attention and if there is the slightest bit of information he can help to provide me with, he does so, provided it is in line with my path. The issue had nothing to do with dowdy dressing or my appearance, as I am a perfectly normal, average looking woman, no different from millions of women in relationships. I have always looked after myself as best I could, because I believe that looking after our bodies and our appearance is an important aspect of self-care and is necessary to live a balanced, healthy life. I put on make-up every day and I do this for myself and because I like it. When I dress up, I do it because it makes me feel good. I do not do any of that for the sake of other people.

So I could go out and buy shoes with higher heels than those I usually wore and pay a little more for designer outfits at more expensive shops than those where I usually buy my clothes, but I knew that all this would change nothing. Now that it had dawned on me that I had to follow the same road as I had done to resolve my anger issues, there was only one way to do this. I needed to keep searching for the answers by turning in. And so it came that almost a year after Akaron had lifted my anger to enable me to download the information I needed to bring me to the understanding that would resolve my anger forever, I finally admitted that I had another block that I could not shift on my own. My anger problem involved ego, arrogance and even a little stubbornness, although in my defence, my own human logic made it impossible for me to change my thinking without Akaron's help even though I had unsuccessfully tried to do that a thousand times. But it was different when it came to relationships, because regarding this issue I simply felt powerless and insignificant, and so very guilty for even attempting to resolve it.

After our walk along the beach, I went home deep in thought. I spoiled myself with a nice home cooked meal and then made myself comfortable, settling down to listen to my favourite meditation recording. I set the intent to engage with my guide during the meditation, in the ten minute quiet time allowed for in the meditation, specifically so that we could discuss how I could go about shifting this new block I had now identified. It felt good to take charge of the situation again. Did he not say in my first channelling of the new year that I should pick up my shovel and 'dig away at the dirt of the past'?

Meditation 16 March 2014: They appeared wearing hooded cloaks … the blue man, my teacher guide Akaron and my primary soulmate. I noticed then that I was also wearing a cloak. I put my case to them, but they turned and walked away. When I asked where they were going, they responded telepathically 'We heard you', but they kept on walking away from me.

The next moment the scene rolled away – it was as if they were walking in a picture that was curling up at the edges, revealing an unbelievably bright white light. Within this light was a light-being - I could sense its eyes and arms, more than see them. I understood that the cloaks were for our protection, due to the high energy and vibrational level of the light-being, which was much, much higher than that of my own guides. I felt the being 'hug' me and communicating to me 'You are loved', before the meditation came to an end.

How do I put into words what I feel when I know that I have indeed been heard? It was as if I had to receive a higher form of assistance, above that which my usual team of guides were able to give me. The experience left me with a profound sense that everything was changing. Something had been set in motion and I would not be able to stop the unfolding miracle even if I tried to. A higher power was now running the show. I had the sense that I could not fail, no matter what I ended up doing.

CHAPTER 32: Meditation – 2 May 2014

I was now in a very different state of mind. The excitement I had felt when I discovered a year earlier that my anger had been lifted, just as my teacher guide had promised, was once again pulsing through my veins. I just knew that something wonderful was about to happen. A few weeks after the meditation during which I had encountered the light-being, still feeling awed and unable to forget about the uplifting experience, I went to a birthday dinner. Incidentally, it was once again the birthday of the same friend whose birthday in the previous year had provided the means for me to discover how to overcome my wheat sensitivity and forever to make my peace with white bread rolls. While writing these pages, I could not help wondering if I have a soul contract with her involving her birthday, as one more year later, her birthday would for a third time coincide with massive shifts in my spiritual life.

On 7 April 2014, the night of my friend's birthday dinner, I sat opposite a friend of hers who during the course of the evening told me about Françoise Lallemand, who had helped him through a really difficult issue. As he mentioned her name, and even before he told me what she did for a living or how she had helped him, my body reacted. I knew that I had to see Françoise. He gave me her number and I called the next day to make an appointment to see her as soon as possible. I had to wait until 27 May 2014 to see her. Patience is not my strong suit when I am pursuing a goal, but there was nothing I could do.

In the meantime, the osteoarthritis in my knees had been getting steadily worse and I was very worried about the realities of my future. My general practitioner had informed me that I would probably need to manage the condition by taking anti-inflammatories for the rest of my life. I need not expand on the visions of knee replacements and hobbling around on crutches that plagued my waking hours. So I decided to head back into the spirit world for some much needed assistance, as I was way beyond the point of merely accepting what a doctor tells me. There was something to my knee problems and it involved much more than the fact that I was getting older. I had already completely forgotten that my guide had told me that I would be free of the agony one day and I would only re-read the transcript of the channelling where he had revealed this to me, during the writing of these pages.

The condition was becoming acute and my movements were becoming restricted. Watching me in a Pilates class, one could be forgiven for thinking that I was moving like someone twenty years older than I was. I recognised the escalation in the condition as similar to that which I had experienced when my wheat sensitivity started getting out of control the year before. That would turn out to be a truly valuable observation, as there would come a time when I would be able to recognise these messages from my body without any escalation being required to draw my attention. When a condition starts to escalate, the urgency of the message is extreme. If the body is heard and immediate attention is paid to removing the root cause of the condition, there is a chance of reversing the condition if that is an option within one's life plan. If the message is ignored, then the learning will have to come in the form of living through the process of managing the condition as it gets worse, forcing changes that allow us to see what we were unable to see earlier. In the end it really does not matter whether we hear the message our condition has for us at a time when we can still prevent it from getting worse or are able to reverse it altogether, or whether the condition takes us on a journey that could lead to ill health or death. The learning is the same. We need not judge ourselves or others for not always hearing the message in time, as our souls are free to choose to have the learning through experiencing the condition to its culmination, and this choice is made even before entering a body.

Initially, at the beginning of my journey, I used to meet my guides in a white gazebo. On the day my anger was to be lifted, the meeting place had changed to a round tower room, but that place was only used that one time. After that, I always met my guide in a particular garden. That garden is the same place where I was taken by my guides at the end of my spiritual regression, when I was told that my soul had been torn. Apart from the stone benches, the amphitheatre and the rolling green hills in this place, there was a huge stone structure in the background that looked a little like a cathedral. I had never been there before and did not know what it was.

Meditation 2 May 2014: During my meditation, my teacher guide and I talked about the state of my knees and I asked if I could be given some healing. We walked over to the stone structure and I saw there were steps leading up to the entrance. He walked up with me and took me inside. Immediately my body changed and as I looked down, I could see right through it. It was like having X-ray vision, but in the form of an infra-red picture. To my astonishment I saw that the interior of the stone structure was made of crystal. I was taken to a separate chamber where I was met by a light-being. I was also looking like a light-being, so I could not be sure whether the way the light-being presented was the result of the crystal chamber's effect, as was the case with me, or whether the being was truly just pure energy and light. The being let me lie down on what I can only describe as a crystal slab and proceeded to work on red spots that were now visible in my knees. It was as if I was looking at an infra-red picture and so I could see the affected areas change as the being worked. They initially appeared red, but as the light-being carried on working, the red areas eventually turned green and then disappeared.

The meditation did not seem to have an effect and I soon forgot about it. As always, the fact that I make notes of everything that happens when it comes to my spiritual journey, later helped me to remember this momentous session when it all started. 'As above, so below'. Once something is fixed in trance or in the spirit world, it is eventually fixed in the physical world, though it might take some time to filter through to the physical plane. That kind of experience was precisely what in the end moved my stubborn soul from a place of anger into one of sheer wonder at the magical, mystical, miracle of life. Everything changed on the day of this meditation, though it would be more than a year before I would be able to see all of it. On that day, three thorns were destined to be removed from my flesh. They would simply dissolve.

CHAPTER 33: Self-hypnosis Regression – 18 May 2014; Meditation – 19 May 2014

While waiting for my appointment with Françoise, my knees remained excruciatingly painful. I was facing a particularly sensitive argument in court. It was the one case that I needed to win at all costs. For reasons of client confidentiality I cannot disclose the circumstances of this case, as the facts of the case were so uncommon that it would be very easy for anyone who knows the family to recognise the people involved. Suffice it to say that it was a terribly sad case involving a very, very painful family dispute.

My young and feisty opponent was clearly grasping at straws. It was the kind of case that did not belong in a court room and would end up destroying the lives of the losing parties. The rift caused by the vicious court battle would be irreparable. The matter really disturbed me, but fortunately, to my mind, our case was rock solid, something which I do not easily conclude when it comes to court cases, as their outcomes are notoriously unpredictable. My belief that we had a very good case made no difference to my stress levels and these were higher than usual, because I could not afford to lose. My client was a very vulnerable member of society who sorely needed to be protected against some of the most unpleasant individuals I had come across in civil litigation. They were also dishonest cowards who actually believed that no one would pick up on their very obvious lies.

The last couple of days before a big matter was to be heard in court, were always hectic. I am a perfectionist and this really made things very difficult sometimes, as I tend to fret over small things that are not perfect. Given the importance of the case for those involved, I found myself suddenly frozen in a state of panic.   I had exclusively been doing litigation work for just short of fifteen years.   I was very well prepared and I knew that once I stood up in court, all fear or nervousness would disappear and I would calmly proceed with my argument. Yet I lost precious hours, because I could not stop procrastinating and pacing my chambers.   That was not good as the last hours of preparation, for me with my perfectionistic tendencies, had to be done.   It was almost ritualistic. I could not imagine going to court without having done the final preparation, which consisted of nothing more than scanning a case I knew almost by heart by then.

In an effort to calm myself two days before I was to argue the matter, I decided on the spur of the moment to see if I could find a past life link to my sudden panic attack. Unfortunately, something went wrong with the recording. I was feeling very stressed and was not in a good space, so what had possessed me to even attempt a regression, is beyond me. I did not, as usual, immediately make proper notes of what I could remember afterwards, as I was in a work-minded space. Directly after the session I felt upbeat enough to calm down and continue with my preparation. The impasse had been broken and I was eager to work; there was no time to type up the notes on a regression. It was only two days later, after the hearing of the court case, that I would sit down to type up my recollections of the session. Unfortunately, even though it was only a couple of days after the session, I had forgotten most of the details, as also happens with channellings and dreams. If it is not recorded or typed up immediately, there is no way to remember what had happened.   The little bit of information I remembered of the details, however, did help me to stay strong over the next two days as I prepared for court.

Self-hypnosis regression 18 May 2014: I recall that at the end of the life I visited, I was confronted with the dying thought that standing up for others is dangerous, as it had led to my death. Although I could no longer recall the details of the life (or death) that led me to this conclusion at the time of death, I recall thinking after the session that this life's conclusion explained the sudden and inexplicable panic I was experiencing in my current life about going to court in the particular matter which was due to be heard in a couple of days. In that life, I was standing up for a truly vulnerable person and died as a result. I was about to stand up for a vulnerable person in my current life.

I would never have been able to forgive myself if something had gone wrong in the case of my vulnerable client. Advocates stand up for their clients every day and often these clients are vulnerable. But my client in this matter, was more vulnerable than most. It was no wonder that an old memory of standing up for someone equally vulnerable had been triggered, resulting in me being more nervous than was normally the case. Fortunately, I had been able to take a hold of myself and after the regression was back to my usual self. We had taken an approach which I had deemed appropriate in all the circumstances, but it fell squarely within the ambit of exercising a discretion based on my experience as counsel. I felt as vulnerable as my client.

My opponents' attack on my approach to the case was as harsh as it was belated. As clever as their answer to our case appeared to be, our reply got them into even deeper trouble. They should have walked away at that stage, but chose to attack us using the dirty tactic of filing an ill-founded application at a very late stage, hoping that the matter would be postponed for many months, because I would either ask for a postponement to deal with the extensive document they had filed, or the judge would not be prepared to deal with the matter immediately, due to the amount of reading involved. They were wrong on both counts.

None of the points my opponents raised had any merit whatsoever and there was no way that they could have been unaware of it. It meant that I had to put my own health and well-being on the line once again, because I had no option but to deal with the points raised immediately in order to avoid the postponement they were trying to engineer. So I decided to get much needed help and settled down for a meditation in order to prepare for the long night of hard work that lay ahead. Meditation had become my daily anchor, a point in each day where I could connect with a tranquil space within, my inner sanctuary where I found peace and quiet strength to carry me through my days. I had a nagging headache and it was not going to get any easier until the end of the case.

Meditation 19 May 2014: I was again taken into the stone structure, where this time I was invited into a 'spa'-room, resembling a crystal cave. I was immersed in water and unseen hands massaged my head, which relaxed my shoulders. My headache disappeared.

Afterwards, I was able to work right through the night in order to finish the necessary work. My client and those of her friends and family involved in the matter who were supporting her, were all very religious people and they were keeping vigil and prayed regularly, especially for extra support for me. I indeed felt as if I was receiving additional strength that night.

To my opponents' surprise, the judge was ready to hear us the next morning and I was feeling calm and confident. My opponents were showing a little discomfort when they realised that I had worked through the night preparing an answer in respect of the late attack they had launched. They now had no chance to reply thereto, unless they exercised the option of asking for more time and tendering our costs. They had picked the fight and had set the impossible time frame, which had now come back to bite them. Again, they should have chosen to walk away at that stage.

In the end, after struggling up the court stairs trying not to wince with every step I had to climb, while my attorney had to lug both our heavy court bags up the stairs to the court room, we spent a long day arguing all the preliminary issues. By the end of the day, the other side had been defeated, rolling over before we even got to the main matter. Their clients ended up not only losing, but they also had to pay the costs for both sides.

I was so grateful for the outcome of the matter. My opponents' clients were hard, cruel individuals who had brought unspeakable pain into the life of my client. I felt that justice had been served, but once the elation and adrenalin rush was over, the matter left me exhausted again. I could feel that I was paying a heavy price for going to war on behalf of someone else, even if it was on behalf of the vulnerable who truly deserved all the help they could get.

I still had a few days to go until I could see Françoise, but the exhaustion I had felt after the draining matter I had argued and won, once again made me wish that there was a way that I could make a living in a way that was less harmful to me. What I had to do on a daily basis was so contrary to my gentle nature. Fighting other people's battles was just not something I wanted to do.

The person who gave me Françoise's name, told me that she does not talk much while she works and that one does not really have to tell her anything. So when I finally got to see her on 27 May 2014, a little over three weeks after my healing session in the crystal chamber and a week after the matter in court, I said nothing about my knees initially and just waited for her to do whatever it was that she does. Within minutes she asked if I had knee problems. I was impressed, because of course I had knee problems. Françoise explained that I had difficulties with my knees, because, according to my body's neurology that she somehow managed to read, I was well and truly stuck in three areas of my life. She listed the three thorns in my flesh as if I had written them down for her. I was stuck in the areas of relationships, finances and career.

Before balancing my energy, Françoise wanted to know if I wanted her to shift all three issues, as it could result in a lot of discomfort for a while. It seems that I am not only over eager and over enthusiastic, but also over confident and so, predictably, I jumped at the chance to have all my issues sorted out once and for all. How bad could the fall-out be?

As Françoise worked, she told me that in respect of relationships I had a ninety nine percent block. I was literally invisible to men. I could not help feeling vindicated. No one ever believed me when I tried to explain that men simply looked right through me. The only men who ever noticed me, were those I was destined to have karmic and less than loving relationships with.

Françoise was able to shift the almost total block down to thirty percent. As I had been able to identify the physical 'feeling' of this block within my body, I could tune into it. I could feel that it was still there, yet it no longer felt 'total'. I have no other words to describe it. Despite that shift, I continued to feel invisible, but I knew from experience that shifts take time to filter through.

After the session, Françoise indicated that I should now be able to enter into a relationship, should I want to. She warned that I would also experience shifts pertaining to my career and finances, which were obviously linked. I was to discover that this was putting it very mildly. She also felt that I might not have to leave my job and that I might in the end find a way of dealing with it differently. I would have to wait and see what the shifts bring about. As I had previously gathered from working with the energy healer, Eric, and from the responses of Li Mang during my spiritual regression, the consensus seemed to be that I might have to stay where I was when it came to my work life. As disappointing as this was, I went home feeling calm and centred and slept soundly that night. There was no sign of any after effects as Françoise had warned there might be.

What is it that makes us think that we can conquer the world when we are merely standing at the foot of Mount Everest? Adding to my inflated sense of achievement at having done the right thing, I was absolutely elated when the infection, pain and discomfort in my knees cleared within a week, roughly one month after the healing session on my knees in the crystal chamber. That was settled then, 'as above, so below'. And it was all so easy! Or so I thought.

In the end, my knees would over the next year remind me every now and again that they had once shown serious and very painful signs of wear and tear. At the time of writing these pages, more than a year after that session, I remain pain free and able to climb stairs like any other person with healthy knees. I take no supplements and only need them very occasionally when I do something silly like carrying a very heavy bag up the stairs. The time when I could barely get myself up the stairs, let alone a small bag of groceries, was all but a distant memory.

CHAPTER 34: Meditation – 30 July 2014

On 9 June 2014 my little goddaughter, Samantha, turned five. Her mother arranged for a teddy bears' picnic in their garden over the weekend before her birthday and all the teddy bears in the area gathered on a lovely, sunny winter's day. As is befitting a godmother, I reported for duty on the Friday before the party on Saturday 7 June 2014. I firstly had to fetch the birthday girl from school, which was a big thing in my life. Having no children, this every day task in the lives of other women, was a very special occasion for me.

When I arrived at her school, Samantha was naturally surprised to see me. They lived in a small town about one and a half hour's drive from Cape Town, where I lived. Samantha's grandparents lived in Bellville, Cape Town, and she was familiar with their address. So as she was skipping along on the way to my car she asked: "But don't you live in Bellville?" I lived in a different suburb, but to her, Bellville was Cape Town. After giving the necessary simplified geography lesson as we negotiated the muddy pools on the pavement, Samantha was clearly impressed and said: "Wow, but you have come a long way to pick me up!" It was my turn to be impressed with the clever little girl who was at the tender age of five able to work out that I had made some effort to get to her school that day in time to pick her up. We spent the afternoon together, bonding while her mother toiled away producing a birthday cake fit for a small teddy bear having a birthday.

The next morning, the place was a hub of excitement as everyone rushed around preparing for the picnic. It was the godmother's task to mix and pour thirty two chocolate milks into small bottles sporting fancy pink and burgundy ribbons and pink and white teddy bear labels. In the end, we only needed twenty six as some of the teddy bears got lost in the woods on their way to the picnic.

My shoulder felt stiff at some point as I was pouring the milky liquid into the bottles. The repetitive movement was tiring, but I forged ahead. At some point Samantha's mother suggested that I should perhaps use a bigger container to mix it all so that I would not have to prepare each mixture separately. Good plan, except that I already had a system going and did not want to deviate. Besides, it was fun preparing them one by one and I liked playing godmother.

When I woke up the next morning, my right shoulder was very stiff. All the muscles in my shoulder had pulled into a painful spasm. These things happen from time to time and I did not pay much attention to it. As I sat rubbing ointment into my sore muscles later that evening, I thought that I might have to visit my chiropractor to get the problem sorted out. Little did I know that something far deeper had been triggered and that a trip to the chiropractor would not resolve my discomfort. There would be a very long and painful journey ahead.

I had, of course, totally forgotten that only a week before the osteoarthritis in my knees had miraculously cleared up in a very short time, after I had been battling with sore knees for years. I had yet to learn that our bodies talk to us and that mine had now established that it could get my attention through pain and discomfort. It was not about to stop talking until I listened.

I spent the remainder of the month of June 2014 visiting the chiropractor every few days. I am a patient and kind person, but my patience was about to be severely tested. My chiropractor, who had always practised in partnership, was a very competent man that I had been seeing for treatments over a number of years. He used to pay attention to his patients and I never had any reason to complain until a new system resembling a factory line was introduced at the practice. Patients were being 'warmed up' by assistants, who never seemed to last long at the practice. The assistants would note a few details on the patient file during the warm up, before depositing the patient in a room where one of the two chiropractors at the practice would see them for three to five minutes maximum. Gone were the days where I could make an appointment to see the chiropractor of my choice, who had been treating me for years. In future the chiropractor who would attend to me would be determined by my place in the factory line. Whereas I previously had the attention of the chiropractor for at least ten to fifteen minutes during appointments, time was suddenly of the essence. There was no longer time to try to explain the problem I was experiencing. The chiropractor would rush into the room while giving the notes made by the assistant a cursory glance, before performing a quick adjustment. Small talk or any deep discussion on the issue at the end of the treatment, would be discouraged as the chiropractor would after the treatment immediately start turning away towards the door, clearly intent on rushing out to see the next patient already waiting in the other room.

When this system was first introduced, my spine merely required monthly maintenance and I did not mind the change too much, but I did not like it one bit when I presented at the practice with my very painful shoulder and was subjected to the same treatment. I had been seeing chiropractors for many, many years. When one is in agony, chiropractors always work towards finding the source of the pain and they spend the time that is required to resolve the issue immediately. I had never been sent away with unresolved spasms. Everyone knows how debilitating back, neck or shoulder pain can be.

During the previous three months, when I had been to the practice for my regular monthly maintenance treatments, I had each time ended up with the other chiropractor, instead of with the more experienced one I was used to. My back had accordingly already been badly neglected by the time I injured my shoulder, as the other chiropractor did not do any of the adjustments I regularly required and merely used a tool referred to as the activator gun, the use of which in a case like mine cannot replace a proper manual adjustment. After quite a number of treatments, I began thinking that it was pointless to keep pouring money into these treatments, only to leave the rooms of the chiropractor in almost as much agony as I had entered. The worst part was that my usual chiropractor, whose practice I had supported for years, was fully aware of what was happening and refused to assist his partner in the practice, who was clearly not coping.

I can understand that chiropractors cannot interfere with each other's patients and they can run their business any way they choose to, but the reality is that no one bothered to ask me if I consented to being treated by a less experienced and definitely less competent chiropractor. So in circumstances where I, as a longstanding patient, could not get the treatment I needed from the chiropractor I had made an appointment to see, because of some internal policy or business arrangement which should not have affected me as a patient, I decided that it was time to go and to find myself a chiropractor who focused on patients instead of on running a business.

As upset and disappointed as I was at the time, I would later remember the perplexing behaviour of my chiropractor. He was a skilled and caring professional who was suddenly acting out of character. Later I would realise that he must have entered into a contract with my soul to help redirect me somewhere that I needed to be at a very specific time, hence the weird behaviour. I still had no idea that I was in the middle of the fall-out of the massive shift that I had so underestimated when I asked Françoise to balance all three aspects affecting my knees. Did I really think that the issues would all be magically resolved, just because my knees had cleared up within a few days? All my knees did, was to alert me to the fact that I had been stuck. Once that message had been delivered and the blocks removed, the knees cleared up as they no longer had any message to deliver. But the three issues that had been loosened up now surfaced and made themselves known, because the blocks had been removed. However, I was too focused on my painful shoulder to keep up with unfolding events and I was in any event very busy steaming about my chiropractor who had acted unprofessionally, in my view.

In yet another series of synchronistic events involving a misunderstanding regarding the date of an appointment with a new chiropractor, I ended up in tears at the office. I was in terrible pain and had just discovered that I had missed an appointment with the new chiropractor. I am too meticulous to make this kind of mistake, but the rude woman running the man's diary was adamant that I had made a mistake when writing down the date. Perhaps I had, but the issue was that I now had no one to help me out of my misery. I dried my tears and went to the kitchen to get some tea. There I ran into a colleague who had been having trouble with his shoulder a few weeks earlier when I had also found him in the kitchen trying to apply one of those fancy plasters that is supposed to relieve muscle pain. He had needed my help to peel off the backing of the plaster, as I had long nails and his were short. So when I saw that same colleague that morning, I remembered the incident and asked how his shoulder was doing. He told me about a young Greek chiropractor he had discovered just up the road from our offices and who had sorted him out in no time.

I was on the phone within minutes. As luck would have it, Dr Aaryn Camitsis could see me that afternoon already and off I went for my first proper treatment in months. Some people are just really good at what they do. But my shoulder had been badly neglected and it would take a number of treatments to bring lasting relief. At least I now had a health care practitioner who actually bothered to spend the necessary time working on his patients. I was not getting special treatment, I was getting the same treatment everyone else did. It was a relief to be in a safe space after experiencing weeks of intense pain.

Something was happening in my world. I felt as if a can of worms had been opened. Perhaps the universe's can opener caused the pain I felt cutting into my shoulder. As the hours of treatment passed, my sympathetic chiropractor and I chatted about life, energy, regression and the wonderful things that interested me, while he stuck needles into the myriad of knots he managed to discover in my shoulder. Our chats were a welcome distraction from the pain and I always felt better after a session, having had a friendly conversation with an open-minded person on topics I could normally not discuss with just anyone. Aaryn was a good listener which added to his patient care skills. It was in stark contrast to my previous chiropractor who had shown such poor judgment in patient care.

Despite treatment going well, I was feeling confused and suddenly had trouble controlling my thoughts. Life felt painful and old issues started arising. I remembered things from my past that I had thought I had put behind me a long time ago. Nothing made sense anymore and I did not like the uncomfortable things that seemed to have been stirred up. I continued to detest my job, but at least court was in a long winter recess and I did not have to go to court often. It gave me time to rest my shoulder, but soon it became apparent that lying down caused a lot of distress, more so than sitting up. Walking was a problem and any kind of exercise would cause the shoulder muscles to go into spams requiring a treatment. Although the shoulder remained quite painful, the regular treatments did bring great relief for intermittent periods and I was less distressed.

If my shoulder improved, my emotional state of mind did not. I had been focused on work and my shoulder for a few weeks, but now the emotional issues were pushing forward. I still had not made any connection between what I was experiencing and the session with Françoise that had resulted in resolving my difficulties with my knees.

My shoulder was supposed to get better with treatment. That was not happening. I simply did not respond to the treatment as I had expected. Aaryn also thought that it was a little odd that his concerted efforts did not produce a better result. I had never had rotator cuff problems before and it turned out that the real culprit was my neck, resulting in spasms extending into my shoulder. I was sent for X-rays to see if we were missing something. He eventually suggested that I should consider seeing a specialist, as my X-rays did not reflect any condition that should not have responded to the thorough treatment I had been receiving for almost a month.

Fortunately, I clearly saw the red flag. I had been a chiropractic patient for long enough to know that I had been receiving excellent care, including a programme with a biokineticist whom Aaryn had referred me to. Nothing about my shoulder difficulties made any sense to me, or to my chiropractor it seems. That was not the kind of scenario I wished to present to any specialist. I had met many medical professionals and admire the work they do greatly. Without them we would be lost, but I do not want them anywhere near a condition that cannot logically be explained.

I went home and thought about my options and decided to write to my hypnosis teacher in London. Perhaps he would be able to make a suggestion or two regarding the way forward. He did indeed have a suggestion, one I should probably have come up with myself. It was perhaps time for a facilitated regression so that I would be able to dig deeper into an issue that was obviously complex. A facilitated regression with a skilled and insightful therapist can always bring better results than a self-regression and at the very least it can bring up more detail which can lead to better understanding. Here and there one might run into a therapist who does not seem to have the knack or who simply misses the point, but that is rare and mostly the experience is good. I was in any event mostly in such deep pain, especially when lying down, that I would not be able to hold trance for long enough to do a proper self-regression.

Later that evening, a few days before the end of July 2014, I sat down and compiled an e-mail to be sent to the regression therapist that my hypnosis teacher had referred me to. After bemoaning the state of my neck and shoulder and giving the background of the problem as I saw it, I stated that I was convinced that there was some underlying issue involved. I could not have known that the next sentence I would type in that e-mail would turn my world inside out. More as a rider than anything else, I added: 'And on top of it all, my career has become a crushing burden I can no longer bear.'

Re-reading the e-mail before sending it off, I felt as if I had just discovered the answer to an age old riddle. How could I have missed this? The shoulder is the part of the body that is associated with weight bearing. We often refer to a heavy weight on someone's shoulders, or we say that a weight has been lifted off our shoulders. The penny had dropped and the sound was reverberating in my head.

For the longest time I had thought I would never be free of my career and I plodded along regardless of my body's complaints, as I suffered through endless throat infections, fevers and even more than one trip to the emergency room with symptoms of a heart attack, which turned out to be nothing more than a stress reaction. And so it came about that I made the decision to leave the bar and to end my legal career there and then. There was nothing to think about. I had only stayed because I thought that it was what the universe expected of me. I had forgotten what Li Mang had said during my spiritual regression about removing myself from a situation that no longer resonates with my soul. I only heard the part where he had said I could work with energy anywhere and thus felt that I had no excuse to leave the bar in those circumstances. Thank goodness my body is much more adamant when it comes to getting a point across.

As it turns out, I did not need the regression session after all. Forty eight hours later, I had set everything in motion to leave the bar and to start up my new healing practice, or rather to transform my casual part-time healing practice into a full-time endeavour. I had found a wonderful web designer who seemed to appear in my world at just the right time and we were on a roll.

Within a week of setting things in motion to wind up my practice responsibly over a three month period without letting any clients down, the muscles in my shoulder started responding to the treatments as expected, but my neck, which was the actual source of the problem extending into my shoulder, continued to trouble me. I thought that it would soon pass and patiently waited for my neck to also start responding.

I paid another visit to Françoise, who was blown away by the change in my energy, something which she noticed the minute I walked through her door. She told me that my soul had taken over since my first visit to her a little over two months earlier. This made a lot of sense to me, as my personality simply would not have been brave enough to make the required changes.

One has to be grateful when things go smoothly. For some reason, I felt the need to spend time with my guides and to express the gratitude, relief and enormous excitement I was feeling. Those who knew me could barely believe the transformation I had undergone. I felt like a bouncing beach ball hopping about on cloud nine. If my soul had indeed taken over, it was much more playful than my own rather serious personality. My shoulder was feeling fine and I was looking forward to my freedom that would be a mere three months away.

Meditation 30 July 2014: All the guides I had come to know were gathered together when I arrived at my usual place in the spirit world. My teacher guide Akaron, the blue man, my primary soulmate, an entity I have come to know as a Reiki angel, as well as my guardian angel were all waiting for me. I knew that the occasion was momentous, as they seldom appeared together.

My guides were really happy with my decision to leave the bar. I noticed that for the very first time I could see the detailed features of my primary soulmate as he chose to present himself to me. I expected them all to focus on my career change, but my primary soulmate had a different message, which he conveyed as the first one to address me that day. He told me that whatever I now needed to do in respect of relationships, would not affect him or our relationship as primary soulmates.

My guardian angel and the blue man indicated that they were always with me and that they supported me. The Reiki angel said that we would be working much more closely in the future, given my career change. Akaron told me to keep moving forward and that I would be looked after. He said that I need not be concerned about the future.

I was already fretting about three cases that I knew would take years to finalise. I could not leave before the matters had been sorted out and one of them had ground to a halt due to the human relationship dynamics of mostly the lawyers involved. The matter was not moving forward, either into litigation or into settlement, as we had reached a stalemate. I asked my teacher guide if there was anything that could be done to ease the difficulties so that the process could move forward, without interfering.

As I continued talking to the other four, Akaron left the group and I saw him in the distance talking to a group of people. To my astonishment I recognised all the souls involved in two of the three matters I had been concerned about. After a little while, my primary soulmate went to join my teacher guide in talking to them. I do not know what was said, but I saw the group talking to each other after my teacher guide and soulmate had turned away.

After that, all five of my guides stood in a circle around me and put me in a bubble of rainbow light, clearing as much of the built up residual negative energy of my career as they could, helping me to move forward to be free of this and to grow as much as was possible.

The next day I started having thoughts of calling my truly impossible opposing colleague to revive settlement negotiations in the matter where we had reached a stalemate. He had the habit of putting the phone down in my ear while I was still talking, so I was not looking forward to it. I also held instructions *not* to try to negotiate with the other side. Eventually, I felt compelled to call my opponent, so I called my instructing attorney to ask for permission, given that I held instructions not to do so. My attorney was suddenly open to trying one more round of negotiations. I called my colleague and discovered that he had miraculously turned into a very reasonable individual. The settlement discussions were revived and we were moving forward again.

There were two other matters that I was gravely concerned about as I could not hand them over to anyone else at such a late stage and I certainly did not want to hang around at the bar until they were finalised. I need not have worried, as both cases settled within days of the meditation.

CHAPTER 35: Meditations – 10 and 24 August 2014

I felt as if I had moved mountains by putting down the burden of my career, but the fact that I had to keep doing the same work for another two or three months, was a real pain in the neck. Now alert to messages my body might have for me, I was convinced that this irritation might be the reason why my neck was not responding as well as my shoulder had done, so I asked my teacher guide about it during a meditation.

> **Meditation 10 August 2014:** Instead of giving me an explanation or discussing the issue, my guide opted to perform some healing work on my neck and worked on all the muscles in my shoulders and the base of my neck by using orange light, specifically attending to the area where the source of the problem seemed to be (to me at least). When my guide was done, he told me that the healing he had performed would be conditional upon my completion of the process of ending my career.

In reality, leaving the bar was not yet a done deal. I had already told everyone I was leaving and had started turning away new work. My briefing attorneys had also been informed of my decision, but I would only need to resign my membership of the bar thirty days before actually leaving. I guess my guide knew that putting my signature to that letter of resignation would not be an easy thing to do. There would still be time to pull back in fear and change my mind, and so the healing was 'conditional'. Perhaps my guide also has a legal background, or perhaps he knew that I would understand and honour the concept of a condition being set.

The healing work my guide performed during the session would, as before, filter through to the physical world a few weeks later when my neck problem would finally clear. As I would realise later, there was still something to be learned before the tension in my neck could be released. These spiritual journeys we are on can get quite tricky. I have no idea how our guides keep up with the process. It is no wonder we each need a whole team. I would also, after the clearing up of my neck problems a few weeks later, completely forget about the condition that the improvement in my neck was conditional upon my completion of the process of ending my career, until about six months after the fact, when my guide would need to tap me on the shoulder.

By now, I had become a regular meditator. It was part of my daily ritual. One evening, as I settled down for my meditation, I felt a little heart sore for no real reason. Some days are just different than others. The pain in my neck was still so draining and it was in fact getting worse. Whereas I had previously been struggling with my shoulder for many weeks until it cleared up, my neck had now become the one thing I never stopped being aware of.

A few days earlier, I had argued a particularly sad case in which the law and fairness came head to head. My client, whom I had never met, as she lived in another province and I was merely arguing her case on review, could clearly not get her head around the realities of the law. Unfortunately, her lawyers in the other province had given her hope and built their case on a skewed version which had been influenced by the client's reasoning, resulting in an argument on the court papers that looked very much like a distortion of the law, mixed up with cultural issues that the draughtsman did not appear to have understood completely. And I was the lucky one who had to argue a matter that I personally would never have taken to court. I would have advised the client differently and would probably have saved her half of the little money she had left. Unfortunately, things ended as I knew they would and I felt sad about how the law, or rather the way it is practised by some, can in fact destroy lives rather than bring justice. It made my heart ache.

Meditation 24 August 2014: In my special place I took a walk to the stone structure I had been taken to before. I stepped inside and engaged with the same light-being that had helped me heal my knees some months earlier. Apart from telling me to be patient, the light-being did not communicate any further, but instead reached into my heart, which started glowing as if a pink light was shining from it. It appeared as if the being was feeding my heart with light. My heart of light started expanding until the light eventually enveloped my whole body. The heart centre was now a beautiful bright green and as my audience with the light-being ended, my whole being exploded and turned into a beautiful circle of bright light, which looked like the sun. I received a telepathic message from the light-being that my heart was now filled with so much love, that I could now draw nothing but love to me.

As always, the meditation lifted my spirits and I slept soundly that night.

A few days later, Aaryn told me for the second time in about a month that he was not sure why I was not responding to the treatment. It was a repeat performance of the shoulder scenario. The muscles in my neck simply kept going into very painful spasms. He suspected that there might be a pinched nerve and suggested, as he had done with my shoulder when it would not release, that I should pay a visit to a specialist. He could see no reason why my neck should continue to be so painful. My reaction was the same. Fortunately, I had a session booked with Françoise that day and I went straight to her practice when I left Aaryn's rooms.

I was feeling absolutely miserable, because I had now lived through three solid months of pain, starting in my shoulder and moving over into my neck. To my horror, it turned out that my neck did have another message for me, but not one that I appreciated. Françoise was able to determine that my subconscious mind was experiencing my decision to give up my career as madness. It perceived my actions as a threat to my livelihood and thus to my safety. My subconscious mind had become convinced that I needed protection against myself. As our subconscious minds cannot reason, it did not know that I intended leaving the bar precisely because my body made it incumbent upon me to do so. All it wanted to do, was to get me to safety where I would have food and shelter. It went into survival mode. The plan of action was apparently to get me to a place of comfort and safety, so that I would feel better and stop doing irresponsible things like ending my career, which would surely result in a lack of food and shelter. My subconscious mind had recorded that the one place in my recent history where I had found great comfort, was at the chiropractor's rooms. That came as no surprise, as for months that had been the only place where I found comfort as the pain was relieved during my treatments. In other words, the pain in my neck had nothing to do with my irritation at having to continue practising law, but was literally 'all in the subconscious mind', forcing me to return to a place where I would be comforted, so that I would stop doing the 'wrong thing'.

It took a little while for me to get my head around that, but clearly Françoise had to have been right, as this time my neck responded to the treatment I had had with the chiropractor that same morning. By the next morning, the terrible pain was gone and did not return again for over four months, and then only due to the fact that I had physically injured my neck by bending backwards over my hairdresser's basin.

And so by the end of August 2014, I was pain free for the first time in three months. I was also almost free of my career. It began to dawn on me, now that I was no longer looking at life while trying to block out pain, that the massive shift that had resulted in the healing of the osteoarthritis in my knees, had also opened the three avenues where I had been stuck up to that point.

A huge change was taking place in my work life and it was not too difficult to work out that with this change there would be a drastic change in my financial circumstances, which was the second aspect to be affected by the shift. Right then, I could not afford to pay too much attention to the hardships that might lie ahead, as I would otherwise not have had the courage to do what I did. I made my calculations, speculated on the risks, tried to inform myself, and then I jumped into the void. It really was the only way to leave the safety of my profession.

The third aspect of my life where I had been stuck, was in relationships. That was much harder to deal with. At the time I doubted that I would ever be completely comfortable with this aspect of my life, or even comfortable with trying to deal with it. Up to that point, nothing much had happened in that area of my life since the shift that had cleared my knees, apart from a great sense of vulnerability that had surfaced, making me feel downright miserable. Perhaps it was just the constant physical pain I had had to live with that made me feel so exposed.

CHAPTER 36: Self-hypnosis Regression – 7 September 2014

About eight days after my last visit to Aaryn and Françoise on the same day, I was feeling great. The relief of not feeling so much physical pain was indescribable. I was also very excited about my impending career change and nothing could bring me down. The events of the past few weeks had convinced me that I could safely put down the heavy burden of my career. Freedom beckoned, but I wanted to be sure that I was not carrying any residual negative energy in my neck or shoulder. Since I was pain free, I felt up to doing another self-regression to see if there was anything to clear.

Self-hypnosis regression 7 September 2014: I was a peasant chopping wood in the forest. Five soldiers passed by, asking for directions, which I gave them. As they were riding away, I saw that they had a captive with them. I could see that it was a young woman, because her hair spilled out from under the cloth that they had covered her with. Her hands and feet were tied and she was hanging over the back of a horse behind one of the soldiers. She appeared to be either unconscious or dead, I could not be sure which. One of the soldiers turned and saw me looking at the woman. He waved a warning finger at me as he was riding away. The message was clear: 'You did not see this'. I nodded my agreement, but later that night I followed the soldiers' tracks to their camp site. They were deep in a drunken sleep and I was thus able to release their captive. She was the daughter of a wealthy man and I helped her to return to the home of her father from where she had been abducted by the soldiers. I returned to the forest where I lived and worked.

The soldiers came to find me and I was taken to the dungeons in the fortress of their lord, whom I had angered by freeing the young woman. I was badly beaten and eventually, a few days after my capture, publicly hanged for my 'crime of interference'. My battered body was left hanging where the people of the village could see it. When the young woman and her father heard of my death, they came to pay their respects at dusk when no one was watching. She laid a wreath near my body. As she did so, she said to her father that she would now never be able to repay the debt of gratitude she owed me. Watching the scene from above, after my death in that life, I recognised the young woman to be the same soul that I know in my present life as Aaryn, my chiropractor.

When I asked my guide, the blue man, if there was another life to go to in order to release any residual energies, I immediately found myself in a place that I knew not to be of this world. I was wearing a beautiful rainbow coloured garment and my hair was all nicely done up. From previous experience I knew that whenever I saw myself dressed up during meditations or self-hypnosis sessions I could expect to be taken to a special meeting or a special place. My teacher guide was there with me and the blue man had gone away. This meant that I was in the spirit world and not in a past life, as my two guides seem to have different roles. Akaron as my teacher guide helps me in the spirit world, while the blue man travels with me into past lives.

My teacher guide took me to a beautiful, but plain stone structure that I had not seen before. There was a sense of anticipation in the air. We entered the structure and walked through a passage into a large room where nine Lords of Karma were waiting. I was able to see the face of at least one of them, namely the one sitting in the centre of a large table shaped like a half moon. My teacher guide explained to them that I would be addressing them myself. The Lord of Karma sitting in the centre addressed me and I could see myself 'putting my case' so to speak, yet most of the content of the communication was blocked, even some of my own words. I was apparently making out a case to them that related to a missed opportunity. I was essentially asking for another chance. I explained that my current personality severely limited my progress, largely because of societal imprints that have imprisoned me for as long as I could remember. I pointed out that my soul had now taken charge and had broken free from the dictates of my fearful personality and I felt that this earned me a second chance. I told them that I at that moment surrendered to any necessary shifts and transformation required to advance on my soul path. The Lord of Karma who was communicating on behalf of them all responded, but again the communication was blocked. I was then taken to a place where a beautiful light was shone on me. The purpose was to cleanse me of negative energy. My teacher guide and I left the room. I knew without a doubt that something momentous had transpired.

There were so many things going through my mind all at once when the session ended. Firstly, I knew exactly where I had just been. It was the place referred to in the work of Dr Newton as The Council of Elders. I had made a similar request once before, long before I had first picked up the amazing books written by Dr Newton. At that stage, I had wanted to break free from a marriage that was literally destroying me, but I simply could not find the physical strength to do what was needed. All those years ago, I was allowed to write a petition and the guide that I have always thought of as my guardian angel then went to the Lords of Karma on my behalf, returning later with a confirmation that I had been set free of the sacred contract my soul had with the soul of my ex-husband. I had written the petition, because I felt that he was not complying with the terms of the soul contract we had and that his actions were damaging me. That was not what I had signed up for and as I felt he would be holding me back on my journey by not sticking to his end of the bargain, in that he was failing to do his own work and learning at my expense, I felt I had a right to withdraw from the contract.

It was thus no wonder that I felt such awe at this time, having been allowed to accompany my guide and to address the Lords of Karma myself. Yet, addressing them personally was actually not out of the ordinary, no matter how special the whole experience made me feel. I have little doubt that they represent what others have referred to as the Council of Elders. I should mention that the people in Dr Newton's case studies certainly do get to address their council personally and the fact that I could personally address what I know as the Lords of Karma, was therefore not an exception. Perhaps that first request to them so long ago was handled on my behalf, because not only my soul was involved. I recall that on that occasion my ex-husband's guide attended the meeting during which I implored my guides to help me get out of my marriage. His guide and mine went to consult the Lords of Karma together, taking my written petition with them. According to Dr Newton's work, each person's council is unique and the council overseeing my life would not be the same one overseeing my ex-husband's life.

Interestingly, after this regression, I looked at my notes on that long ago meeting in the spirit world and noticed that after I had been set free of the sacred contract with my ex-husband, my guide had returned to the place where I had been waiting without my ex-husband's guide, although they had left together. My ex-husband's soul arrived at the meeting shortly after my guide's return, to tell me that he simply could not believe what I had just done. He was not happy. Clearly, he had been informed of my petition. Who knows, perhaps he even had a chance to answer to that petition before our respective councils came to a conclusion which had allowed me to be set free from the sacred contract. I will never know. What I do know, is that after our divorce my ex-husband and I have managed to remain in each other's lives as a firm support whenever needed. Our souls, it seems, did not abandon each other after the particular sacred contract, and subsequently our marriage, was terminated. I suspect that both of us still managed to learn whatever it was that we needed to learn from our relationship.

This regression also reminded me of my basically failed journey into the spirit world during my facilitated spiritual regression in the life between lives session I had eleven months earlier. I did not get to go to the Council of Elders, nor did I get to meet my soul group in that session. Given that the communication this time round was also blocked, there clearly still is something that I am not ready to hear or know. I know from previous experience as well, that if communication in these sessions is blocked, it does not mean that you do not receive the information. It is stored in your subconscious mind and will rise up into your consciousness when you need it. What matters is that I know that I have been heard. I can safely leave the contents of the communication in the hands of the universe and synchronicity. Whatever it is, it will come to me when I need it.

As I sat down and typed up the contents of the session immediately afterwards, I noticed the somewhat surprising aspect of my chiropractor's soul appearing in one of my past lives. Although the past life of the brave peasant who had rescued a young woman was very interesting and the link to my chiropractor even more so, my memory of my journey to the spirit world would occupy my mind for the next few days, as a visit to the Lords of Karma tends to overshadow anything else. It was only after my pre-occupation with the visit to the Lords of Karma had passed that I was able to make a few very interesting connections.

The intent with the session was to clear any residual energies in my body relating to the neck and shoulder problems my chiropractor had been treating for a couple of months. During this time, I had several treatments lasting an hour each and to distract myself from the discomfort, I spent the time chatting to Aaryn, who obligingly listened to all my stories about energy work and my particular interest in hypnosis. He served to witness the transformation in me as a person, as I entered his practice as an advocate and left it as someone intent upon following a soul path working with hypnosis, Reiki and meditation. It was a transformation that he greatly encouraged.

During these two months, Aaryn in the role of my chiropractor was very supportive and helpful. Apart from being a kind and cheerful type of person who loved his work, he seemed to want to help me with my journey into the unknown of a new venture. He lent me a book to read, which I found to be exactly what I needed at the particular time. His encouragement and conviction that I would be able to make a success of my new career was heartening. He even handed out some of my business cards to persons whom he thought might benefit from working with me. Why would he be so helpful to a total stranger that he actually knew very little about?

Another aspect was the fact that I have had problems with a straight neck for decades. As it turned out, Aaryn specialises in restoring the curvature of the neck in cases like mine where it has been compromised by injury, poor posture or a combination thereof. His techniques were directly opposite to those used by other chiropractors I had visited for almost thirty years. And his techniques worked. He was therefore, out of about eight chiropractors who had tried to help me, the first one who actually sorted the problem out. How did this relate to the brave peasant, hanging from his neck so long ago, because he had freed a helpless person?

I once read somewhere – I think it was in a text book on forensic medicine during my legal studies – that it takes someone about eight minutes to die by hanging, unless the neck is broken during the hanging. From what I have seen in my own sessions, it seems that our bodies absorb the memory of our suffering during moments when we know that we are about to die. Those memories are the ones that are imprinted on new bodies we take in later lives, for release in such lives. In the life of a Franciscan monk I spent a few days fearing for my life as I was hiding amongst the wheat stored in a barn. At the time of my death, while I was being tied to a cross, the wheat was burning. I knew I was going to die and the memory that came with me was that at age forty five the presence of wheat would mean death. At age forty five in my current life, I developed a severe sensitivity to wheat and all products containing wheat.

So what was the significance of the fact that the peasant was hanging from a rope, with the knot tied at the back of his head, pulling his neck straight in the moments of death, which might not have been immediate? And how did this tie in to the presence of the soul who felt it owed a debt of gratitude to that peasant, and who would in another life as a chiropractor restore the curvature in the neck of the new body occupied by the same soul who had long ago been that simple, kind peasant? To my mind, the hours spent by my chiropractor in restoring the curvature in my neck and relieving the terrible neck and shoulder pain I had experienced, as well as the helpful and supportive chats we shared and his other small acts of kindness and helpfulness, indicated that our souls were balancing a karmic event. The soul of my chiropractor got to repay the perceived 'debt' of gratitude, which I simply see as a balancing of energy, not as the repayment of a debt. I had indeed needed the help of someone knowledgeable to help me to sort out my physical difficulties and to relieve my pain so that I could make one of the biggest decisions of my life and see it through. Let's be honest, without the support and help of people like Aaryn and many others, I am not sure that I would have been brave enough to just walk away from all I know to do what I knew to be right for me.

I shared the story of the peasant with my chiropractor, who said that it somehow all made sense to him. For me, this entire chapter of my life served to shift me into a space where I am no longer able to doubt my path. I stopped caring what others think about my 'strange' beliefs. I truly understand other people's hesitance when it comes to things like past lives and I do not spend much time trying to convince anyone of anything. After all, I firmly believe that we all have a team of helpers who look after us and that they will always find ways to guide us, no matter what we believe and regardless of whether we follow any kind of path that would include communication with them. Our lives never go wrong, even when they appear to, no matter what our belief system or religion.

In the months to follow, the insights of this profound session would open me up to see many of the obstacles in my way. It is tough to make progress if you feel that something is holding you back, but you do not know what it is. Once you can see the obstacle though, you can sit down and make a plan either to scale the mountain, climb the ladder, or to find a way through the river. Sometimes waiting things out is the best option. But you need to know what you are working with.

I did not know it yet, but the way had been paved to lead me to the last bit of information I needed to bring me to a place where I would never again have to pick up the burden of being angry with my Creator.

CHAPTER 37: Visions and Dreams – 11 - 17 December 2014

As time went by and I extricated myself from my legal career, I started meeting new and wonderful colleagues. It was so exciting to work with people who understood the things that I was passionate and excited about. I was able to share my insights in respect of all kinds of things and would learn new things from them. It was a magical time.

Removing myself from a profession that no longer resonated with me, resulted in huge improvements in my health and mind set. I started meeting more and more wonderful, likeminded people and my circle of support grew wider. My old friends and my family were already a huge support to me and adding new people to that positive support structure, became one of the great joys of my journey.

With my mind now free to concentrate on what mattered to me, instead of what mattered to my attorneys and their clients, I finally had the time to dig into the deep recesses of my soul. I also had the wherewithal to notice small things that might before have passed me by in the pursuit of another deadline. When a topic pops up more than once in the space of a couple of days, I pay attention. Since leaving my chambers, I had developed the habit of going for long walks along the canals near my home, listening to uplifting audiobooks, usually on behavioural psychology or some other enlightening work. I had just returned from a trip to Pretoria where I had met a NLP practitioner. A former client had put us in touch as she thought that we would have much in common, and she was right. As we shared insights and experiences, my new contact mentioned to me that she was part of a group who met on a monthly basis to study *A Course in Miracles* by Dr Helen Schucman (scribe).

Just the week before, I had been listening to an audiobook in which the authors made reference to *A Course in Miracles.* Suddenly references to this work popped up everywhere, for example on Facebook. It had clearly been around for a long time, yet I had never heard of it before. I decided to investigate, because I could hardly be seen not to know anything about a topic that most other people in my line of work seemed to be aware of. As it turns out, the next time I picked up the iPod to listen to an audiobook, I discovered that *A Course in Miracles* had already been loaded on it! A friend of mine had lent me her iPod on which she had loaded a large number of very interesting audiobooks and these were the audiobooks that had accompanied me on my daily walks for many weeks. I had been working my way through them and had not yet reached *A Course in Miracles.* It seems that I was bound to come across this work. It was almost inevitable.

It was just as well that I was introduced to this work through striking coincidence. I knew I had to listen to it, but, given my attitude towards religion, it was an effort to listen to the first couple of chapters of the audiobook version. I probably would have switched it off and abandoned the whole thing if it had not been for the synchronistic events that had led me to listening to it in the first place. I decided to push through, reminding myself that most people dabbling in the spiritual practices that fascinate me so much, had read it. I told myself that I was doing research. Since I was now making my living by doing energy work, I needed to read and understand all that is out there.

A Course in Miracles is a very long audiobook and by early December 2014 I had been listening to it for many weeks during my long daily walks in nature. I soon realised that the book, although all about God, the Holy Spirit and the Son of God, had absolutely nothing to do with religion. It seemed also to deal with many of the delusions and misconceptions many people suffer from when it comes to religion and pointed out the terrible abuses of power and limitations that were imposed out of fear and the need to control others. In fact, as I understood it, it dealt with the delusions of the human condition in general without making anyone right or wrong. The book seemed to draw me in, as it meticulously did not take sides and no one was made out to be wrong or bad.

As I listened, many things started making much more sense to me. Everything had already changed when it came to my career and thus the very basis of my financial security and how I made a living had changed. I had moved into a space of exhilaration when it came to my work life. When it comes to money, the shift brought me out of a space where I had to work myself into the ground for the sake of my clients and attorneys, only to then have to beg and plead and fight to get paid for many months after finishing the work. I was now getting paid as I worked. No one expected me to save them and then to wait to see when, or if, I would be remunerated for my efforts.

I recalled how my journey had started in March 2013, when I knew that I would have to face and deal with my attitude towards my Creator, an attitude that had been feeding a deep rage that I could do nothing about, except to suppress it, until it came looking for me. After the miraculous disappearance of my anger with the help of my teacher guide, who had understood that I would never be able to break out of that prison without help, my healing journey became so much more than I could ever have believed possible. Slowly, but very surely, I began to see life, really see it. And the more I observed, the more I realised that it was indeed a miracle. It was magical and mystical and there to be lived to the full. Had the anger not been lifted, I would never, ever have been able to see that.

The lifting of the anger had sent me on a crazy ride between channellings, self-hypnosis, regression and meditation sessions, which had in turn brought me to Françoise, who had shifted the next thing in my way, namely the three blocks in respect of money, my career and relationships. On the latter, I had made zero progress. Regarding money and my new career, I could foresee many challenges ahead, but I found these exciting and for the most part tried to see them as opportunities. How many people can start with a clean slate, with complete freedom to do whatever presented itself as an opportunity? What a privilege. This attitude saved me from feeling sheer terror at what I had done by pulling the rug from under my own two feet myself.

But shifting money issues does not mean that one becomes a millionaire overnight, or ever. It means that the system within which one's financial well-being is determined, is healed. I was now rendering a loving service in support of humanity and getting paid for it. Nothing remained of the terrible exploitation affecting my health that had been the system within which my financial well-being had previously been determined. The joy of entering my new career was complete and the shift had manifested immediately, the moment I made the decision to put down the burden of my legal career.

So what remained unresolved, was firstly the issue of relationships and secondly the fact that I kept wondering whether I had done enough to comply with my teacher guide's instruction on the day he lifted my anger. I had never forgotten that he had told me to download the information that I needed to stop being so angry. Perhaps that is what drove my frenzied efforts when it came to channelling, meditation and self-regression work. I really tried to do what I could to understand how it all worked. I was able to do this, because I had been angry for years about the fact that my prayers had never been heard. Now I had been heard and given an extraordinary opportunity. It was my duty to make the most of it. Good thing I am a real goody two shoes.

I think my guides must have known that I would need something to finish off that particular chapter of my growth. The anger was gone and I had been downloading as they had instructed me to do. Things seemed to fall into place. But surely I should be getting some sort of certificate, along the lines of 'It is hereby acknowledged that Cathy Mc Donald had made peace with her Creator on this day'. What if I ever needed proof, even if only to remind myself? As always, I received what I needed, when the time was right.

As it turned out, both remaining issues resolved themselves in a very short period of time. I remember those precious moments when I first realised that these last two major issues had finally been resolved. It was almost as if I had been someone trying to break the code on a safe keeping the great secrets of my life, carefully listening for the right amount of clicks in the right order that would allow the heavy door to swing open. I could almost hear the click in my head as these larger than life aspects of my little world simply seemed to work themselves out in my mind. These are those intensely private and mystical moments that you can share with others, but in many ways, it will always be between you, your soul and all that is sacred to you, because you are the only true observer of the actual moment in time.

On 4 December 2014, I was finally able to make my peace with the Creator. I had been looking for this peace for almost twenty years. It just happened and there was no drama involved. I went out for my morning walk as I do on most days and the peaceful reality simply slid into my mind as I walked along listening to *A Course in Miracles*. This major shift in my consciousness came about more as a process of 'knowing it is alright now', than of making peace. Nothing was expected of me. Things were just okay. No action or drama was required. All was well between us now and I understood my place in it all. Most of all, I was totally at peace with that place and fully accepted it. When I got home, I made a note of the date on a big sheet of paper and left it on the pile of things to be attended to – 4 12 2014. I smiled as I looked down at the numbers of the date. Even the date was special, because it contained a pattern of numbers and I never fail to notice patterns in dates. Those who take care of me really do know me very well. And I knew that I would never be the same.

A few days later, I found myself once more face to face with an insight that quietly entered my mind as I walked along the canals, still listening to *A Course in Miracles*. I finally understood relationships and could clearly see their purpose and their place. I also understood that in my current life I have no further use for a human romantic relationship. This I had known for a long time, but I still sometimes 'wished I had someone'. I now even understood that. I suppose it will always be a dream to share life with someone who really loves you in the same way as you love that person. It is part of the human condition. In my case, I already knew that my relationships had all had a purpose. These relationships were lessons, karmic balancing opportunities and learning curves, all involving sacred soul contracts with souls who had agreed to help me achieve the learning I had set out to accomplish. I suspect that my primary soulmate and I had chosen not to incarnate together in my current life. It made perfect sense looking back over my life. I would not have grown into a strong and independent woman with my primary soulmate's awesome strength, energy and integrity there to support me. I had to go it alone. Perhaps I needed to toughen up as a soul. Perhaps there is another relationship I shall have to work through, but it will come if it is in my life's plan. And perhaps, if I accomplish what I have set out to do, I might indeed get to meet up and spend some time with my primary soulmate after the work had been done. I remember that I gained the impression during my spiritual regression that the particular issue of whether or not we will be meeting each other in this life, seemed to be 'undecided'.

During or shortly after the time that I realised that I had in fact achieved what I had set out to do in March 2013, I had five strange experiences; experiences that are certainly not everyday happenings in my world. They were strange enough for me to realise that they might be significant and so I jotted down the details as I always do, because if it were not for the notes I made, I would soon forget that they had happened. As we do with our dreams, we simply forget the precious information we receive in those fleeting moments of awareness.

The first such experience was when Christ came to meet me during a meditation I did on 11 December 2014. He took me to a valley and as we looked down on it, I saw a happy community going about their daily lives. He told me that the valley was a representation of the results of all my contributions to the well-being of others on earth. I felt profoundly humbled as I looked at the ordinariness of the activities in the valley. Those people were free to live their lives and appeared happy and content. It made me feel valuable to have been able to contribute to that.

Later that evening, I realised that it was probably really significant that Christ had appeared in my meditation. After all, with peace now restored between me and the Creator, the avenues were opened. I suddenly realised that *A Course in Miracles* had restored my connection to the Holy Trinity by totally removing religion from the connection. I no longer connected God, Christ or the Holy Spirit to the religious teachings that had brought me so much distress. The connection was pure, and certainly did not involve fear, judgment or limitation in any form.

The second experience came during the following night, on 12 December 2014, when I dreamt that a snake was trying to bite me. I was fending it off and eventually managed to get hold of it just below the head so that its fangs could not reach me, but it just extended its head and bit deeply into my hand. Naturally, I felt less than happy when I woke up. A search of the internet dream diaries revealed that dreams of snake bites often relate to periods of spiritual growth. Given my enormous shift regarding the Creator, the dream was pretty spot on and I immediately felt much better. Things were moving along quite nicely. I just loved symbolism and I was enchanted by the sheer magic of the small things occurring in my life confirming the culmination of the journey.

The next day, on 13 December 2014, out of nowhere, a very clear vision flashed into my mind for a few seconds before it vanished. I saw the most beautiful night sky filled with bright, flickering stars. What was amazing about the vision, was the fact that I was right there. I could almost feel the vision, because I was seemingly out there in the night sky. The clarity was unreal and intense. It was a good thing that I had made a note of this third experience, because a few days later I would realise that everything I saw in my mind's eye during meditations, were suddenly totally clear. It was as if my ability to see visions with clarity had been even further enhanced since that night. I have stated before that I had begun to notice that I could see things in my dreams and meditations with much more clarity than before, but now the clarity had increased to a point where I had the experience of actually being present in the vision, of actually seeing it. About six months after this, I would return to this place in the midnight blue sky. It would be the moment my soul had waited for.

The following day, on 14 December 2014, I had another flash vision. This time, I saw a bridge between two worlds. I was in the process of walking across it, halfway between the two worlds. I am not sure what the vision meant, or if it was supposed to mean anything, but it made me feel that I was making good progress.

The Christmas holidays had started and, as always, our small family got together at my parents' home in Hartenbos. My parents spend the whole year preparing for our annual visit and although I get to see them more regularly than my sister does, because I live closer to them, the three weeks that my sister's husband is able to take leave so that they can take a holiday, are the highlight of our year. With everyone settling in, I continued my daily walks, but I was now able to walk along the promenade, drinking in the early light of dawn, marvelling at the peaceful atmosphere hanging over the sleeping tents and caravans hugging the long stretches of pristine beach. I was happy.

A few days later, on 17 December 2014, I had another flash vision. Perhaps this vision had been inspired by the fact that I was now at home with two truly talented artists, namely my sister and my father. My little nephew was already showing promise of stepping into the big shoes of his grandfather and his mother. This time, I saw with astonishing clarity a beautiful painting of a white vase, filled with the most beautiful aquamarine blue flowers hanging over its side, standing on a white table. In the background, three grey, blue and tan rectangles were set against an even lighter grey surface, each of a different size and one placed vertically and the other two placed horizontally. I drew a picture of it immediately, adding in the colours, so that I could recall the details later.

Seeing flashes of paintings was something that had happened to me before, but somehow, I just never had the inclination to paint what I had seen. Perhaps my stressful career simply squashed all my creativity. Once before I had tried to paint what I had seen in visions, but my perfectionistic streak would not tolerate my inexperience and I soon got bored with the effort of trying to get it 'just right'. I had so much happening in my life at that time and had started those paintings just before my divorce. After leaving home, I did not really have the time, energy or inclination to follow through and finish them. My failed marriage signalled the end of my initial spiritual journey and the flashes of the paintings I had seen, were part of that. And so I had closed that door, locking away my creativity with it.

This time though, I intend picking up that paint brush the day I type the last word of these pages. I hope I can get the aquamarine colour 'just right'. And when I do, I know the door to another part of my soul will swing wide open. I shall walk through it.

CHAPTER 38: Meditation on Inner Healing – 24 December 2014

My mind was now a peaceful place. The weeks working at home after closing my law practice had worked wonders. Even though I had been busy starting up a fulltime practice seeing clients for hypnosis and Reiki sessions and spending time writing meditation scripts, I had ample time to learn to control my thoughts. I embraced the simple principles in Robin Sharma's *The Monk who sold his Ferrari*. Incidentally, this was the book that my chiropractor lent me just before I left the bar, as mentioned earlier. After reading it from start to finish in two days, I returned his book and went out to buy my own copy. I summarised the jewels I found in its pages and it forms part of my daily meditation ritual to this day. The greatest gift I found in the pages of that book was the technique of oppositional thinking, whereby a negative thought is stopped in its tracks and immediately replaced with a positive one. After three days, my brain got tired of producing negative thoughts and stopped trying. After a while, I found that I had to remember to plan to attend to aspects in my life that might need attention, because I no longer had the ability to worry about anything. If I worried about things, they would get done, but if I stopped worrying, there was no automatic reminder in the form of a worried thought spinning in my mind, ensuring that I pay attention to important things.

In the months after leaving the bar, I found great pleasure in writing. My new website had a blog that allowed me to play. I could write about everyday things and pretend to myself that, even if no one bothered to read my blogs, every blog would touch at least one heart. In the months to come, I would find people crossing my path who were struggling with the very issues I had been blogging about in a hopefully light hearted fashion. It was amazing to be able to send the link to a particular blog to such a person and to receive a note later telling me that what I had expressed in the blog was spot on. In a small way, I found a way to share how I see life and energy dynamics with those who are open to it. It was wonderful to use words to spread love and kindness, looking at the world through gentle eyes, instead of using words to tear people's lives apart in an effort to win a legal battle. The choice I had made to leave my career and to jump into the void had been the right one. In fact, it was the very first thing I shared in my blog, that first exhilarating jump into nothing.

Jumping into the void

I have often wondered what it takes to jump into the void of not knowing what to expect but following your heart anyway ... One hears stories about people taking this seemingly courageous step and landing on their feet, living their dream, regardless of how impossible it all seemed to those looking on from the outside. I always felt a tiny bit envious and fervently wished that I had the courage to do just that.

As it turns out, I ended up jumping into the void with much less thought than I figured would be required before doing something like that. Courage was not involved at all! For the record, I am still in free fall and it seems like the ideal position from which to report on the issue – just in case there is someone out there wanting to jump into a void of their own!

For the most part the actual jump is a bit of a blur right now. Perhaps later I shall remember more of the 'details', and probably embellish a little! What I do remember is that I felt swept up in ... something. Synchronicity? No idea. But it felt right. More than that, it was right. Jumping was in fact the only option. That first step out into the void, if it is taken when it is meant to be, happens almost automatically once the clear sense of knowing settles into the mind ...

Given that I tend to be overly analytical, I feel obliged to dissect the section of the jump between stepping out and where I think I am now – in free fall. It seems to me that what brought about that almost involuntary reaction to jump is a mixture of clear intention, absolute passion, a sense of knowing what is right at that very moment and a total absence of fear. If one's passion can shape one's intention clearly, the resultant exhilaration produces a state of mind that pushes out all fear, because in the end all will be well.

So much for stepping out ... Once over the cliff, it is encouraging to find cloud nine drifting by and it is not too difficult to adopt the behaviour of a bouncing beach ball. For a while everything is just fine, but one soon bounces right off the cloud and for the first time a little catch in the throat makes one think ... oh my word ... Happily, by then it is too late and as there is no turning back, tumbling further into the void is inevitable anyway.

Much to my surprise I found that the very act of jumping into the void is an act of creation which seemingly produces what feels very much like tiles under one's feet. So far so good. The very fact that tiles have been slipped under one's feet of course suggests forward movement, and one is left with the amazing belief that if such tiles appeared once, more tiles might magically appear. The thing is though, feeling the tiles under one's feet brings a sense of being looked after and with that, trusting that more tiles will be slipped under one's feet just before one tumbles into free fall, becomes easier.

Of course every now and again a little free fall is apparently part of the path through the void when the next tile is nowhere to be seen. At this stage I am not sure whether I am really in free fall downwards towards goodness knows what, somehow having missed a tile, or whether I am being swept along through the void stepping on invisible tiles I am not able to perceive. What I do know is that the chance to jump would not have come again, because I know that when I jumped, the time was exactly right. And somehow, this knowledge manages to dissolve all fear.

I found that the writing of each blog healed a small part of my soul. A few months later I would stumble upon the statistics of how many people visited the blog on my website. I could not believe my eyes. Maybe I could hope to touch more than one heart!

Another new passion that I had discovered, even before I left my career, was that I simply loved writing guided meditations. I would spend hours researching topics and then come up with a script that would take the meditator on a magical journey. I started incorporating my techniques as used during my own meditations, hoping to share with people the amazing reality that we can all call upon and receive help from our guides, simply by entering the meditative state. Anyone can do this. There is simply nothing to it. Holding group meditations led to a compilation of quite a number of guided meditations, which I recorded and used for myself on a daily basis. As much as I found healing in the practice of meditation, others seemed interested, but not quite as taken with the idea as I was and I often ended up doing group meditations for only two or three people. It did not matter. What mattered was how it made me feel to be able to produce a meditation that could transport someone to a healing space. That, to me, was magical. I felt as if I was taking people on a journey to sacred sites. And is that not what the deep recesses of our minds are?

On any given day I could pick any topic to meditate on, as I had a long list of recordings to choose from. And so it came that on 24 December 2014 I settled down for a long meditation after my early morning walk along the beach. Everyone was still asleep and the house was very quiet. The birds were happily chirping away, as excited about the new day as I was. I had chosen to use the *Inner Healing* meditation. The particular meditation had very special meaning to me. I had originally written a hypnosis script for a dear friend of mine who was in the process of working through cancer. The script was deeply moving and I felt inspired to adapt it for meditation. I had last used this meditation for myself somewhere towards the end of November 2014, a few days before I had made the shift in respect of my relationship with my Creator. As I settled down that morning, I recalled that last time when I had used it, as I had received profound healing towards the end of the meditation. As I was standing in the violet light which at some point is part of the imagery used in the meditation, I felt my body rise up and the light simply enfolding me. It was as if my soul itself was being cleansed. It was a truly moving experience. Perhaps that was the actual moment of restoration of the relationship between me and my Maker, which I would only truly realise a few days thereafter.

I initially struggled a little to relax into the meditation, mostly because I had been eating unhealthy stuff during the holidays – too much sugar! Yet I eventually settled into it and spent time in the quiet space when the guiding voice stops speaking and the meditator can do his or her own work while gentle music is playing in the background. I felt that the forest of my life as it usually appeared to me in the meditation when prompted by the imagery used, needed changing. I made it lighter and greener and then decided that I wanted to have cherry blossom trees in my life's forest. Instantly, Li Mang, my energy teacher in the spirit world, appeared. He sat waiting on the stone bench under the cherry blossom tree where he always meets me when I go home after an incarnation. After a friendly greeting from him, I told him I needed more power in my hands so that I could bring more healing. He felt that this could be given to me. I was then transported to a waterfall amongst beautiful green ferns, where Christ was waiting. He sat on a rock and I washed His feet using the water from the waterfall. He reached down and touched my hands. I knew He was giving them more power. I continued washing His feet and 'healed' the wounds in them, though I was very much aware that this was a symbolic healing only, and merely a demonstration to help me see that I would now have more strength and power to heal in my hands. Christ told me that with this gift comes tremendous responsibility, namely the responsibility not to interfere in the lives of others.

I returned to Li Mang, who told me that I would be given certain meditations, which I should share with others. Thereafter, every now and again, I would get an idea for a meditation and the words thereof would always somehow just flow out of my fingers when I started typing.

I should point out that apart from hypnosis, the energy healing modality I practise, is Reiki. As many people might know, Reiki is the universal life force energy, accessible by anyone who chooses to accept the attunement to the symbols releasing this energy. The practitioner has no personal power at all and is simply a conduit for the energy, and a very privileged one at that, as the energy travels through the body of the Reiki healer before entering the body of the recipient. I have no idea why I asked Li Mang for more power in my hands during the meditation. Since this had been agreed to and apparently effected, I thought that after the meditation I might have become able to draw more of the energy for transfer to the recipient, but of course I would have no real way of measuring the effect of the change, if any.

Shortly after this meditation, I worked on two clients. I suddenly felt drawn to using a different technique, one that

I had seldom used before, mostly because I preferred using another technique with which I got really good results. Both clients took the trouble to carefully note how their lives unfolded in the weeks following their Reiki treatment, as I had asked them to do so. Both experienced truly major shifts in their lives. One was finally able to draw a line in the sand when it came to a bullying business partner. His attitude, previously closely resembling that of a bad tempered elephant bull, changed completely. She found that she was being left in peace to get on with her work and that her workload was halved. The other client was a cancer patient and her journey required every ounce of her courage. During the hardest part of her truly difficult journey, she found a sense of quiet strength and profound peace within. She suddenly had access to the courage and faith that one only finds in a place of total surrender. She later told me that she first became aware thereof directly after her Reiki session during which I used the new technique.

As always, good results with clients make me feel utterly humble. Mostly because I fully understand that healing comes through us, it is not given by us. What a privilege it is to be able to work with a loving energy that makes people and their lives, hearts and souls whole. And if the additional power I had symbolically been given during my meditation had in the physical world merely translated into me brushing off and using an ancient technique I had known about for a long time, it all still made perfect sense to me, and it was still a miracle.

CHAPTER 39: Meditation – 25 December 2014

As Christmas Day dawned over the majestic Outeniqua mountains in the distance, I felt my heart open up as I walked along the paved pathway. The sea to my right was so calm that the waves seemed almost apologetic as they crept up the shoreline. I could breathe deeply and freely and just felt blessed. The voice of the narrator of *A Course in Miracles* droned on in my ears and so it came that I started thinking about forgiveness.

I have long had a problem with all terms connected to religion. In my own way though, I had always employed the mechanism of 'putting down' things that other people had done to me. If I had to hold on to all the wrongs that had been perpetrated against me in circumstances where I gave nothing but kindness and love to those who relished bringing harm to me, I would not be able to get out of bed. That, I suspect, is true for many people. Letting go of these things is essential.

I just never liked the word forgiveness and in many ways, the use of the word still got my hackles up. I am pretty sure that the word somehow just had a negative connotation for me. In principle therefore, I accepted and agreed with the notion that forgiveness sets us free. I also understood the rider that comes with the use of that word, that forgiveness is all about setting oneself free and does not mean that one condones what the other person has done. Yet somehow the word still felt too mushy to me. I preferred putting things and people who have harmed me behind me by putting down the burden of hurt and pain they placed on my shoulders and walking away, never again to honour them with so much as a thought.

Thinking about it that morning, I suddenly realised that the problem that I had always had with the word forgiveness, was that from an energy dynamics perspective I felt that forgiveness in fact also sets free the forgiven person, not only the forgiver. Did that mean I did not want some of my perpetrators to be free of what they had done to me? I had to admit that that was exactly what it meant. I have always thought that once I had put someone or something down, I was free. To my mind, they would still have to deal with the karmic fall-out of their deeds, as we all have to. Frankly, putting down my perpetrators was easy, as I was doing it for my own benefit. The Triad, despite the enormous harm they did to me, were insignificant and utterly forgettable people who were definitely not worth remembering. Yet I knew that despite my letting it all go and putting them down, they would never be free of what they had done to me and that they would have to balance the distortion they had caused in the karmic pattern at some point. Perhaps that was why it was so very easy to put them, and what they had done, down.

As I was walking along the promenade, I wondered if forgiveness, instead of just letting go and putting perpetrators down, could change what they had done in the sense that it would absolve them from having to deal with the karmic consequences of what they had created. I had no idea. The issue of forgiveness would again come up in my world a few months later and at that stage I would finally see that forgiveness, to my mind at least, sets free the forgiver as well as the perpetrator. That still did not mean that the forgiven would not have to deal with the karmic fall-out or that their actions were condoned. It just meant that, after having been set free by the forgiver, they would more easily be able to start extricating themselves in a healthy way from what they had done and find forgiveness for themselves, thereby healing the karmic distortion created by what they had done and had subsequently been forgiven for.   In other words, forgiveness results in an energy release of the perpetrator. This realisation finally explained to me why I preferred to put certain people down and leave them behind, not bothering to forgive them.   Not a nice attitude to have, I suppose, but moving towards forgiveness is a process and it begins with setting oneself free.   Later, it might be possible also to release the perpetrator. In some instances I suppose the process is shorter and it is easier to get from the point of leaving something behind to full forgiveness and it can even be done simultaneously. But some things are close to unforgivable; such things take much, much longer to forgive, because in terms of the physical laws governing energy, forgiveness does hold an undeniable benefit to the perpetrator in my view. In fact, their energy shackles are loosened, allowing them to free themselves as the forgiver had done.

That morning, however, I was still a long way away from working out the intricacies of the mechanism of forgiveness. I just knew that the term was usually used in an over-simplified sense and this remained something that irritated my analytical mind.   During my walk the word forgiveness was repeated a number of times in the chapter of *A Course in Miracles* I was listening to.   As with all things dealt with in that book, the narrative managed to strip every sentence of any connotation and interpretation linking what was discussed to societal boxes, limitations and admonitions.   I found the words easy on the ear. Perhaps I was just ready to hear them.   By the time I walked back into the quiet house where my family slept peacefully, I felt that it would not do any harm simply to make sure that I had indeed put down all the people who had harmed me in the past, by releasing them one more time. I suppose one could say that I felt able to employ the term forgiveness as used in *A Course in Miracles*.

When I reached the quiet time of my morning meditation, I called in nine people, including The Triad. With their energies present, I thanked each one for their part in my journey and told them that I forgave them. The minute I did this, I felt my vibration increase, almost as if I was taken into a vortex.

CHAPTER 40: Meditation – 12 January 2015

The new year had quietly entered our lives. For me, it was the first year of freedom. I had been freed from a prison that had managed to dim the light of my soul for so long. In the years before I became a lawyer, I was in a different kind of prison. My entire life had been filled with pain and I had spent all the years of my adult life trying to repair myself and the damage that had been done to my mind and body. Becoming a lawyer in the first place was a major repair job. And it worked, until it became my prison. But so it is when our choices are not authentic. And yet, even the choice to try to repair myself turned out well. There are no mistakes in the paths we follow. Even my choices that were ostensibly wrong or poor worked out well in the end. The key factor, however, was that there would always come a time when change was required, and then it would take courage to make that change. Without change and without the courage to change things, we would stay stuck in the space created by choices that no longer serve us.

My new endeavour suddenly looked crazy. Did I really think I could make it as a hypnosis practitioner, Reiki Master Healer and meditation coach? Yes, I did. But my societal conditioning and training as a lawyer dictated that my enthusiasm might not be enough. The day before I was due to see my first client for the year, I felt quite down. In fact, the entire day was hard and I suddenly felt that I might not make a success of this. The strict voice in my mind was clear: catch a wake up, stop dreaming, and start working. As in 'Get a job!'

Fortunately, I knew that my poor conditioned subconscious still struggled to accept my new habits and approach to life.

I had not forgotten the crazy stunt it pulled the previous year to get me to a space of comfort so that I would stop destroying what it saw as my only possible livelihood, jeopardising my survival. I resigned myself to the fact that I might have to be diligent for a while. I would have to check up on the scared protector that is my subconscious. It means well, but it has no spirit and no sense of adventure. It does not do risk. It is boring, but safe. It definitely cannot dream of a better future and living an authentic life. And so I came to equate 'safe' with prison. I had already taken an enormous risk to break free from my shackles. I might as well finish the ride.

I decided to meditate on the matter and to see if I could find the reason for the block that was holding me back from my new venture. This time, I employed a technique that I had learned from Christie Els so many years before. As I entered trance, I just allowed my mind to bring me the information. And I loved the picture it showed me. Somewhere in my mind is a brilliant movie director who simply loves symbolism. The mind movies that had played out in my mind under hypnosis years before in Christie's therapy room, had all come true. Every single aspect of those symbolic visions manifested in my life. They were always hopeful, uplifting and positive. They helped me to believe in something when I had nothing to hold on to. I truly believe that we were created with unbelievable wisdom stored within, ready to be accessed at a moment's notice. We really just have to ask, and reach up. I shall dedicate the rest of my life to sharing this truth with as many people as may be willing to listen to my overly enthusiastic chatter about this miracle.

As my mind began to drift, I started seeing pictures from many lives in rapid succession. Once more I was struck by the absolute clarity of what I was seeing. Something in me had shifted a few months ago and since then my visions had become clearer, but after the flash visions of December 2014, they had become startlingly vivid. Is that what happens when one's vibration lifts? I do not know, but I sure hope that it is the case. The visions were no longer just dreamlike images, as when one recalls a memory.

The series of visions of my many lives stopped coming and suddenly a beautiful black chess board appeared. I knew that it was the Game of Life. It seems that chequered floors and chess boards are highly symbolic to me, because they had been part of my mind journeys from the beginning. I recall seeing similar symbolism for the Game of Life on the day my journey began. On that day, 8 April 2013, I saw a round tower room with a chequered floor and an ornamental pillar in the centre thereof, representing the Game of Life. This time though, I saw a meditating dark grey Buddha sitting in the middle of a square chess board. I asked my guides to help me to interpret the vision. I really, really wanted to know what was holding me back from moving forward into my new career.

The Buddha in the centre of the chess board opened his eyes. The colour of his almost yellow human eyes was startlingly clear. He asked: 'Which one of the pieces on the board is you?' As I stared at the pieces, the King became illuminated in light, while all the other pieces remained in shadow. Then he asked me: 'What do you want?' I said: 'I want this!' I meant that I wanted my new career. The Buddha disappeared and all of the other chess pieces flew off the board. Only the King remained sitting on the chess board and grew to become life sized. As it got bigger, it took on my human form until I stood alone with the sun rising brilliantly over the chess board, the game of my life, as I absorbed the golden rays.

Unlike before, the symbolism in these visions was instantly clear to me. I no longer needed to look up the meaning of any aspects of the vision. I knew that it was now all up to me. I had to choose, and choose with utter faith and conviction. It was my life and mine alone. I could not worry about society or concern myself with the opinions of others. But most of all, I could not waste any time on my own fears. It also struck me that in the original round tower room with the chequered floor resembling a chess board, representing the Game of Life two years earlier, the round pillar in the centre had appeared to me to be out of place at the time, presenting an obstacle hampering my ability to play the game. I was so right. At that stage I had been unable to play the game of my own life.

It was good to see the symbolic change that had taken place in the intervening years. What was now at the centre of the game of my life, so to speak, was the regular practice of meditation, as symbolised by the Buddha, which enabled me to make decisions with much more clarity, knowing my true place in the order of things. Through the practice of meditation I had been able to remove the pillar in the centre of my Game of Life. Was the pillar a symbol for my anger? Perhaps, but only now did I realise that the pillar could also have been symbolic of all the things that had been holding me back, including my anger. No wonder I had felt stuck.

In the months that followed, I would have to face my doubts many times over. The fear and the constant nagging of a deep survival instinct, in the end, proved to be my worst enemies. I could control my thinking and keep negative thoughts about failure at bay, but I had to do it in a responsible way. I had to remain capable of making sound and objective decisions, instead of walking off with my head in the clouds, only to wake up at the bottom of the ravine amongst the remains of my shattered dreams, because I had failed to remember that I was living in the real world where one still has to pay the bills. Steering my dream remained absolutely necessary.

And so I learned that my wonderful friends and family understood that I could not always answer their questions on how things were going, because it would mean that I would have to tell them that things were a little tight. They also knew that it was a risk I had been willing to take for the sake of living an authentic life. One does not make massive changes in one's life without some discomfort and uncertainty along the way. The amazing thing is, as much as discomfort and uncertainty follow like shadows in one's brave footsteps, hesitantly moving forward, so miracles literally pave the way. Just at that moment when all seems lost, and a difficult decision has to be made, like selling a home that had been a safe and healing haven for years, the miracle required materialises.

It became a matter of perception. I started seeing that I wanted my new life to contain all the safety mechanisms that I had constructed during my old life. I clung to a home I loved. Until I saw that it was not the ideal space for my healing practice. Then I no longer felt as if I needed to give it up, I felt that I needed to move to a better and more comfortable space for my new practice. The minute my perception changed, I found the courage to let go of what I had built up and of what had been my anchor for so long. Within days I managed to find a purchaser, who paid my asking price. She approached me through an agent charging five and a half percent less commission than any other agent, releasing funds I would otherwise not have had access to. Suddenly, the additional hypnosis courses I was dying to take, became accessible.

My survival instinct kept plaguing me and I had to manage it as a reality in my life. In time, my subconscious would settle down and see that I was going to do just fine, and then it would stop worrying on my behalf. There is a purpose for every struggle and my concerns about survival in uncertain times led me on a very short path of almost venturing back into a space where surviving in society dictated how I would spend my energies. Would it not be better just to do all this part-time and spend the daytime hours working for a basic income that would enable me to do what I loved in the rest of my time? In my case, definitely not, but I had to discover that by going through the miserable process of applying for jobs that I did not want and prayed that I would not get. I hated the idea of returning to a field I had already experienced to be toxic for me. As much as the law has an important place in the world, it no longer had a place in mine.

Sometimes one has to stay open to what one does not want, allowing all resistance against it to fall away, because resisting something will draw exactly that which one resists into one's world. But in the end, I knew that I had the courage it would take to forge ahead and to follow the path I knew with my whole heart and soul was the right one for me. It nevertheless took a gentle reminder that I had chosen to follow my soul path and that veering off that path, would not be good for my health. On 10 August 2014 my guide had performed healing on my neck while I was still practising as an advocate and told me that the healing was conditional upon my completion of the process of ending my career. My neck only released some weeks after that healing and only after my subconscious and I had a little misunderstanding about how safe it would be to end my career. After that, it was fairly smooth sailing as my neck kept improving. But at some point about four months after I had left the bar, my neck started giving me painful reminders that it had once been injured. I put it down to the fact that once injured, one tends to be vulnerable. It took a few weeks for me to realise that, just as my subconscious had almost derailed my career change a few months earlier, I was now consciously jeopardising the change myself – by applying for jobs I knew would destroy my soul, simply because I was worried about survival. It seems that completing the process of ending my career was much more than just leaving the bar; it was about fully and fearlessly engaging in my new career. That would require trust, faith and a whole lot of courage. I had plenty of all three. I just needed reminding.

And so the journey would continue as I learned to, and to this day continue to learn to live in trust, having faith that once one finds one's passion and chooses to follow one's soul path with courage and conviction, serving one's fellowman in doing so, the universe smiles upon one's efforts. Wounds heal, lives change, doors fly open and dreams come true. In short, miracles happen. My neck soon loosened up, but only once I allowed my dreams to grow wings in order to fly to a new space that had been prepared for me. Once I embraced the move to a different region, far away from the jobs I had applied for, the rigidity in my neck and body finally began to relax with the help of a very talented myosteopath. I suspect that my body will always be sensitive and attuned to whether or not I am on my soul path. I have no doubt that should I veer off course, I shall be reminded.

As I wrote the pages of this book, so many pieces of the puzzle of my life fell into place. I could see the entire tapestry, woven together from strands of carefully recorded recollections of meditations, channellings and regressions, all but forgotten in the recesses of my mind, until I took them out, looked at them, and allowed them to speak to me through these pages. I realised that if all I had done came to nothing more than me having had the space within which to complete this story, even if I were to be the only person to ever read these words, it would still all have been worth the while. As this realisation dawned on me, I began to see that the months since I had ended my career, had in fact been the sabbatical I had been dreaming of for years. I would never have taken six months off work to write a book and to devote myself to energy work. Yet, this was exactly how it worked out. In the end I spent six months writing this book, while further honing my skills in hypnosis, Reiki and meditation work when I was not seeing clients. It was so much more than starting a new venture; I was on a sabbatical. I just did not know it until about five months into the six month sabbatical. And what a privilege this was. I will never be the same. The learning, insights and clarity I received in these few months, changed me forever. All because more than two years earlier, I had decided to choose to heal.

CHAPTER 41: Self-hypnosis Regression – 9 February 2015

As much as things were finally flowing and I was learning how to live in the moment, watching things unfold while also quietly planning and staying open to opportunities, one thing remained. It felt as if there was one place in my soul that was still not completely healed, although I now had complete understanding and acceptance of the greater order of things, especially in my life. It was buried so deep that I was unsure that I could ever reach it, or whether my soul would let me come close enough to examine the wound.

Despite all the work I had done, I had never regressed to a life that I had spent with my primary soulmate. As I said, I had reached a place of full understanding of the place and value of relationships. I also knew that I was now hiding behind that insight, avoiding what I did not want to feel. It was time for one more regression. What had transpired during my spiritual regression eighteen months earlier, when the therapist asked a question about my primary soulmate which resulted in the journey suddenly ending with the revelation that my soul was torn, remained unresolved.

I owed it to myself to finish my soul's work, no matter how painful and so I visited two lives in one session that deeply resonated with me. Finally, I was able to reach deep into a place I did not even have the words to describe.

Self-hypnosis regression 9 February 2015 (first life): In an ancient and still fairly barbaric time, I willingly left my village to live with a man that my family referred to as a half breed barbarian. He had a light brown skin and clear grey eyes, just like the eyes of his white mother. He was a beautiful man with long brown hair and an athletic body, a horseman living in the woods with his tribe. I happily transformed into one of them. We were very happy and very, very close. One day, I felt I needed to return to my village just to tell my people that I was happy and that I had left them willingly, otherwise they would worry and might be looking for me. I wanted to avoid trouble, but my partner would not let me face my village alone and accompanied me. There was a young man in the village who had been my childhood friend. He had been in love with me all his life. He knew about the man in my life and hated him, not only because I was with him, but because he was not 'one of us'. The young man stayed hidden while he watched me talking to the people of my village. My partner was sitting on his horse next to mine. My young friend tried to kill my partner and shot him with an arrow from where he was hiding. Although he had meant to kill him, he only wounded my partner. We left the village in a hurry and raced home to the woods. It was easy for the villagers to follow us, as my partner had been wounded. A skirmish erupted, but I walked out into the middle of it and stopped the fight, telling them all just to let it be. The villagers left and my partner healed. We were so very happy. I was still young when I died of a fever. As my partner held me, my dying thoughts were that no one would ever be able to hold me and love me the same way he does. After my death, my partner became distraught and bitter. He eventually died in his old age, still not having been able to let me go.

What can I say?   Now I understood why none of my relationships had ever worked out. The men I had loved were simply not a match for the man with the clear grey eyes. As soon as the scene unfolded, I recognised the powerful energy of my primary soulmate that I had come across so many times during my meditations. My primary soulmate presents very differently during meditations and does not resemble the man with the grey eyes, but the energy is the same. How do I know that? Because the integrity I sense is absolute. It has nothing to do with his physical form.

By now I knew how karmic bonds are formed. I recalled the life of the peasant and the young woman who had felt that she would never be able to repay her debt of gratitude to him. In much the same way, my dying thoughts as a young woman in a happy union with her primary soulmate were that no one could ever love me in the way that the man with the grey eyes did. I presume that would be true, unless my primary soulmate and I decided to share an incarnation, in which case he would indeed be someone who could love me the same way the man with the clear grey eyes did. But if I decided to incarnate without him and with a different purpose, like sharing my life with other soulmates for karmic or other reasons, I certainly would find myself in relationships that could never measure up to what I would be able to share with my primary soulmate.

Was this why the facilitator of my life between lives spiritual regression had not been allowed to ask any questions regarding me meeting my primary soulmate in my current life? Was this what I needed to discover? Whatever the answers to these questions were, I knew that I needed to heal these aspects. If I need to enter another karmic relationship in my current life or another life for purposes of balancing something, or for purposes of learning something, then the bond my dying thoughts created to the man with the grey eyes might block this, even though he was my primary soulmate's incarnation. It might even block me from meeting up with my primary soulmate again in a new incarnation, or even in my current life.

I was able to register all these things while still holding trance. Everything was so clear and so detailed, just like the visions in my mind journeys, meditations and dreams. The ability to see with such clarity helped me to hold the trance, while doing what I needed to do in trance to resolve the issues. And so I called upon the man with the grey eyes to let me go, so that we could both be free. He agreed and I encouraged him to find someone new after my death, which he was able to do. I changed the outcome of that life to one where he died a happy man and while he had very good memories of me, these did not hold him back. Then I purposefully released the thought that no one could ever hold me and love me the way my long ago partner did.

What happens now is not important. All I know is that there are no longer any blocks to learning through relationships that might be required to finish my soul path. Time will tell.

During the session I moved straight from the one life into the next.

Self-hypnosis regression 9 February 2015 (second life):
I entered the life standing in a room. I had white paint on my toe nails and was wearing a white shift. I guessed the time period to be somewhere in the seventeen or eighteen hundreds. I was living on a farm with my two foster parents and I was probably around seventeen years old. I was extraordinarily beautiful, with blue eyes, dark brown hair and an olive skin. I had the type of beauty that absolutely no man could resist. I was aching to have a partner of my own, but no one ever came for me. We hardly ever saw other people. And so something inappropriate developed between my foster father and me. My foster mother found us together in the barn. She was torn apart with grief and the whole incident brought shame to all three of us. I could not live with what I had done to someone who had done me no harm and who did not deserve to feel so much pain. We were so isolated and I had no hope of someone ever coming for me. I felt dirty, because I knew how sensual and attractive I was. This had brought me nothing but shame and I felt guilty about my looks. And so I hanged myself in the same barn where my foster mother had discovered us together.

Sometimes I wonder if the day will ever come when I would no longer be amazed at the powerful shifts that regressions can bring. As in the first life I had visited that day, I recognised the tapes playing in my mind instantly. I have always felt that no one was ever going to 'come for me'. This is the very reason why, each time I met someone, a filter came down and I did not see that the match would be entirely inappropriate. Because what if no one else ever 'comes for me'?

Sadly, this was not the only thing that carried over from that life lived so long ago. I have always felt excruciatingly uncomfortable at the mere suggestion that someone might find me interesting or attractive. I could not talk about it. The words 'I would like to have a partner' could not leave my mouth. It was ... 'not done'. It was not right. The sickening feeling in my stomach would get stronger if anyone tried to convince me that there was nothing wrong with me. Now I recognise that feeling. It was how I felt in that life, filled with shame and seeing my ability to attract men as something dirty. No amount of reasoned thinking could change the feeling in the pit of my stomach. It was that block that made me feel invisible, the one I had described to Françoise and that had the shape of a steel pole driven through the centre of my being, almost skewering my soul.

Before terminating my trance, I made my peace with my foster mother, hoping to ease her pain. I apologised to her and asked her to forgive me. I was able to explain to her how I had felt and why everything happened the way that it did. I also made peace with my foster father and helped him to let go of his own shame. Then I allowed someone to 'come for' the seventeen year old girl that I was in that life and allowed her to live a happy life with someone appropriate.

The details of this particular life went to the root of what I had been experiencing in my own relationship life. Since this release, I have been able to move into a space of quiet contentment and I seldom register that I am living my life alone. I believe that my original conclusion that my current life was probably better lived alone, was correct. None of the learning in my life would have happened had I met and married a good man when all my friends did, or even later in life. My life was about learning to work with energy and, above all else, learning to heal my wounds using energy and exploring the recesses of my own mind. On this journey I found my Creator, in a way that is far more authentic than any relationship I was able to forge with Him as a religious person. I was able to release a myriad of karmic blocks, some of them involving my failed relationships, which were all things I am sure my soul had brought with me this time around for the very purpose of releasing them. Being with my primary soulmate would, without a doubt, have detracted from my ability to learn and shift as much as I had done in my current life.

A memory stirred deep inside and I remembered something that was said to me in a very long channelling that was done for me in 2005 that I already mentioned earlier.

Channelling 18 February 2005: *Your life makes perfect sense. You have chosen to experience things in this incarnation in order to rise above the karma that you have accumulated in many previous lifetimes. You have chosen not to take one or two small things, you have chosen to take big, huge, important things. In many other life times you took the smaller ones and you managed those and you managed them well, but when you were on the other side of the veil where we are, you looked at it again and you thought that perhaps you* *were a little bit timid, because you are now progressing so slowly.*

And you had been wanting to move ahead more quickly for a long time now. On the first occasion when you wanted to bite off a bigger chunk of things to chew, you were counselled against, because it was thought by your advisors that it was too much for you and you had to build up incrementally as it were to the point where you could cope with more. This time you have chosen to take on the maximum that you can cope with in this life time and you knew that the challenges would be difficult. But you also knew that the rewards, the rewards on a soul level, would be great.

Thinking back to the lives of the Native American Mo'an and Andrew the Boston journalist, I could now easily see what the channelling was meant to convey to me. I had indeed lived a few lives where I could only be described as timid. Andrew had certainly made no great shifts. Although Mo'an was a good father and lived a happy, contented life, he certainly did not do much karmic balancing in that life while hunting rabbits.

In my current life I have met challenges that are not even mentioned in these pages. I do not like focusing on the past or on the things I had spent a lifetime trying to heal and overcome. But looking back over my life, this channelling makes complete and utter sense. Up until now I really would not have had the time to spend in a happy relationship. There are many, many people in very happy relationships who are still able to move mountains and change the world. Not everyone needs to be alone in order to live an authentic and meaningful life, but I do. The problem is that I know that if I should share my life with, say, my primary soulmate, he would become my focus. I would focus on our happiness, not on my life's work. I would become Mo'an. Perhaps Mo'an did not have much to shift at that time in my soul's journey, but I certainly had tons of things to shift and work on and with my current personality, I am afraid there was only one way to achieve that, and that was to go it alone.

Now I see why the two things that had kept me in a single space for most of my life, namely my deep belief that no one would 'come for me' and my inability to see myself as attractive without feeling nauseous, were the last things on this journey that I managed to access and to shift, apart from resolving the link to the man with the grey eyes. They remained in place so that I would stay mostly single and have the space that my soul needed to learn and to complete its work.

I should perhaps mention here that I learned the technique of changing a past life *memory* into something different, in order to symbolically repair the damage, from other therapists. There is another school of thinking that teaches that one cannot change what happened in a past life during a regression session in this way, as that would be interference. I respect that view and the different methods that are employed to clear karmic patterns and to leave behind anything that no longer serves the subject without changing the facts, work very well. However, I understand the laws of energy that I believe are applicable here, a little differently. When the statement is made that one cannot change the facts of a past life, that is of course correct. But I believe that one can change the *memory* of those facts, thereby changing the neural pathways that cause us so much distress in our current lives. Memory changes all the time in any event. This is why memory is so unreliable in our current lives. One just has to cross-examine a few people to understand that a memory is seldom an accurate reflection of reality. Furthermore, if one considers the theory that past life recall is perhaps merely something the brain produces to help us heal, instead of being a memory of a real past life, then changing the imagery the brain brings is really only a method to help us heal, as there would be no true facts to change in any event.

The method of 'changing the facts' when resolving past life issues in trance, merely involves symbolic repair and to my mind this is totally in line with the age old principle of 'as above, so below'. It is about energy, not about facts and thus there is no interference. Changing the memory of the facts, or the memory of what happened in a past life, only changes or releases the energy imprint that the current body carries and this brings healing into the current life, where the memory lives. Is the purpose of the current life not to heal old hurts? So why would changing the memory of events in a past life, simultaneously changing the neural pathways in the current body to achieve healing, result in interference when all it does is heal? The methods that do not change the facts also bring healing in the current life and leave behind what is no longer needed. In other words, the issues are resolved after the karmic consequences have been lived through and probably resulted in the client entering therapy in the first place. The methods changing the facts also bring the client to therapy after the karmic consequences have been lived through. The only difference is the method by which the healing is achieved. Neither method changes what happened in the past life. Symbolic repair does not change the facts of a past life. To my mind, both methods work equally well, though not everybody responds equally well to either method. It would always be best to use a technique that resonates with the particular subject, as well as with the therapist.

CHAPTER 42: Final Connection – 5 April 2015

The days passed and I stayed busy steering the course of change through new territory. I was nearing the end of writing these pages, but it was as if I was waiting for something. How would my story end? Certainly life would continue to flow after the end of the book, but I had the feeling that the particular journey I had been on, would soon draw to a close.

As I continued writing, the pieces kept falling into place as I read through the raw material I had arranged in chronological order. And so the day came that I re-read my experiences in the last two regressions. I now understood things perfectly and I felt an inexplicable and deep need to share my success with my best friend, my primary soulmate. I know that he had helped me to plan this life before my incarnation. I felt as if I had gone on a field trip and had accomplished a dangerous mission going solo, just as we decided would be the best way for me to accomplish my goals for this life. Except for mentioning the fact that my soulmate told me during the meditation of 8 April 2013 that it was 'almost over', I omitted the fact that my primary soulmate, during each and every appearance he made in the meditations along my journey, told me that I was almost done. Sometimes he would add that I would soon be home. On three occasions my teacher guide also encouraged me to hurry up as there was not much time left to complete my work.

I do not know what these statements by my guide and my primary soulmate meant, because they could really mean anything. They have been telling me that there is not much time left for the last year, yet I am still here. There is no time in the spirit world and any references to my having to hurry up would have been in relation to earth time. This could for example mean that I still had fifteen years' worth of work to be done, and only had fourteen years and six months left within which to do that work. I do not believe that we are told before the time that our lives are about to end and I do not think this is what they meant. Yet I have to admit that I started feeling a really strong connection to 'home' after this journey. If my life had to end now, I would be happy that I had not left the hard work undone.

But something was telling me that there is still much to do for me on this planet, whether it involves further learning, shifting imbalances, simply working through another karmic romantic relationship, or even meeting up with my primary soulmate. Who knows, he might have incarnated in this life as a good friend that I have yet to meet. I believe that a part of our souls stay home while another part incarnates, and just because I had access to my primary soulmate's energy in the spirit world during meditations, does not mean to say that he is not wandering around on the planet at present, perhaps happily married to someone else and busy with his own lessons.

My enthusiasm boiled over as I realised nothing stopped me from sharing my joy about all I had learned with those who had been guiding me on my journey, including my primary soulmate. I also felt that it would be okay at this stage to seek a little confirmation from those who had accompanied me and had been looking after me on my journey, that all that I had experienced was 'real'. I am not sure whether it was my energy dynamics expert soul or the earthling scientist whose body it currently occupies that came up with the idea to ask my primary soulmate to find a way to let me know that he is real, but I liked the sound of the idea. In doing this, I wanted him to use a song. As I said before, my guides had been able to bring me solace in difficult times by playing the tune *White on White* in my mind when they needed to comfort me. This made me feel really, really special and I was curious to see if my primary soulmate could come up with something similar. I had no doubt that I would somehow just know when it happened. I soon forgot my request and carried on with life. Of course only after making a note of the date and the content of my request!

Two days later, I had been busy writing some of the pages of this book until after midnight and was exhausted by the time I finally put my head down on my pillow, ready to pass out. I had been thinking about the ending of the book and I still had the feeling that I was waiting for something to happen. As my head touched my pillow, I clearly heard a tune playing in my mind … my eyes flew open. Immediately another, different tune followed. I focused, trying to listen and by now I was wide awake. I only heard one short phrase in each tune and I recognised the tunes more than the words, as I am simply terrible at remembering lyrics, let alone the names of the songs and the artists singing them.

I was beside myself with excitement, because this was the moment I had known I would recognise when it came. It was my primary soulmate's answer. He really knew me so well, because the two tunes kept repeating, slowly, one after the other. It was like a musical quiz show on television where the same tune is played a few times so that the contestant can identify it. Believe me, no self-respecting producer would ever let me near such a show, but I was the one who had chosen this particular mechanism for my primary soulmate's communication that he is real. I was merely getting what I had asked for. So I strained to latch on to the two phrases as I lay listening to the tunes playing over and over in my mind, concentrating as hard as I could. Despite the effort, I could only place the phrases 'all my love' and 'harbour lights'. What would I have done without Google? I got up and switched on my computer. I could hardly search for the melodies I had heard, but I was able to search for the two phrases I remembered. On the first one, Google came up with the lyrics for a song sung by *The Seekers*, sometimes called *The Carnival is Over*, but at other times listed as *Harbour Lights*. The part of the tune I recalled, matched the last four lines.

Say goodbye my own true lover

As we sing a lover's song.

How it breaks my heart to leave you,

Now the carnival is gone.

High above the dawn is waking

And my tears are falling rain,

For the carnival is over.

We may never meet again.

Like a drum my heart was beating

And your kiss was sweet as wine,

But the joys of love are fleeting

For Pierrot and Columbine.

Now the harbour light is calling.

This will be our last goodbye.

Tho' the carnival is over

I will love you till I die.

I ignored the tears streaming down my face as I typed in the next phrase in the search line. It turned out to be part of *All my Love*, sung by Cliff Richard. The part of the tune I recognised, matched the first line of the lyrics.

All my love, came to nothing and oh! my love

When I woke up to find, you were no longer mine.

All my love, thrown away after all this time

Now there's no place for me, in the future you see.

I don't understand you,

I've done all I can do

Tell me how could I give you more, more than ...

All my love, came to nothing and oh! my love

When I woke up to find, you were no longer mine.

All my love, came to nothing and oh! my love

When I woke up to find, you were no longer mine.

Although the words were rather sad, I instinctively felt that the words were not what it was all about. The two songs were tunes from the same era as *White on White* by Danny Williams – or at least I think so. They fit the mould. I had asked him to use a song, and he did. The point was that, as had been the case the first time I had heard *White on White* playing in my mind, I had not heard these two songs for many, many, many years. They were songs I had grown up with. And, like *White on White*, they were both songs I liked and that somehow always touched my heart when I heard them. I had been confident that I would know when I received confirmation from my primary soulmate that he was indeed very real. He did not disappoint me. I would never doubt his existence again, because he knew exactly what to do to convince me.

I downloaded the music of all three songs and sat listening to them in the small hours of the night, looking over the lyrics I found on the internet. They were all about losing love, even *White on White*, the song that was supposed to lift me up. As I read the words of *White on White*, I wondered whether the lyrics of the three songs perhaps reflected the sadness of a separation in a life so long ago, or the sadness of a separation now imposed for the sake of a life mission to be accomplished in solitude.

White on white, lace on satin

Blue velvet ribbons on her bouquet

White on white, lace on satin

My little angel is getting married today

Here she comes in her wedding gown lookin' like a queen

She has been my only love since she was thirteen

I've been dreaming of this day and how proud I'd be

When she came walkin' down the aisle and held out her hand to me

White on white, lace on satin

Blue velvet ribbons on her bouquet

White on white, lace on satin

My little angel is getting married today

I'll be waiting to kiss the bride when her name is new

Standing oh, so close to her silently saying "I do"

I'll be holding back my tears till she's gone away

'cause she'll belong to someone else when the organ starts to play

White on white, lace on satin

Blue velvet ribbons on her bouquet

White on white, lace on satin

My little angel is ge-e-etting ma-a-rried today.

I sat thinking about the long road behind me and looked at the time. It was after midnight on 5 April 2015. Exactly three days short of two years since I had first started out on the journey to heal my life.

CHAPTER 43: Group Hypno-meditation - 31 May 2015

I attended a course on group hypnosis over the weekend of 30 and 31 May 2015.   The preceding week had presented me with a difficult situation in that I had heard that I had been shortlisted for one of the legal advisor positions I had applied for some time before, when I was in survival mode. I knew that I did not want the position, but that it would be irresponsible not to go for the interview. I felt as if I needed to keep my options open and so I decided to attend the interview. I was still in Cape Town, which had been my home for sixteen years, but I had in the meantime packed up all my stuff and had sent it ahead to the Southern Cape, where I had decided my new home and practice would be. By the time I got the news that I would be invited to a job interview, I had only a few casual outfits with me, as I intended staying in Cape Town only long enough to finish a weekend course and to say goodbye to a few friends. Any clothing remotely suitable for a job interview, was now safely stored away in a numbered box in a storage facility situated in a small town in the Southern Cape.

My body started feeling stiff and tight and my gut felt uncomfortable.   I became irritable and small things managed to upset me a lot. In short, I felt trapped. The disappointment that surged through my body at the very moment I got the message that I had been placed on a short list, was undeniable.   Amazing how we get conditioned into believing that we can never be free. In the end, feeling suffocated by the obligation I was starting to feel, I decided to decline the invitation to attend an interview. I would be turning away an opportunity to earn a very big salary, but I knew that if I went to the interview and was selected for the position, saying no to the position, if it was offered to me, would be much harder. I also knew that if I ended up taking that position as a legal advisor, I would have traded my soul path for gold, and I would not recover from having disappointed myself. I knew without a doubt what was right for me.

My life had been disrupted by the sale of my home and the move to the Southern Cape, more so because I had to stay in Cape Town to finish a few courses that I had been enjoying tremendously. My wonderful friends all opened their homes to me and I spent a few days squatting with some of them, while I attended to the last of my commitments in Cape Town. It was, however, a truly exhausting experience living out of a suitcase and travelling non-stop. It is amazing how unsettling it can be not to have a home space, no matter how comfortable or welcome one is in one's temporary lodgings.

As I drove to the course venue on the cold Saturday morning of 30 May 2015, I told my teacher guide that I had made up my mind not to go for the interview, but that it would be nice to have some sort of indication that I am not being irresponsible in passing up the opportunity. I knew that he would find a way of letting me know his thoughts on the matter.

Later that same morning, the instructor dealt with the aspect of using metaphors in hypnosis scripts. He read us an example, which in short boiled down to a little bird sitting in a gilded cage with ample food and water and all the comforts a feathered creature could require, except for the freedom to use its wings of course. One day, the little bird's owner left the house in a hurry and forgot to close the door of the cage after cleaning it and feeding the bird. The cage was standing in a room with an open window through which freedom now beckoned. The little bird spent the day contemplating its options and thought about the dangers the free world might hold, weighing them up against what it had easy access to in the comfort of its familiar cage. It was still weighing its options when the owner of the house returned and closed the door of the little bird's cage.

I knew that the little bird's story held a message that was meant for me. I had already left the cage and was sitting on the outer windowsill of the open window, looking out at the beautiful free world that I had already decided to make my home. The invitation to the job interview was not a test; it was a possible outcome I had created by applying for a job at a time when I felt financially vulnerable. Since completing that job application, I had figured out that the slump in my practice had nothing to do with survival; I had simply been given the time and the space to complete the writing of this story. My ultimate financial survival was never an issue, although I could not see that at the time. I realised that I was only now, after writing these pages, truly ready to be free, to leave the windowsill and to finally fly away into the free world.

The invitation to a job interview was not an authentic opportunity. It was an opportunity created from a space of fear and lack of faith in myself, my soul path and the universe. The road to change had not been easy and resulted in all kinds of truly difficult situations. Yet each and every time the universe provided the helping hands I needed along the way. It was my turn to learn to accept help, instead of always being the one to carry others, giving without taking.

When the official call came the following Monday, I had no difficulty turning down the invitation to attend the job interview. If I turned back to answer the call from somewhere inside the cage at that stage, I would have felt deep disappointment in myself. I would have earned a big salary while feeling like a total failure, frustrated and tired all the time. Eventually I would have spiralled into a depression I doubt that I would have had the strength to pull back from.

The weekend was not over and the next day would bring something even more profound. The instructor led the attendees into a hypno-meditation, focusing on forgiveness. I have already earlier in these pages alluded to my thinking on this issue. I do not agree that forgiveness only sets the forgiver free. Forgiveness is often 'sold' as something that one does to set oneself free and the difficult task of forgiving is sugar coated by adding something to the effect of 'it does not mean that one condones the actions of the perpetrator'. Forgiveness, to my mind, does much more than setting the forgiver free. It allows, or rather makes it possible for the forgiver to actually wish the perpetrator well. The type of forgiveness where one merely leaves something behind, putting the burden down and not holding anything against the perpetrator, is not quite the same to me. There were three people in my world that I had forgiven many times, but the cold feeling in my gut when I think of them, would never allow me to wish them well. I did not wish them harm, but I could not wish them well. The Triad truly did not deserve it – in my biased view of course.

The instructor's voice urged us to enter a room where we were to be met by the people we still had to forgive. And there they were. The Bishop, The Pawn and The Rook. I should mention that I had heard only a few weeks earlier that these people are still spreading their slanderous untruths in an effort to try to justify their actions of a quarter of a century ago, despite the ample proof that they were dreadfully mistaken about me.

As I looked at these miserable energies as they appeared in my mind's eye, I could only feel pity for people who are utterly incapable of seeing the truth of what had happened, or their part in it. I found myself bored with their presence and suddenly, I felt the need to rid myself of them forever. And so I wished them well – and I meant it! For the Rook I wished a life of courage instead of cowardice and the ability to resist manipulation. I wished that The Bishop would have a life free of jealousy and the destructive need to control a loved one. I hoped that The Pawn would learn to live life free of envy so that it would never again be necessary to destroy the object of his envy at all costs.

I had heard that life has not been overly kind to these people. Something told me during this meditation that they needed the full extent of my forgiveness to set themselves free, not merely the forgiveness I had so far been able to extend to them; this was why their energies had presented themselves in the meditation. They were still trapped by what they had done. I knew they were not strong enough to ask for my forgiveness even if they would be prepared to admit that they needed it, or that they were wrong, which I highly doubt as they are still sticking to the story they had been telling themselves and the world for twenty five years. They would certainly not have the insight to see the error of their ways, nor would they be courageous enough to admit it. And so I gave them my forgiveness anyway. I really do hope they are now free of what they had done and that they will no longer need to keep telling themselves their own vicious tales. Because I am certainly now free.

I heard later that the meditation guided the others in the group to two more rooms where we were given the opportunity to be forgiven by others and to forgive ourselves. I must have tuned out of that, because after I left the room wishing my old enemies well, I ended up in the spirit world where my primary soulmate was waiting. He was overjoyed at what had just taken place and for some reason I seemed to feel pretty proud of myself. It was almost as if the two of us were celebrating something. The voice of the instructor was calling me back to full consciousness and I had to leave, but before I left, my primary soulmate asked: 'So can we now meet up in this life time?' I had no problem with that.

As I drifted up through the layers of awareness after this deep group meditation, I heard his voice in my mind: 'I'll come to find you.'

Was this the 'undecided' factor that I had been made aware of during my spiritual regression, when I felt that it still had to be decided whether my primary soulmate and I would meet up in this life? It is possible. Perhaps I had to fully forgive those who had injured me so unfairly and so unnecessarily in my youth in order to fully complete the tasks my soul had set for me. I am looking forward to whatever life now brings. There is a part of me that would like to look up one day and recognise my primary soulmate's energy in a normal human being, but there is another part of me that hopes that I will be able to live in total freedom until my last day. Either outcome will be just fine, though I must admit that I have found so much joy and depth in my aloneness, that it would be hard for me to give that up. Whatever body and personality my primary soulmate would have chosen to carry his soul this time round, I am pretty sure that, if we do meet up in this life, we would like the same music!

After moving to the Southern Cape, I had been busy settling in and unpacking, so my exercise regime had been limited to a daily walk instead of completing both a morning yoga routine and going for a walk later in the day. When I rolled out the yoga mat for the first time since leaving Cape Town, a few days after these two experiences I had during my training course group sessions, on the exact date that I injured my shoulder at my godchild's birthday party the year before, I realised as I went through the yoga moves, that the pain which had previously extended down into my arm from either my neck or my shoulder had finally released to the point where I was able to perform my regular yoga routine with no difficulty. Had I put down the remainder of the burden when I turned my back on the last open door to the legal world? Only time will tell.

CHAPTER 44: The Reconnection – 28 June 2015

I suppose I should not have been surprised that the pages of this book at some point started taking over my life. It was as if certain aspects were left unattended and the story could not be complete without the resolution of those matters. I had reached a stage where I was content that I would probably never really be able to resolve the mystery of my stiff frame and perhaps I would always have a bit of a problem with my shoulder and my neck. After all, the injuries were old and once a body has sustained an injury, it is asking for a miracle to expect total healing to take place.

Life was hectic and having committed my journey to paper, I could relax into the realities of moving to a new region where I had decided to settle and to start a healing centre perhaps. I had no fixed plans and felt like going where the flow would take me, not caring much where that would be. I would end up at the right place; that much I knew. It is a wonderful feeling to be able to trust life. I was content.

For a while, after the sale of my home, I had to travel up and down between Cape Town and my new home in the Southern Cape to finalise my hypnosis training through the South African Institute of Hypnotism, as I still held only a British qualification, having completed my initial training through a London based school presenting courses in Cape Town. Just before I left Cape Town after having attended a course, I found myself in a space where I was forced to inhale cigarette smoke in circumstances where I could not simply get up, take my car keys and leave.

For eighteen years I have been keeping quiet about what happens in my body when someone lights a cigarette in my presence. I hate offending people and I have made my peace with the reality that I share this world with smokers. They had a right to smoke, especially in their own homes. I had a right to be healthy, but it was up to me to avoid their smoke. I could not expect them to stop smoking for my sake. When confronted with a situation where I had no option but to inhale cigarette smoke, unless I was prepared to offend someone or hurt their feelings, I usually quietly swallowed an anti-histamine to try to reduce the impact of the smoke inhalation and simply lived with the consequences that would usually last at least a week, sometimes two. I never told the smokers involved about the infections that I had to live with after exposure to their cigarette smoke.

I have met many smokers over the years who are very considerate and who try to accommodate non-smokers, but others are either not prepared to accept that passive smoking can have a detrimental effect on the health of others, or they do not care whether this could be the case. Over the years, whenever someone's cigarette smoke caused me to sneeze and my nose to run, I got used to some smokers' confident explanations that 'it must be a virus' or 'it must be the pollen in the air'. Trying to explain that my lungs instantly contract when I catch that first whiff of cigarette smoke and that my sinus cavities start burning within seconds of inhaling it, was simply pointless. I was in any event quite comfortable with my decision to manage my space as best I could and to be tolerant when it comes to smoking. As I said, smokers are often truly considerate people who smoke out of choice. I was quite happy to accommodate them and to take responsibility for limiting my exposure to smoking as far as I could. Perhaps my attitude on this issue was shaped by what I experienced at the time of my sinus operation, eighteen years earlier. I was coughing up blood at the time, but the three chain smokers who shared an office with me, could not care less. I learned then that it would always be up to me to protect my own health.

But this time around my presence in a smoke filled room for an extended period triggered an experience I could not have foreseen. The infection that I developed as a result of my exposure to cigarette smoke shortly before leaving Cape Town after one of my courses, was raging in my aching head as I made the four and half hour trip to my new home in the Southern Cape.   I had taken the medication I usually take after I have been exposed to smoke, hoping for the best. Whenever the exposure was prolonged, I developed painful sores in my sinus cavities that took weeks to heal. During such times I felt a little less tolerant and I often wondered why I was so considerate towards some people who were so inconsiderate towards me. The answer was of course that my health was my responsibility, not theirs. I am considerate, because that is in my nature. What others do does not affect the fact that I believe in being considerate to all human beings, even the ones who appeared to be less so.   I was the one who never told smokers what their cigarette smoke was doing to me. It was just the way I had chosen to handle my sensitivity to cigarette smoke many years before. Perhaps my boundaries were not strong enough on this issue, but how does one draw a boundary without judging someone else's habit?

In the days to follow the onset of the infection, smokers suddenly seemed to follow me around as if they were on a mission to seek me out. All of them were lovely, likeable people who were extremely considerate and who tried their absolute best to accommodate me, but the infection steadily got worse as even a slight whiff of cigarette smoke further inflamed my sinus cavities even more than they already were.

Inevitably, the night arrived when my fever was so high that I could not measure it with the thermometer I had at home. By the time I started vomiting, shivering with fever, I knew that I had to get to the hospital.

Spending two days in hospital usually gets one's attention. As I lay there in my hospital bed, I was fretting over the possibility that I would be too sick to travel back to Cape Town to attend a particular hypnosis course I had been looking forward to. The needle of the intravenous drip in my hand was uncomfortable, the medication made me shiver and I developed night sweats in a freezing cold hospital. Forgetting that I never blame smokers for the fact that I am not prepared to walk away from their smoke, choosing to take medication to deal with the after effects instead of hurting anyone's feelings, I spent some time feeling sorry for myself and fuming over the unfairness of what I had to endure when it comes to cigarette smoking as I turned over my pillow in an effort to find a dry patch.

Fortunately, once we develop the habit of not blaming others for what happens to us, even if it would appear as if they were the cause of our misery, it is hard to shake. Habits can be really helpful. It therefore did not take long for me to revert to my habit of not blaming others. I stopped fuming and was able to figure out that the whole thing had little to do with others disrespecting me or with me not setting the necessary boundaries to protect my own health. I was missing something, there was something that I needed to see. My body was delivering a message. It was the first time in eighteen years that the infection got so out of hand that I ended up in hospital. Where did all the smokers suddenly come from?

So I decided to switch into gratitude mode, staring at the ceiling above my hospital bed as I listened to the elderly patient snoring at the end of the passage. I silently thanked the infection for the message I could not yet see. I expressed my gratitude for the learning that would come from the painful experience of having a needle stuck in my bruised hand, causing me great discomfort every fifteen minutes when the intravenous drip line that was connected to the needle had to be unplugged so that I could go down the icy passage to make space for even more fluid to be pumped into my body. The change in my attitude instantly made me feel much better and even the clumsy nurse, who had little regard for the bruising and pain caused by the frequent unplugging of the connection between the intravenous drip line and the needle in my hand, started being a little more gentle.

I managed to convince my doctor to release me two days earlier than he had planned to do and I enlisted the help of my parents to help me to pack for a two week trip back to Cape Town. I was in no state to do it myself. What made me think that I could get into a vehicle to make the four and a half hour trip to Cape Town after having been released from hospital that morning, I cannot explain. Everyone tried to reason with me, but I just ignored them. By the time I eventually got behind the steering wheel a few hours after leaving the hospital, I felt as if I was in trance. I have never been able to make the trip without stopping halfway. This time, I had very little time to get to Cape Town before dark and stopping along the journey would not have been wise, especially as my still very sensitive lungs would not respond well to the cold.

I arrived in Cape Town four hours later, just after dark, without having made one single stop. The focus and sense of peace I experienced during the trance-like state I was in for the entire journey was uncanny and it reminded me of the time my guide had allowed his energy to envelop mine when he was showing me how to hold my body when I climbed stairs in order to relieve the discomfort in my knees at the time. I knew that I was being protected. It was as if someone was in fact doing the driving for me, holding the steering wheel and getting me safely to my destination. How could I have known that that would be the most important trip I had ever made? Nothing would be the same after that particular weekend. My presence at the course was a date with destiny and my soul, and it seems my guide, were not about to let anything keep me away from that appointment. I know I was not alone on that journey.

Sinus infections invariably end up affecting one's throat and lungs and I had developed bronchitis, which was still a long way from getting better, especially since I had been discharged two days earlier than my doctor had advised. So when I sat in the course the next morning, grateful to be there, I noticed the discomfort of the other people attending the course. Not only was my constant coughing a distraction for everyone, but it appeared to me that they were concerned about possibly being infected themselves. During the tea break I approached our course leader, Claudia Klein, Director and Principal Lecturer at the South African Institute of Hypnotism. I asked her just to explain to everyone that my condition was not contagious. I told her about my condition and the reasons for my hospitalisation and I found myself explaining the background of my sinus infection to her, quite unnecessarily. Claudia took note of the fact that many years before, I had a sinus operation after sharing an office with three chain smokers during the years before the use of tobacco was controlled in our country. When I finished giving her the background of my difficulty with cigarette smoke, she asked whether I liked these three chain smokers very much and I responded by saying 'Not very much!'. I have an image in my mind of a tiny seed that at that very moment must have recognised that it was time to wake up and to grow into what it was meant to be.

As the morning wore on, the group of students went through a few processes while in trance, practising the skills we were learning. I became very emotional at some point while the group was working on the issue of healing. The visualisation we were taken through in trance was beautiful and moving and it touched me deeply as Claudia created a space for us all to work on healing aspects in our bodies. I felt my lungs expand and open up and the raw coughs that had been tearing through me for days on end faded away. I hardly coughed for the remainder of the weekend. I had been aware of every painful breath up to that point, but I could suddenly breathe freely. One cannot help but feel special when a natural process like hypnotherapy works, effortlessly assisting one to heal oneself within the healing space that one can access when in trance. I was very aware of my body's ability to heal itself, but I knew without a doubt that its little tantrum involving my sinuses, was no coincidence.

As the group trance session was coming to an end, I invited the message I could not yet see to reveal itself to me. What was it that I was not seeing? What was I missing? And there he was: The Bishop. Had I not forgiven The Triad just a couple of weeks before? What did he want from me this time? It was still hard for me to confront The Bishop's image in my mind. I really did not particularly like seeing any reminder of his existence. So what had happened to the forgiveness I had extended two weeks earlier? It was all quite disturbing, but as I came out of trance I decided to focus on the lightness of my breathing after the healing I experienced during the session. For the moment the new found freedom to take in as much air as I needed without coughing, was enough.

Claudia and the group had in the meantime decided that I would be the best person to be used as a subject for the weekend's demonstration, which meant that I was to be hypnotised by Claudia in the presence of the group and that she would then demonstrate a particular technique to the group in an effort to find some answers around my sinus problems, just as she would do when working with one of her own clients.

There is no such thing as coincidence. The day was perfect and produced all the conditions required for me to heal the issue that was clearly up for consideration. The energy of the people around me was perfect and their compassion and kindness were at a level that would give me the comfort I would need to face my issue, without intruding into my space and my privacy. No one there knew anything about my past history, and neither did Claudia. It did not matter. The details of the things that actually happen to us on this planet eventually turn out to be utterly unimportant in any event.

The discussion during the course turned to the amazing work of Louise Hay and the links that she has made between dis-ease in certain body parts and the connected underlying causes. Her booklet listing various ailments and what their presence in our bodies conveys to us was passed around the group and I looked up the meaning of 'sinusitis'. I had looked it up before, many times in fact. But that morning it really meant something to me when I read the words 'Irritation with one person.' One person. Just one.

The seed inside was growing. It was running around my brain waking up neural pathways to places I had forgotten about. The necessary information was retrieved and the links cleared out for me to be able to finally make those connections in my conscious mind. I cannot recall the exact moment when it happened and perhaps it was the moment I looked at Louise Hay's book that morning, but it dawned on me quite a while before my demonstration was due to start, and a short while after I had had the healing visualisation clearing my lungs and calming my throat and lungs, that my old enemy was that one person, the 'original smoker', the one who irritated me so much that I developed severe sinusitis. The Bishop was a chain smoker and although cigarette smoke during the time that I knew him had absolutely no effect on me and I only developed sinusitis years later when I shared an office with three chain smokers, I recall that The Bishop's habit of smoking in the kitchen used to irritate me. It made everything feel 'unclean' and I seldom enjoyed a meal prepared in such circumstances.

I suddenly understood why The Bishop entered into my visualisation earlier in the day. If he was the original irritant that was at the heart of my sinus problems and I was attempting to heal that aspect, then naturally The Bishop would be part of the process. I was intrigued. I had finally managed to forgive him fully just a few weeks earlier. This process was followed by an almost immediate journey where I ran into smokers everywhere I went, ultimately resulting in my hospitalisation. I recalled how my body tends to go a little overboard when it is trying to get its messages to me. I can be a bit of a drama queen sometimes if I am not careful and my body is apparently also very good at being dramatic. Or perhaps it has just learned over the years that I do not listen unless it makes itself heard loud and clear. I smiled to myself as I remembered the sneezing fit I had before I met the Franciscan monk whose life in northern Spain held the key to my sensitivity to wheat. Something was coming up and it would be wonderful.

The next realisation that day was that I was actually not too unhappy with the presence of The Bishop. Before, I would have tried to give The Triad as little energy as possible as they had forfeited the right to take up any space in my life and my thoughts a long time ago. I would have loved to write them out of this book if I could, except that they kept pushing themselves into these pages. I eventually accepted that they were part of my journey and that I could not just wish them away. I had no idea when I started writing that I still had anything to work on when it came to them, as I had dealt with it years ago during trauma counselling and had all but forgotten about them until I ran into someone recently who told me that The Rook was still sticking to the same slanderous tale of twenty five years ago, as mentioned earlier.

The connection that The Bishop was the 'original smoker' and irritant was surprising. Oddly enough, I cannot remember his first name. I had so completely put The Bishop from my mind so many years ago that the slate had been wiped clean. Perhaps it is significant that I had forgotten his name, because he was an insignificant person and yet someone who had managed to almost singlehandedly destroy me. Perhaps a part of me felt that The Bishop did not deserve to be remembered and that is why I had forgotten his first name to this day. Now I knew, before my demonstration started, that the root of my sinus infection was connected to the events that transpired between The Bishop and me. So now that I knew that, what would be left to work on during the demonstration?

I had completed the forgiveness process some weeks earlier and the link to The Bishop had now come up and had revealed itself as the root of my sinus problems. We had a healing session during the morning that I knew impacted on my lungs and sinuses and I also knew that I would now be getting much, much better, very quickly. The day was to prove to me once again that we are living a miracle. We are amazingly complex, beautiful souls having a human experience which is meticulously planned and while we are having it, we are guided, guarded and loved. Nothing is left to chance.

The time came for us to do the demonstration and despite my feeling that I already had all the answers, I sensed that the universe was about to turn to me for a short while and deal with me with the intensity of a laser beam. I would be changed forever. My heart could tell.

As I settled into trance, one of my fellow students performed the induction, putting me into trance. Her lovely voice resonated with me and she was the obvious choice when I was given the opportunity to choose the person to do the induction. She used a deepening script written by one of Claudia's students that Claudia had remembered about that morning and which she thought would resonate with me. Over the series of courses I had attended in previous months, Claudia had observed all of us and she knew enough about me to understand what would resonate with me. Claudia's choice of script was perfect. It was one of the most beautiful sets of imagery I had ever heard. It managed to achieve a few things, the most important being a total dissociation between my conscious and subconscious mind, something that had never happened to me before. That script had been written for me and it was waiting in Claudia's office to be used that day. Of that, I am sure.

The dissociation resulted in my conscious mind drifting off on its own, leaving my subconscious utterly free for the first time. I remember 'seeing' my conscious mind and feeling a deep sense of caring and compassion for it, because I had moved into the realm of my soul. I was looking at my conscious mind as one would look at a small child, with indulgence and understanding, feeling such compassion for the naïve little person who has so much to learn. The script invited me to consider the miracle of my body and its functions. I suddenly felt grateful for my conscious mind, silently thanking it for all its hard work and how it had guided me and kept me safe. Basically, it was given a gold star for good performance. It was almost pathetic to see my conscious mind puffing itself up, drifting off with an air of self-importance, star struck by the beautiful gold star it could not stop admiring.

In that moment, I knew that I had been bullying and criticising my beautiful mind as a matter of course since I started learning about hypnosis and the power of the subconscious mind. I totally missed the truth about the importance of the thinking mind. Concern over negative thinking and what these thoughts create, caused me to forget that there is a master plan. And the conscious mind is an integral part of that plan. As my fellow student's hypnotic voice droned on, lightly moving me along to another world, I was taken on a journey deep into my body, my genes and my cells and even into the atoms of my body. She could not have known that as she was guiding me into inner space, my soul was floating freely and that I could only see the light of who I am drifting in outer space where my six companions had gathered. The presence of all my guides and my primary soulmate made me realise that something momentous was about to happen. They waited patiently among the stars while my soul explored the depths of my body. There was a moment where I saw with clarity that what was inside my cells, was a space that was identical to the vast space my soul was occupying. Outer space and inner space was the same place. I was meant to see that. Once that was clear, I saw that my body has always known that. It was acting in accordance with that knowledge. My body, my soul and my conceited little conscious mind, still staring at its prize while off floating on a cloud of its own, were working in perfect harmony to get the blue print of my soul's plan for this life executed in a way that would benefit my journey. Nothing, but absolutely nothing had ever gone wrong.

Claudia's voice took over from that of my fellow student and gently guided me further along into the deepest recesses of my soul. It was as if my soul was sharing its experience with the silently watching group of students present, explaining in my voice that my guides had gathered because today was the day of my reconnection when my soul would be able to connect to its full power for the first time since incarnation into my current body. While my conscious mind was still drifting off to the side, mesmerised by its prize and my body was feeling as dissociated from what was happening as my conscious mind was, my soul aspect seemed to be fully present. It was that aspect of me that was overcome with emotion as my eternal self admitted to my waiting guides that I had never been sure that I would ultimately be able to get to the point of reconnection during my current life. I had the impression that such reconnection would be considered to be quite an achievement and that there had been some uncertainty all along as to whether my soul would be able to complete the journey to reconnection.

In one moment, it all made sense. I felt the shift as my soul joined the source of all joy, surrounded by friends in the physical world and by eternal companions in the spirit world. As Claudia started asking me questions, intuitively knowing exactly what was needed, I found my soul aspect responding. She was aware that I was in the process of finalising this book and she asked about it. I responded that the book I was writing was 'the heart of the process'; it was the heart of the reconnection. She asked me 'To which rhythm does this heart beat?' I replied that it has joined the heartbeat of the universe.

Claudia gave me some time to do what was needed while the rest of the group held the space. In the privacy of my mind and somewhere off to the side, the soul of The Bishop was waiting, presenting himself in the body of the person I used to know. I called his soul to me. I looked at the wrinkled face and into those eyes as I remembered them; eyes I had avoided remembering for a quarter of a century. If I in that moment was connected to my body, I would have thanked The Bishop from the bottom of my heart, but I was experiencing only my soul and I expressed to his soul a profound gratitude that only a soul is capable of feeling. I conveyed to him that I was eternally grateful that he had established the disconnection in the physical world, which had enabled me to conduct this experiment of reconnection. I had wanted to be disconnected, so that I could see if I could get back to love, to life and to my Creator, while cut off from almost all support and the source of my power as a soul. The Bishop had undertaken to be the soul who would, after my incarnation into the physical world, cut the cords that connected me to my faith, my inner strength, society, humanity and basically, to all that one usually needs to go through life with a semblance of normality. It was an unpleasant task. Yet The Bishop had agreed to do it. As my gratitude telepathically crossed the energy field between us, I could almost hear him say: 'It was a pleasure, my dear.' As for The Rook and The Pawn, they were mere minions, dutifully doing as they were told; there was almost nothing to forgive. They were just in service of the soul who had agreed to cut me off, doing his bidding.

As the scene between me and the soul of The Bishop took place in my mind, the tears were streaming down my face and Claudia waited for me to collect myself. I was finally able to see that my inability to do more than put The Bishop down for so many years, was necessary. If I had been able to forgive him years earlier, in other words not only to put him down, but also to set him free and to wish him well, engaging in forgiveness in its fullest form as I understood it, I would not have managed to reconnect. The reconnection required such extraordinary growth and learning, that I needed decades to push forward. In a way, my inability to forgive completely was the fuel my reconnection rocket engine needed to get home. Only after I had completed the myriad of other learnings that became necessary after my disconnection, would I be near enough to my end goal to tackle the issue of forgiveness. The rocket engine's turbo could be disengaged and I could slow down enough to allow three people back into my consciousness where I could attend to the last of the learning involving them and to full forgiveness. At the end of the session and on Claudia's prompting I was able to share with the group that I felt at peace and quietly blissful.

Once forgiveness was complete, the scene had been set for reconnection and this was the cue for my sinuses to deliver the message it had been keeping safe for so many years, reminding me of the original chain smoker who was so inextricably involved in my soul's plan in this incarnation.

Interestingly, the place where my soul reconnected, was the same place I saw in a flash vision in December 2014 during a series of strange experiences. At the time I was just aware that I experienced the vision as if I was in it, as if I was actually out floating in space looking at the night sky. I did not know then, so shortly after I was able to make peace with my Creator, that I had been shown the place that I would return to six months later to restore and finally to heal my torn soul.

Of course these events brought immediate clarity to the perplexing way in which my life between lives spiritual regression failed to bring me the answers I needed at the time. I finally understood that that session had in fact been perfect. It gave me just enough information to help me move forward, but without limiting my growth and progress as a soul. That insight expanded my soul more than I can put into words. Some things one cannot share in words, but going forward I shall live the truth of what I have learned and of who I now know I am. I can only share the immensity of what has happened to me by living my life expressing the feelings and emotions that seem to fill up

my entire being, spilling over in endless joy which I shall
never stop sharing.

CHAPTER 45: Conclusion

While I was busy writing the previous chapter, I was thinking about the script that was used during what I have come to think of as my reconnection session. I recalled Claudia telling me that day that the script had been written by one of her former students, Mae Naude. I made a mental note to ask her for Mae's details when I returned to Cape Town for my next course, so that I could contact her.

I returned to Cape Town about a week later to attend another course and when I walked into the venue, I saw a blonde woman whom I had not met before. I walked over to her, but before I could introduce myself to her, she said 'I know you'. I knew we had never met, but when she told me her name, I knew why she felt that she knew me. It was Mae. Although she had already qualified and did not need to take more courses, she had decided to attend the weekend's course as a refresher. I think we were supposed to meet. Her words transported my soul to its appointment with destiny. She had to have known me to be able to write words that resonated with me on every level of my being. Our souls are old friends I suspect. With her permission, I duplicate here the beautiful script Mae had written for a client of hers who was a scientist. Claudia, who had a copy of it, knew that I had studied Physics and remembering the copy of Mae's script that she had in her office, thought it would work well for me on the day. She was so right.

Connecting to Resource State through the Atom©

Mae Naude

And from here ... where you are feeling so comfortable, connected and relaxed, I invite you on a little journey through consciousness to explore those processes which are the real wonders of this world ... those processes that all too often remain beyond our everyday conscious awareness. And if you would you can picture, visualise or imagine ... if you could imagine ... looking at your conscious mind which is still hovering somewhere close to your physical body ... where it feels most comfortable ... Your conscious mind can listen and it will remember whatever it needs to remember so it does not really matter if you choose to leave it behind or bring it along, but you know that it will slow us down if it does come along ... so you might prefer to leave it here ... watching from a distance ... knowing you are in a safe and supported space ... and when you are ready to do so you can just nod your head ...

That's right ... and as this journey continues I would like you to recognise that your everyday awareness is only a tiny fraction of your total consciousness ... and on this journey we begin exploring the infinite quality of your consciousness, which can be anywhere and everywhere at the same time ...

Perhaps you already know that the subconscious mind is deeper than the deepest ocean, bigger than the greatest galaxies and broader than time itself. And though you travel often through your subconscious you might only just have realised that you have many different ways of travelling ... and ... for now I'm inviting you to visualise, imagine or pretend that you are travelling deep within yourself, diving through the levels of your infinite consciousness ... until you eventually reach that point of absolute peace and perfection where you are perfectly protected and where anything is possible. And as you start on this journey and allow yourself to go deeper still ... you may be surprised to find that the deeper you go ... the lighter you feel and the lighter you feel the clearer you become ... so that the deeper you go the more aligned you are with your deepest truths ... It may feel like you are lifting veils or unlocking records or accessing reservoirs of information in some other way.

So just imagine ... picture or pretend ... that you could enter this consciousness by going deep within your body and ... starting in that rather dense level which we experience as so real but at this moment is quite dissociated ... and having already left your conscious mind in that world of matter and matters, where it feels most comfortable, we can start to travel freely ... through the realms of our own inner wisdom. And something wonderful happens when we get so in tune with ourselves ... the more in tune we are ... the more assured we become ... and the safer we feel. Now being so in tune ... you could sense the deep awareness within your body ... and for a moment you could ... if you would allow yourself ... admire the miracle of your body which fine-tunes the functioning of the organs that work together to ensure perfect balance ... so that oxygen reaches muscles, toxins are cleared, temperature is maintained and nutrients are fed where nurturance is needed. And with this realisation you may find a new appreciation for the deep wisdom, intelligence and complexity of your body ... And as you go even deeper ... right into the cells of your body ... you may be surprised to find that this awareness expands even further ... as each cell communicates with every other cell at every moment in this unit we call our body ... and at some level every cell knows exactly what needs to be done to maintain the perfection that is you ... and you may come to realise that the knowledge and wisdom contained within each cell within each organ within each body within the world ... which at this point seems so very far away ... is equal perhaps to worlds themselves ... and so you could begin to see that worlds exist within worlds within worlds ... and you are free to move between these worlds ... And going even deeper ... deep within the cell you could ... if you wished ... enter a gene where you could sense the wisdom contained within that sacred helix. You may even find that you are curious and you could use that curiosity to explore and ... whether you have pictures or sounds ... or words ... or just some other way of knowing ... that's OK ... because we all know that each gene contains instructions from generations past and information about generations future. And yet … you can go still deeper … past the molecules … right into the atom and … just before you cross into it … you may wish to marvel at the fact that at any given moment your body could house atoms that were once shared by the Christ, the Buddha or the great blue whale. And … with an attitude of awe and deep gratitude you can allow yourself to pass right into the atom … right into the awareness that in-forms the atom to form the matter … that we tend to think matters … and as we enter these deeper levels of awareness … where density does not exist … where matter no longer matters … and where all there is … is infinite infinity … notice the sensations you may or may not have and just become aware of the lightness … the lack of density … the infinite potential …

And some people experience an unspeakable sense of peaceful freedom as they find a connection with "all that is" – whatever that "is" may be. And other people report an almost overwhelming feeling of love as they enter the emptiness of this infinite potential … and here in this space of infinite possibility, this space of utter love where everything is designed to keep you safe and fulfil your wishes and needs, this space where there are no limitations and where everything is possible … you can just take a moment … to enjoy everything … that everything has to offer… and just before we continue on this journey … if there is anything you would like to prepare, whether you wish to invite someone or something in to support you even further or whether you want to clarify your intentions for this journey ... you can do so ... now ... And when you have brought in whoever and whatever you need and when you feel that you are ready to learn that something about yourself that you wish to learn, you can just let me know by nodding the head.

Having had a while to allow the insights of the profound experience when my soul reconnected to its full resources to filter through into the physical plane, I was able to understand the full lesson behind it all.

I had suspected since my life between lives facilitated spiritual regression that my soul was somehow 'disconnected' from whatever it is that provides souls with the energy they need to move forward.   From that experience I gathered that the disconnection had occurred before my incarnation and was apparently part of a plan, which had not been revealed to me during the spiritual regression.   In fact, the only thing that had been revealed to me at the time, was that my soul specialises in energy dynamics and that my incarnations are chosen to promote my learning in this field.   At the time it took a while for me to figure out that my soul was probably busy with some sort of experiment that had to do with 'coping while not connected to the source' – whatever this source is.   I had no other explanation for the uncomfortable spiritual regression experience and so I made peace with that explanation and put it behind me, as I felt very disappointed at the time, because I had to my mind been blocked from entering the spirit world of life between lives fully. I now understand that I was still making choices at that time that would have affected the outcome of the 'experiment', had I known what was going on.

As it turned out, this book turned into more than just the story of my journey to healing. It became the story of the journey I had been on to reconnect my soul, although I remained completely oblivious to this fact until I lived the last two chapters.

But before my soul could reconnect and heal, I had to forgive someone and I had to make many, many different connections, before any of it would make sense to me. I know now that forgiveness holds gifts. When someone forgives another, the energy dynamic involved results in both the forgiver and the forgiven being set free. This bi-directional flow causes the gifts of forgiveness to become available to the forgiver. Ultimately, the forgiveness experience I had gone through approximately two weeks before the reconnection experience, resulted in many different things shifting and my body bringing up the physical link to an old injury of twenty five years before. This link could only come up for consideration and healing after I had forgiven The Bishop, simply because it is a gift that could only be made available after forgiveness. The energy dynamics of the whole business required this.

The gift that flowed from the moment of forgiveness came wrapped up in a hospital visit. I would have missed it, had I not been guided to use the energy of gratitude to reveal that gift to me. I expressed my gratitude for the gift in the experience, although I could not see it at the time. After my discharge, I was then able to make it to the appointment my soul had with its destiny during the course I was due to attend. For some or other reason, Claudia instinctively had all the keys to unlock that opportunity for me, as over the weeks of observing me at other courses, she was able to press the right buttons in preceding weeks and was also able to use her insight into my way of thinking to give me what I needed that day. That too, was a gift that was only made available after the forgiveness experience.

During the reconnection experience I was able to make the connection that the one person who had almost destroyed me, was in fact the soul that had before our incarnation agreed to do a very difficult thing for me. I had before incarnation been disconnected from a number of my resources as a soul and I became aware of this during my spiritual regression when I saw the orphaned aspect of my torn soul waiting to incarnate in circumstances where I at the time felt that I had been locked out from where I wanted to be. In those moments I was also aware that another aspect of my soul was dispassionately waiting to ensure that I enter my current body. During my reconnection experience I finally understood that when the time was right during my current incarnation, it was The Bishop's job to disconnect me from my resources in the physical plane by cutting me off from society, from the ability to have faith in anything and from the ability to trust. 'As above, so below'. I believe it is possible that the disconnection that had occurred before my incarnation resulted in my soul being torn, causing the deep pain that I have always been aware of. This would have created a substantial energy distortion that I would have been born with and that could have resulted in the mechanism that ultimately drew The Triad and their vicious actions into my life, so that The Bishop could complete the disconnection in the physical plane and I, as an incarnated soul, could start the journey back to reconnection. The journey home.

I was never able to give The Bishop 'space' in my life, especially not in the sense of 'perpetrator' as used in the beautiful poem *A Soul's Journey*, as quoted earlier. I had put him down as I could not carry the burden of remembering The Bishop on my shoulders. I pushed him from my mind – he did not deserve any place in my life, nor did he deserve a place in my soul's journey as 'perpetrator' carrying out a sacred contract between our souls. I would not give him any energy by even thinking about him. And yet, once my soul was reconnected that day and I knew for certain that it had indeed all been a carefully planned experiment, I was able to thank him during the session for his part in my plan merely by connecting with his energy. Between us as souls, there is now peace. The Bishop was indeed one of my 'perpetrators'.

During the session I also understood that had I forgiven The Triad earlier, I would not have had the 'fuel' to propel me forward to my reconnection. My soul could only reconnect after I had forgiven The Bishop, and I could only do that after completing a myriad of other journeys. The timing of both the forgiveness and the reconnection was perfect. I will never again judge anyone when it appears as if they are 'not getting it' or are 'not aware' or are 'unable to forgive' or 'unable to let go'. If people are on some or other destructive journey, then it is probably precisely what they need at that moment and for anyone to judge another's journey or perceived lack of progress is beyond arrogant and presumptuous. I will not forget this lesson – I have always known the truth of it, but I now really 'know' it is true.

I remembered that Claudia had asked us to write a message to ourselves that morning before my reconnection, while in trance during a healing session.

The message had to begin with 'Dear me' and we were asked to give ourselves an affirmation to take forward. Here is what I wrote:

Dear Me, I like you and your spirit and how you never give up until you know how to make it better.

My affirmation was as follows:

I trust all that is completely.

Given what followed during the session, I now understand why I have always been so driven to find answers and to understand how things 'worked'. I never thought that I had the option to give up. A part of me, my soul I suspect, knew that if I could understand the energy dynamics of what was happening in my life, I could resolve all my difficulties. I finally got to the point where I could trust, an ability I had lost many years ago. The restoration of my trust was also one of the gifts that flowed forth from the forgiveness experience and that finally propelled me forward to the reconnection of my soul.

So many things changed in my life from that day. I feel like I have been operating on the strength of a pen light battery my entire life. Now I am connected to a power source that resembles that of a super nova. I almost do not register my body's weight, because walking is now so easy. I have had a very stiff frame all my life. For a few weeks after this session my entire skeleton felt as if it was well-oiled and my shoulder muscles no longer cried out for a massage, staying soft and loose. The stiffness returned to some extent after a few weeks, but probably due to long hours sitting in front of my computer, completing this book. I believe that the condition of my neck and shoulders will always be a good indication of whether I am taking care of my health and living a balanced life. It is up to me how good I want to feel.

My skin feels different and I do not see the same person in the mirror that I used to see there. I look different, like a really happy twin of myself with a totally different personality. I find that my thoughts are clear, precise and logical and I cannot think a negative thought even if I tried. The world truly looks magical to me and every second of every day is filled with excitement, no matter how mundane the task I am busy with. I never understood how people could be happy and actually like life and as mentioned earlier in these pages, they used to irritate me. I am now one of those people! Hopefully my joy will not irritate people, but will inspire them, because nothing can stop me from sharing what I feel inside. It just flows out. Suddenly everything I need at any given time flows into my world almost instantly. I feel completely safe, guided, guarded and protected. I have absolute faith that all is well and I am able to trust from moment to moment, not worrying about anything for even one second. I am able to enjoy every single minute of every day, feeling either gratitude or joy. And in between, as I drink in the perfection of my days, I feel a deep humility. It is all so simple and yet it took me five decades to work out.

I have learned three important things along the way. The first important thing I have learned is to respect the paths of others. It would be disastrous to think we can teach each other anything. No one knows better about your journey than you. You are the expert and your soul is in charge. It is pointless judging someone for 'not listening', 'not seeing' or not doing what we want them to do. If we focus on what someone does to offend us, or to irritate us, or we fail to understand why they are tearing themselves apart in such seemingly destructive ways, then we are already missing the point. What we see in others, points to something in ourselves. It does not mean to say that a drug addict in our world mirrors an addiction within ourselves. It simply means that the plight of that drug addict brings something to life inside us and if that is an uncomfortable feeling for us, then it is best to forget about the drug addict and his problem and to follow that emotion within. It will lead us to what we need to heal in our own lives.

The second important thing I have learned on this journey, is the power of gratitude. It functions on every level. It moves mountains. If your life presents you with something painful, bring your focus to that matter and be grateful for the message that you cannot yet see. The universe will move the earth to bring to you what it is that you need to know.

The third important thing I have learned, is that true forgiveness is a difficult journey. The energy of forgiveness, or rather the mechanics of the energy dynamics involved in the process of forgiveness, unlocks gifts that only become available as a result of the completion of the process. Once the dynamic has played out, the gifts are revealed. These gifts are unique to the forgiver involved. These gifts are only available when the forgiveness is authentic. And authentic forgiveness is a sacred journey that no one has the right to judge. It cannot be rushed as its timing in each life is as crucial as it is perfect. Instead of urging others to forgive, live your own journey towards authentic forgiveness while being patient and gentle with yourself and let others do the same, for how can anyone know the plan for any other soul?

I know that joy resounds through eternity when a human learns to trust and to accept the journey its soul has decided to embark on. I know there was joy in the higher realms where those who guide and guard us exist, each time that I made a connection or managed to recognise a pattern in the darkness of my human existence that eventually led me home safely. And that joy found a way of enfolding me. Once I gave it a space in my heart, it grew strong and all I needed flowed to me at the right time.

In the end, all we have is the present moment. It sounds so simple and we have all heard it being said so many times before that we no longer really take the meaning of this truth to heart. Tomorrow will come, but then it will be our now. When it does, we had better hope that when yesterday was now, we chose well and took responsibility for that moment, living it fully and creating with all the power it gave us, because we move from one present moment into the next and in each moment we build on that which our presence produced in the previous one. Hoping that tomorrow will change things for the better is only natural, but it only makes sense if we can also have faith, in that moment of hope, that good things will come, as it is in that moment of faith that we create the possibility for what we believe can be, to flow into our present moments, piggy-backing on the moments that were our yesterdays.

Bibliography

1. Brown, Les. 2011. *Dream Blocks, Removing Yours.* Made for Success, Inc. [Audible Audio Edition]

2. Newton, Michael, Ph.D.. 1994. *Journey of Souls.* Llewellyn Publications

3. Newton, Michael, Ph.D.. 2002. *Destiny of Souls.* Llewellyn Publications

4. Newton, Michael, Ph.D.. 2004. *Life between Lives Hypnotherapy for Spiritual Regression.* Llewellyn Publications

5. Roman, Sanaya, and Duane Packer. 1987. *Opening to Channel.* H J Kramer Inc

6. Sharma, Robin. 1997. *The Monk who sold his Ferrari.* HarperElement

7. Weiss, Brian L., M.D.. 1988. *Many Lives, Many Masters.* Fireside

Recommended Reading

Tomlinson, A., *Healing the Eternal Soul*, From the Heart Press, 2012. 'This is a definitive reference work in regression therapy, for both past life and life between lives. Andy shares his valuable experience in detail and uses concrete case studies to illustrate his points and techniques. This book is a must-have for any regression therapy practitioner and will captivate any reader interested in the subject.'

Tomlinson, A., *Exploring the Eternal Soul*, From the Heart Press, 2012. 'Andy takes the reader beyond the death experiences and gives a wide and comprehensive explanation about Life Between Life therapy. He puts the content into a structured way that is easy to follow and understand what is happening. This is a highly recommended book to understand about our life choices, and also for readers who are curious about what lies beyond death.'

Mack, P., *Healing Deep Hurt Within; The Transformational Journey of a Young Patient Undergoing Regression Therapy*, From the Heart Press, 2011. 'Dr. Peter Mack is a Neurosurgeon who after years of frustration incorporated regression therapy into his practice and helped a patient with a debilitating illness unresponsive to mainstream medicine. This is a book hard to put down once it's been started.'

Mack, P., (ed) *Inner Healing Journey - A Medical Perspective*, From the Heart Press, 2014. 'The book tells the stories of eleven patients whose medical doctors were prepared to use past lives and regression therapy when tradition medicine did not work, and shows the amazing transformation that can take place using a holistic approach. It is written to be an absorbing read and bring new hope to the public, and to inspire medical professionals.'

www.ingramcontent.com/pod-product-compliance
Lightning Source LLC
Chambersburg PA
CBHW062041080426
42734CB00012B/2522